# Lobbying for Social Change

## Third Edition

# Willard C. Richan

Willard C. Richan

# Lobbying
# for Social Change
## *Third Edition*

## More pre-publication
## REVIEWS, COMMENTARIES, EVALUATIONS . . .

"This book provides individuals, groups, and organizations with an arsenal of tools and techniques that can be used to enhance their ability to affect public policy at every level of government. Through the provision of numerous case examples, Richan not only illustrates the strategic steps required to effect change on a variety of horizons, but also the opportunity for role-playing. He provides a blueprint for understanding the general mindset of most policymakers; for gathering evidence for successful lobbying through case preparation; and even on how to best use the power of the mass media.

Scenarios of practical application draw heavily upon the translation of basic principles identified in the early chapters of this book. Students interested in taking on the 'System' through direct action are afforded a guide for such a journey; faculty interested in teaching community organization will find that the very generous information in Part II provides helpful hints for the aspiring advocate; and for grassroots organizers, Richan's recount of a life and death lobbying campaign is a must read. The campaign reflects an honest portrayal of a welfare reform lobbying effort by a small but determined grouop of people operating on a shoestring budget. I recommend *Lobbying for Social Change* to all who are eager to learn some of the many tricks of the trade as well as their own personal strengths and limitations."

**Rufus Sylvester Lynch, DSW**
*Dean, Whitney M. Young, Jr. School of Social Work,
Clark Atlanta University*

"This is a handbook for students, activists, and ordinary citizens trying to make a change in the confusing and frequently intimidating American political structure. Drawing on diverse academic literature, as well as his experience as an activist seeking to affect Pennsylvania welfare legislation, Willard Richan explains the challenges facing activists and offers suggestions for organizing and lobbying. He makes the policy process comprehensible, and he provides a step-by-step guide to affecting that process. His advice, which ranges from how to write a brief to how to speak to the media, includes both broad strategies and specific suggestions. This is an important source for students learning about the policy process for the first time or citizens organizing for social change. It is lively, informative, and accessible for those with little experience in politics. The book itself performs an important social mission as it educates citizens about how to affect their government, a process that is crucial to any democracy and sadly lacking in America today."

**Anya Bernstein, PhD**
*Harvard University Lecturer and Director of Undergraduate Studies; Committee on Degrees in Social Studies, Harvard University*

## NOTES FOR PROFESSIONAL LIBRARIANS AND LIBRARY USERS

This is an original book title published by The Haworth Press, Inc. Unless otherwise noted in specific chapters with attribution, materials in this book have not been previously published elsewhere in any format or language.

## CONSERVATION AND PRESERVATION NOTES

All books published by The Haworth Press, Inc., and its imprints are printed on certified pH neutral, acid-free book grade paper. This paper meets the minimum requirements of American National Standard for Information Sciences-Permanence of Paper for Printed Material, ANSI Z39.48-1984.

## DIGITAL OBJECT IDENTIFIER (DOI) LINKING

The Haworth Press is participating in reference linking for elements of our original books. (For more information on reference linking initiatives, please consult the CrossRef Web site at www.crossref.org.) When citing an element of this book such as a chapter, include the element's Digital Object Identifier (DOI) as the last item of the reference. A Digital Object Identifier is a persistent, authoritative, and unique identifier that a publisher assigns to each element of a book. Because of its persistence, DOIs will enable The Haworth Press and other publishers to link to the element referenced, and the link will not break over time. This will be a great resource in scholarly research.

# Lobbying
# for Social Change

*Third Edition*

*The Haworth Press*
Haworth Series in Social Administration
Simon Slavin, EdD, ACSW
Editor

*Research and Utilization in the Social Services: Innovations for Practice and Administration* edited by Anthony J. Grasso and Irwin Epstein

*Social Work Ethics on the Line* by Charles S. Levy

*Performance Evalation in the Human Services* by Wayne Matheson, Cornelius Van Dyk, and Kenneth Millar

*Human Services Technology: Understanding, Designing, and Implementing Computer and Internet Applications in the Social Services* by Dick Schoech

*Lobbying for Social Change, Third Edition* by Willard C. Richan

# Lobbying
# for Social Change
## Third Edition

Willard C. Richan

The Haworth Press
New York • London • Oxford

For more information on this book or to order, visit
http://www.haworthpress.com/store/product.asp?sku=5782

or call 1-800-HAWORTH (800-429-6784) in the United States and Canada
or (607) 722-5857 outside the United States and Canada

or contact orders@HaworthPress.com

Published by

The Haworth Press, Inc., 10 Alice Street, Binghamton, NY 13904-1580.

PUBLISHER'S NOTE
The development, preparation, and publication of this work has been undertaken with great care. However, the Publisher, employees, editors, and agents of The Haworth Press are not responsible for any errors contained herein or for consequences that may ensue from use of materials or information contained in this work. The Haworth Press is committed to the dissemination of ideas and information according to the highest standards of intellectual freedom and the free exchange of ideas. Statements made and opinions expressed in this publication do not necessarily reflect the views of the Publisher, Directors, management, or staff of The Haworth Press, Inc., or an endorsement by them.

Third edition of *Lobbying for Social Change* (The Haworth Press, 1991).

Cover design by Kerry E. Mack.

**Library of Congress Cataloging-in-Publication Data**

Richan, Willard C.
    Lobbying for social change / Willard C. Richan.—3rd ed.
        p. cm.
    Includes bibliographical references and index.
    ISBN-13: 978-0-7890-3165-5 (hc. : alk. paper)
    ISBN-10: 0-7890-3165-5 (hc. : alk. paper)
    ISBN-13: 978-0-7890-3166-2 (pbk. : alk. paper)
    ISBN-10: 0-7890-3166-3 (pbk. : alk. paper)
    1. Lobbying—United States. 2. United States—Social policy. I. Title.

JK1118.R53 2006
324'.40973 —dc22

                                                                    2006015165

Anne Bernstein Richan
1933-2000

She never gave up on a worthy cause nor on any human being.

# ABOUT THE AUTHOR

**Willard C. Richan, DSW,** is Professor Emeritus at Temple University, where he taught social work and social policy for nearly a quarter century. Since his retirement in 1993, he has been actively involved in lobbying and education. He was co-founder and chair of the Delaware County (PA) Coalition to Save Our Safety net (DCCOS), a grassroots lobbying organization described in this book. More recently he has worked on issues related to urban education. Dr. Richan is on the Advisory Board of the Widener University Center for Social Work Education. Since 2003, he has made his home in Chester, Pennsylvania, a city with severe economic and social problems and a public school system that ranks 501st out of 501 school districts in Pennsylvania. He is co-chair of the Board of Chester Eastside Ministries, an urban mission in the Presbytery of Philadelphia. His writings include five books and many articles in the professional social work literature. He is the recipient of many awards, including Pennsylvania NASW Social Worker of the Year.

# CONTENTS

# Preface to the Third Edition

It has been less than a decade since the second edition of *Lobbying for Social Change* appeared, yet we live in a world remarkably different from that of 1996. Information technology continues to change at a dizzying pace, transforming the art of persuasion in the political arena. But perhaps the most revolutionary change of all was started on September 11, 2001, by nineteen men armed only with box cutters and the willingness to die for a cause they believed in.

This latest edition is meant to fill that gap. Throughout the book I have sought to update the material, to bring in contemporary developments as they bear on the subject of lobbying. Many of the original case examples are still there, because they are as relevant today as they were in 1991 and 1996. The underlying principles, I believe, are still as valid as ever. I shall let the reader be the judge of that.

None of the three Pennsylvania legislators profiled in Chapter 6 of the second edition is still serving in Pennsylvania's legislature. Senator Roxanne H. Jones died in office. Representative John E. Peterson moved on to become a congressman. Representative, later Senator, Allen Kukovich now serves as the governor's representative in southwestern Pennsylvania. I have chosen to leave these three profiles in place, however, because they illustrate so well the kinds of lawmakers you will encounter and the competing pressures under which they operate.

On a personal note, Senator Roxanne Jones's tragic death was a special loss to countless people. Her ascendancy from welfare mother to respected Pennsylvania state senator is a reminder to all of us of the possibilities in any person, however humble his or her beginnings. I have worked closely with a number of people who knew her intimately. After she died, a reporter visited her apartment. On her bedside table was a copy of *Lobbying for Social Change*.

*Lobbying for Social Change*
© 2006 by The Haworth Press, Inc. All rights reserved,
doi:10.1300/5782_a

In the third edition there is a new chapter on confronting the system through direct action. A new section added to this edition is the case history of a grassroots lobbying effort on welfare reform in one county in Pennsylvania. It allows the reader to go through the stages of forming an organization and lobbying at different levels of government by a variety of means. Also new in this edition is the case of a troubled urban school district, which we visit at a number of points along the way to illustrate lobbying principles.

# Acknowledgments

There are countless people who have helped to make *Lobbying for Social Change* a reality. For this third edition, I owe a special debt of gratitude to Joanne Bikle, Yvonne Fraley, Ann Hubben, and Linda Walker. They are the four social workers who helped launch the grassroots lobbying campaign described in Chapter 10. Niles Schore was a particularly helpful source on the use of electronic media in the political arena. Terry Rumsey and Robin Lasersohn, seasoned activists, provided invaluable insight into direct action and related tactics. Also giving helpful feedback on part or all of the manuscript were Martin Berger, Bernice Sisson, Constance Smith, and Anne Vaughan. Thanks also to the series editor, Simon Slavin, for his stewardship of the project. As always, however, any mistakes are the sole responsibility of the author.

*Lobbying for Social Change*
© 2006 by The Haworth Press, Inc. All rights reserved.
doi:10.1300/5782_b

# Introduction

These words are written at a time of deepening pessimism among those who believe that government has a responsibility for promoting social justice. Always implicit if not explicit in our national mythology, social justice has been approached ambiguously at best in this country since its very beginnings. The writers of the Constitution included "promote the general welfare" among their mandates yet turned a blind eye to that most shameful injustice, the enslavement of hundreds of thousands of people of African descent.

Government responsibility for its most vulnerable citizens has been steadily eroding in recent decades. It is easy to conclude, therefore, that there is little point in trying to stem the tide. This is not a conclusion shared by the author. I hope this book will not only give you some useful tools for fighting for social justice but also help you see that the cause is not hopeless.

Are things bad these days for those of us who care about what happens to people? You bet. Are things likely to get worse before they get better? Much worse. The political landscape as of 2006 can look pretty dismal if you are of the blue-state persuasion, user-friendly if you prefer red states. Except that nobody feels like a winner these days. The religious right can feel just as victimized by the powerful elites arrayed against it as the iconoclastic left does.

This book is a guide to that mysterious world where our state and national policies are made. These policies determine the kind of air we breathe, the sort of treatment we and our loved ones can expect from the state if we get into trouble, the many ways government impinges on our lives every day—in short, the very quality of life itself. I am writing this without assuming the reader has a lot of prior knowledge of the world of public policy, only that he or she would like to be able to affect it.

They say a book should be written with a particular reader in mind. My imagined reader is someone who cares about what happens to

*Lobbying for Social Change*
© 2006 by The Haworth Press, Inc. All rights reserved.
doi:10.1300/5782_01

*1*

people and wants to make a difference in the world but is not sure how to go about it. I have used as my model the hundreds of social work students I taught these principles to for many years and the other professional and laypersons who have taken part in short-term workshops. Many of these people were at first intimidated by the whole process, certain they could never persuade policymakers to do what they wanted them to. It has been exciting to watch their confidence grow and with it their actual ability to make a difference.

My imagined reader knows those are real people in Washington and the state capital making the decisions that rule our lives, yet the public policy arena seems like another world, far removed from the mundane existence most of us know on a daily basis. In that other world there is money—much of it. It is a world where power brokers can lard election campaigns with cash and summon huge pressure groups at a moment's notice. The people whose names and faces dominate the news media are of course the real movers and shakers. While you and I rush around trying to meet deadlines in our unglamorous jobs and studies, wondering why we keep getting into stupid arguments with loved ones, and worrying about an aging family member, they, that mysterious "they," are out there pulling the strings. If this sounds at all like the way you see things, then you are the reader I had in mind.

First we must get rid of that vision of two separate worlds—one world inhabited by people like you and me and the other by those larger-than-life public figures. They, too, sometimes get bored and restless in their jobs, have pointless quarrels with loved ones, and feel the frustration of their own powerlessness in the hands of some other "they." There is always another "they" to taunt us. Were that not so, the rate of alcoholism among members of Congress would not be so high, and promising politicians would not jeopardize their whole careers with a fleeting adventure in a motel room. They are human like the rest of us—a bit frightening when one stops to think of the power they wield.

Powerful they are. This is not necessarily because they are smarter than we are. There are ways in which they do differ from the average American, however. One way is the driving ambition that got them where they are. That ambition—which you can also think of as commitment—leads them to use their time in acquiring the knowledge and skill that is the true key to gaining influence in the policy arena. To a great extent this kind of information is free of charge. This means you and I can begin to wield more influence. We may never achieve public office, but we do not have to in order to affect public policy.

It is my firm belief that the major reason more people don't become actively involved in advocating for social change is not a lack of interest. How could anyone not care about what happens to their tax money, the air they breathe, and the quality of life they bequeath to future generations? What deters most of us is a belief that what we say or do will make little difference. This is part of a general lack of confidence in our abilities; we don't want to look foolish. Understand that this set of beliefs did not just happen. It is drummed into us from our first breath to trust people more powerful and wise than we are. If this book teaches you to be less trusting in the wisdom of people in that other world, and more trusting in your own ability to think and to use basic good sense, it will have gone a long way toward achieving its goal.

If the idea of becoming an advocate in the public policy arena is overwhelming, it may help to know about other people who felt the same way. Lois Gibbs, for example. She was the last person you would expect to be a lobbyist. She was a shy, retiring housewife—but then her quiet suburban community known as Love Canal became a seething cauldron of toxic chemicals. That crisis transformed Lois Gibbs into the leader of a national crusade that took her into the offices of mayors, governors, and members of Congress. In the process, this young woman with only a high school education learned two cardinal principles of advocacy: You have to do your homework and know what you are talking about, and you can take on the so-called experts on their own ground without being one of them.

Jennie was a more typical first-time advocate. Her first taste of lobbying was as a student in a social work course. She had spent months studying the problem of truancy from school and was ready to "educate" a state senator. Her goal was to get a state education system to keep statistics on truancy in its local school districts. Although not an earthshaking issue, perhaps, it is important if one considers the critical role of public education in preparing future citizens.

During her meeting with the senator, Jennie made an important discovery: His sixteen-year-old son was a chronic truant. Drawing on her social work skills, Jennie helped the senator think about strategies for improving the chemistry between his son and the school. Yet she knew enough not to get permanently sidetracked from her original mission. Before she left she had extracted a promise from the senator that he would talk to the chair of the Senate Education Committee about her concern.

Marty was once told he would spend the rest of his life in and out of mental hospitals, but he refused to let that grim prediction stop him. He became the head of an organization of mental health consumers. In this role he frequently lobbied public officials and taught other "mentally ill" persons how to be advocates. There are people we label as "mentally retarded" who tell state legislators about the plight of the developmentally disabled in a way that you and I could not. They receive a respectful hearing and, more important, results.

If you asked Ann if she had done lobbying she would probably deny it. She, to my knowledge, neither buttonholed her representatives in the capitol corridors nor carried a sign in a street demonstration. But Ann did lobbying in every sense of the word. Self-effacing by nature, uncomfortable when speaking to a group, she preferred to work behind the scenes in the grassroots lobbying group she joined. In so doing, she made it possible for others to twist lawmakers' arms with a kind of clout they would not otherwise have had. When the group needed bylaws, she borrowed a set from another organization she had been a part of and helped adapt the language to fit the new purpose. Ann took a lead role in organizing the group's annual dinner meetings. Later, when they found themselves without a chairperson, she stepped into the breach. In lobbying, it's not what you do but how what you do helps make a difference in public policy.

The title of this book talks about advocating for social change. Are advocates always seeking something new? In recent decades, under the impetus of attempts to reduce government's social welfare functions, human service advocates have frequently found themselves fighting off changes they considered negative.

So you may at times want to lobby *against* social change, not for it. The principles you will employ in a resistance movement will be the same as those used in promoting affirmative changes. Given the nature of our political system, however, the task of the advocate is typically to call for new approaches, not simply hold on to old ones.

At times our government drags its feet, in the face of a crisis, as in the weak and belated response of both the administration and Congress to AIDS and environmental pollution. When government does act, it may meet the needs of only certain people. Most of us would probably agree that the problems facing ordinary citizens should take precedence over those of defense contractors, that the plight of people with very limited means has priority over that of the very affluent. Not that the pain of personal crises is any less wrenching for the rich than the poor, but intuitively we sense that the former have fewer such crises and more alternatives for dealing with them.

## THE CONTEXT

In recent years two trends have had a major impact on every aspect of the political process. One is the growing fear and frustration among middle- and working-class Americans as they watch their economic position erode. The reaction to downward mobility in the economic sphere has been compounded by a crumbling of old status relations among races and genders and rapid changes in lifestyle values. The second trend is a revolution in the technology of communications. The Internet has opened up the political process to many of us in ways once undreamed of. We are able to gather information and send out our message in new and efficient ways, to tilt the balance between the haves and have-nots.

### The Politics of Frustration

Not long ago, the notion that the United States might dispense with the welfare state altogether seemed downright absurd. Even in the wake of the "Reagan Revolution," that conservative sea change of the 1980s, the basic social welfare institutions that emerged during the Great Depression were intact. Surely, it was thought, social security, that most sacrosanct of safety-net protections, was here to stay. I was among those who once believed that government responsibility for basic survival and human decency would continue indefinitely because of its urgent necessity.

Now, suddenly, everything is on the block. Yes, including social security. Even public education, that fundamental right of every child in America, with roots going back to the very beginning of the nation, is being debated.

Actually, not so suddenly. Beginning in the 1980s, the world of work changed drastically for many Americans. Rapidly evolving technology was transforming the production of goods and services, eliminating the need for many workers, including some in skilled occupations. It wasn't just automation in the factory. New technology made it easier to export jobs to developing countries where labor costs were much lower than those in the United States. Corporate mergers and buyouts compounded the problem, by shrinking the workforce and often moving jobs around the country.

People who had played by the rules and assumed their futures were secure found themselves out on the street. Those who were able to make the transition to a new job frequently did so by taking a cut in both employment status and income.

In 1990s, the downsizing of the work force extended into the ranks of middle managers and professional and technical workers, parts of the job market that had at first seemed immune. Adding to the insecurity and frustration was the lack of clearly identifiable villains. You get a pink slip along with a curt "Please have your things out of here by tomorrow." Who did this to you? Do you start by blaming yourself? Your boss? Your fellow workers who are not getting axed? The company? An exploited child laborer in India or Latin America? A large corporation you never heard of? An amorphous "they"?

Social scientists tell us that rising expectations among the havenots tend to be accompanied by a move to the left politically. Conversely, those who were presumed to have made it economically and then find themselves losing ground are more likely to look rightward for answers (see Smelser and Lipset, 1966:49; Germani, 1966). Add to this the fact that the people who were feeling the frustration most keenly were the ones traditionally cast as winners in this society: young white males. It is not hard to see why issues such as affirmative action and women's rights and a broad range of programs to help the nonworking poor have become such an explosive mix.

## *No, Toto, We're Not in Kansas*

Maybe we can all be forgiven for feeling a little like Dorothy when she landed in Oz. It's certainly not the world I grew up in. Old assumptions about government and social welfare are falling by the wayside at a hectic pace. And, sure enough, we have more than a few Wicked Persons of the West. But we're going to have to do more than click those ruby slippers together to get out of this one.

Which brings us back to the subject of Kansas. Thomas Frank (2004) has written a fascinating account of what has been happening in his home state of Kansas. The state has a long tradition of populism, ranging from antislavery militancy under John Brown to farmers' protests in the 1930s. But now, says Frank, the populism has been turned on its head, with people at the lower end of the income ladder voting to keep their oppressors in office. The anger is still there, but it seems to be aimed at the wrong targets—and, Frank generalizes, this is happening all over the country. Hence, powerful corporate interests hold sway in Washington, free to cheat the rest of us and destroy the environment in the bargain, while the oppressed masses crusade against moral decay. Frank faults the Democrats for trying to look Republican on economic questions, while alienating the masses with their stance on the so-called social issues.

Much can be said for the theory that the working class in this country is easily diverted from voting its economic self-interest by anger over other issues. It is a phenomenon with a long history, well exploited by savvy politicians. For example, generations of poor whites in the South allowed themselves to be alienated from their natural allies, poor blacks, keeping economic resources in the region safely in the hands of the well-to-do.

But it's easy to overstate Frank's thesis. Take, for example, the notion that, like Kansas, the country as a whole has been "going red." No question: The country returned George W. Bush to the White House in 2004 with increased Republican majorities in both houses of Congress. Yet we need to remind ourselves that Bush received fewer popular votes than Al Gore (Democrat) did in 2000. Although Gore could in no way be categorized as a flaming liberal, his views on both economic justice and a sustainable environment were a far cry from his opponent's. The 2004 election was also a cliffhanger. Again, the outcome hinged on the vote of a single state.

Then there was 9/11. Frank barely mentions the issue of terrorism. Yet this event, thrust on the country from outside, probably had as much to do with Bush's reelection as the entire array of domestic "social" issues combined. I for one am not persuaded by exit polls showing that voters were driven by "moral values" more than other concerns. Christian conservatives have been quick to seize on these findings as showing a trend toward their political views. That is a huge logical leap, given the fact that we really don't know what the respondents to those polls meant by "moral values."

September 11 changed the political landscape in fundamental ways. In the bargain, it precipitated a war on terrorism and made the invasion of Iraq more palatable to Americans, thus contributing to the wholesale diversion of government spending away from social programs.

If we look at the state level of government, the question of party dominance becomes more ambiguous. At first blush, the Republicans, with six more governorships than the Democrats in 2005, including the biggest states, would seem to have a clear upper hand. But things get a little more murky when we look at state legislatures. The Republicans controlled twenty-one legislatures, the Democrats nineteen, and the remaining states were split or nonpartisan. When it comes to numbers of state legislators around the country, the two parties were in a virtual dead heat.

Yet there is no question that the country has moved to the right, and there is every indication that it will continue to do so in the near future. Even the way we talk about left and right has changed. "Conservative" used to mean inclined to keep things as they are, opposed to change. Now the term gets attached to people urging drastic rollbacks in everything from our personal liberties to social safety nets. "Liberal" gets confounded with "elite," so that a word once used to refer to the wealthiest and least generous segment of society is now used to label people who want to reduce the gap between the rich and poor.

Another 9/11-type catastrophe—freely predicted by people on all sides of the political spectrum—could push the country even further into a garrison mentality, with social programs taking the brunt of the damage. There is no sure way to prevent such crises from happening.

Instead, we should find ways to create a different climate in this country.

That is where you and I come in. Every time we speak up for social justice and protection of the environment into which our children and grandchildren will be born, we make the political climate a little more positive, a little more able to withstand negative pressures. Every time we remain silent, we yield the stage to those with a different kind of agenda.

## The Information Revolution

"Revolution" is not too strong a word for it. In the past decade an explosion of information has dwarfed the information explosion in the decade that preceded it. It's getting to be too much for the average person to comprehend or absorb. Here's a case in point: I typed "information overload" into a popular search engine on the Internet and got more than 700,000 citations. If you tried to pull up and examine every one of those, spending a couple of minutes per citation, for twenty-four hours a day, seven days a week, you would still be at it two and a half years later. Now that's what I call information overload.

Of course nobody does read all that information. Instead, we make selective use of the information that inundates us. How that selection process is conducted makes all the difference. Do I rely on the Internet citations with the most hits? Or articles that are repeatedly cross-referenced in other articles on the same topic? Or sources that I consider politically correct? Or people I spend a lot of time with? Or the magazine or newspaper that "everybody" says is *the* source of good information? Or word of mouth from people I trust? Probably a little of all of the above.

You and I, we conduct our own independent search for the truth, wherever it may lead. As does everybody else, right? Especially harried policymakers who don't have the luxury of endless searches for information but must rely on whatever they can glean in the few hours or minutes before they have to make a critical vote.

Howard Dean's 2004 bid for the presidential nomination demonstrated the power of the Internet to bring a relative unknown to the head of the pack in fund raising and make him a serious contender.

Though he was left in the dust by the more established John Kerry and some of his own miscues, he managed to change presidential campaigning forever.

## THE POLICY CYCLE

There is a logical sequence in thinking about social policy that is different from the chronological sequence. The logical sequence starts with analysis of a social problem, which leads to formulation of policy, enactment of the policy in modified form, rules for implementing the policy, programs to carry out the intent of the policy, and, finally, evaluation of the consequences. In reality, the problem-policy-program sequence is a never-ending series of interlocking cycles, one stage leading to others. It is a little like the old question, Which came first, the chicken or the egg? In this case, the answer is "Both."

A social problem is not just adverse circumstances. It must be circumstances that affect a significant segment of the population and appear amenable to change. It must also be perceived as a problem by a significant part of society. There was a time when slavery was not defined by the majority of Americans as the evil we know it to be, so for them it was not a "social problem."

There are personal troubles that individuals want to rid themselves of and which they try to resolve, with or without much real planning. Unless the trouble is seen as more than idiosyncratic, however, it is unlikely to be defined as a social problem. When people began to realize that AIDS is more than a rare disease that happened to befall a few isolated individuals, it became a social problem.

Sometimes a personal problem is recast as a social problem. It can start with one individual or family. The most obvious examples are those involving public figures. A president has a stroke, and the affairs of the country are placed in the hands of his wife and an unelected circle of advisers, as happened at the end of Woodrow Wilson's second term. Bill Clinton's sexual liaison with a young woman nearly ended his presidency.

In the spring of 2005, the fate of one woman in a Florida hospice precipitated a national controversy that dominated the attention of the president, Congress, the governor and state legislature of Florida, courts at all levels up to and including the U.S. Supreme Court, the news media, and millions of people in this country and abroad. Was the plight of Terri Schiavo a social problem? Only if it became defined as something affecting many people and lending itself to a policy solution.

Problems have different histories. When we first became aware that toxic waste disposal posed a massive threat, it was such a new problem that no country had answers for dealing with it. The closest approximation to this kind of (human-made) disaster at the time was natural disasters such as floods and tornadoes. As a result, there was a question whether the toxic waste disposal problem fell within the existing legal framework. Compare that with welfare reform, which has almost too rich a history. Old solutions and old debates make it hard to take a fresh look at poverty and chronic unemployment.

Our society is spawning new social problems all the time. For example, we are developing a generation of young adults, many of whom will be wearing hearing aids before their parents do. The serious damage to young people's hearing caused by rock concerts, boom boxes, and headphones is predictable. Changing definitions will also create new problems in the coming years. Not too many years ago, lack of skill with a computer was not defined as a social problem the way illiteracy was. Now computer illiteracy among inner-city high school students is coming to be seen as a serious social problem. As people get older, certain symptoms are so widely shared and appear so inevitable that they are simply accepted as part of life. If science finds ways to maintain people's eyesight, hearing, and gastrointestinal functioning—to say nothing of life itself—far beyond what is now considered "normal," the aging process as we know it will also become a "social problem."

Being strictly tied to a linear conception of problem-policy-program can get in the way of seeing the true nature of the policymaking process. In the 1990s, President Bill Clinton defined "ending welfare as we know it" as an urgent national priority. Welfare dependency was the same chronic issue it had been for decades, yet Clinton's pronouncement set in motion a drive that resulted in a fundamental change in income maintenance for families with children. If there was a crisis at the time, it was a shortage of entry-level workers in the service industry, for which enforced entry of thousands of women into the workforce could have been one solution.

This was not the first time welfare reform was suddenly shoved to the front burner. In 1988, some public officials had a problem— namely, getting reelected. These officials saw welfare reform as a safe issue on which to mount a crusade, around which one could rally conservatives bent on getting the chiselers off the welfare rolls, hu- manitarians wanting to integrate the very poor into the economic mainstream, and feminists angry that absent fathers were getting away with not supporting their families. So, with the help of authors who had achieved prominence writing about welfare dependency, they turned welfare reform into a major issue. The welfare rolls had been declining, and the total cost of welfare transfers had been declin- ing even more. In short, the problem of getting people off welfare and into jobs was no more urgent at that point than it had been for years. Note two points: There was not a new social problem of welfare de- pendency, and the policies being debated dealt not with a single social problem, but several.

Food aid policies deal with two quite different problems: increas- ing the nutrition of needy populations and aiding agriculture. Some government housing programs have had the dual functions of in- creasing poor people's access to shelter but also creating business for the construction industry.

You have a great deal of control over the extent to which you be- come active in trying to change policy but little control over where in the cycle you enter the fray. Let us say that you are employed by a community mental health agency that must trim back its services be- cause of federal budget cuts. The challenge you and your agency face is salvaging programs that you believe are helping people in need. The etiology of mental disorders is relevant, but you don't have the luxury of stopping to design ideal solutions. The issues in the debate on funding are probably already well defined, so your task is to arm yourself with the best available information with which to argue your point of view.

Or say your state legislature is considering a bill that would restrict access of minors to abortion services. The problem for one faction is abortion itself, which they consider to be murder. The opponents say the problem is denial of freedom of choice to young women and risks to their physical and mental health. During the debate you may find yourself arguing about the cost to the taxpayers caused by either outcome.

On the other hand, you can get involved at the beginning of the policy cycle and contribute to thinking about AIDS or toxic waste disposal in new ways. It's always preferable to be able to examine social problems in fundamental terms and prevent crises instead of mopping up after them. Preferable, but not often possible. Meanwhile, a large number of decisions with impact on many lives will continue to be made. You can have input into those decisions or abdicate the field to others.

This book doesn't deal with the whole policy cycle. The process of policy formulation may involve months, or even years, of searching for solutions to social problems. We pick up the process at the point when someone is proposing solutions. A pro and a con are already emerging.

## *TAKING ONE STEP AT A TIME*

Any task that is at first overwhelming becomes less intimidating if it is broken down into specific steps. This is certainly true of lobbying. Thus, this book is divided into three parts. Part I, Basic Steps, outlines a series of tasks the advocate must carry out in preparation for lobbying— regardless of who is to be urged to do what and under what circumstances. Although this may sound like a rigid formula-for-all-occasions, the steps are really guidelines that allow one to exercise a great deal of discretion.

The first step is assessing one's strengths and limitations, the subject of Chapter 1. We tend to underestimate our strengths and exaggerate the limits of our power. This chapter should be a useful antidote to that tendency. Next comes setting the agenda for action, the subject of Chapter 2. From the agenda, all else follows. As this chapter points out, it is usually easier to say what one does not want than to decide what one wants. Chapter 3 deals with the analysis of the target of one's lobbying: the policymaker. We must first decide who will be the target, then try to understand how that person views the world. This *definition of the situation* is what the advocate seeks to change, as a way of getting the desired action. Chapters 4 and 5 go hand in hand. Chapter 4 tells you how to put together your case for action. Chapter 5 tells you how to find the evidence to support your case.

In Part II, different kinds of action are discussed, not just lobbying in the narrow sense of direct work with a particular policymaker. We look at several strategies, including such indirect approaches as speaking to community groups and using the mass media. Taking one's message directly to the policymaker, the topic of Chapter 6, is lobbying in its purest form. We look at ways of adapting one's message to the particular target's definitions.

Testifying in a legislative hearing is the subject of Chapter 7. It can be an intimidating task. Knowing the territory and taking the task step-by-step help to demystify the process.

In Chapter 8, the use of mass media is discussed. Television, radio, the Internet, and the printed page are playing an increasing role in advocacy for social change, and it behooves us to learn how to get maximum mileage out of them. The electronic media have added a whole new meaning to "mass."

A different, more confrontative, brand of politics is the subject of Chapter 9. Especially as the country moves further to the right, and our very ability to participate in mainstream politics becomes more constricted, many advocates feel compelled to engage in direct action against the root causes of social injustice. Efforts to dramatize issues or disrupt proceedings, with tactics ranging from street demonstrations to civil disobedience, can indeed be powerful tools of advocacy. They also carry with them certain risks and must be approached thoughtfully.

In Part III we follow the history of a grassroots lobbying campaign in one Pennsylvania county. The subject was welfare reform, but it could have been one of any number of issues. Chapter 10 presents the historical narrative. Chapter 11 seeks to extract the lessons from the experience, both the good and the not so good parts.

Decisions and regulations coming out of Washington and your state caital are continually affecting you and your family and friends. Even those decisions about the troubles of "somebody else" may well affect you indirectly. If you work in a social agency, your work is impacted every day by public policies. Many of us have elderly family members who are facing dilemmas regarding their living arrangements or their need for adequate medical care. You may know some-one who has AIDS or is hooked on drugs or alcohol. Problems of domestic abuse, mental illness, and economic distress, however remote they may seem, affect all of us directly or indirectly. Public policies have a major impact on all professions these days, so if you are a professional practitioner or training to be one, you have a stake in the decisions being made in the public sector.

In short, you can't avoid social policy even if you want to. I hope you will do more than simply "live with it." I hope you will try to have an impact on social policy. In a real sense it means getting a little more control over your own life.

# *PART I:*
# *BASIC STEPS*

In this part of the book, we look at the step-by-step process the advocate must go through, regardless of the specific kind of lobbying involved. The process begins with a careful assessment of what you have going for you and the limitations on your ability to influence policy. The more obvious sources of political power—large sums of money, blocs of votes, and connections in high places—are probably not available to you. But that doesn't mean you are totally lacking in power. In Chapter 1, you will discover hidden strengths. At the same time, it is necessary to be realistic about power in the political arena. You should come out with neither an inflated view of your ability to bring about change nor an underestimation of it.

Chapters 2, 3, 4, and 5 move you from settling on your action objectives to identifying the person or persons toward whom your lobbying should be directed, and mapping a strategy for persuading your target person(s) to act.

# Chapter 1

# Assessing Your Strengths and Limitations

It's hard not to be cynical about the possibility of changing anything in the policy arena these days. I will assume at the outset that you are not an elected official or a cabinet-level appointee, so you don't have official status to trade on. Do you have thousands of dollars with which to seed election campaigns, hire lawyers and other experts, and send out massive mailings to computerized lists of voters? If not, money is not one of your strengths. Can you deliver a thousand votes on election day? Hundreds? One hundred? If not, blocs of voters are not one of your major assets.

## APPRECIATING YOUR STRENGTHS

Rather than focus on what you can't do, let's look at your assets. It turns out they are considerable. So what do you have going for you? Let's look at five assets you either already possess or can acquire regardless of who you are: commitment, time, allies, organization, and information. The first of these, commitment, is the one resource that is entirely in your hands. It is also without doubt the most underrated. There is, finally, a sixth asset that builds on all the others and in some ways is most crucial: confidence in your ability to be an advocate.

### Commitment

In the beginning, Lois Gibbs, the lady from Love Canal, had nothing working in her favor except fierce commitment. Painfully shy,

*Lobbying for Social Change*
© 2006 by The Haworth Press, Inc. All rights reserved.
doi:10.1300/5782_02

lacking any formal education beyond high school, firmly believing that a woman's first duty was to look after her children and keep her husband happy, she sneered at "women's libbers." Politics was a strange and intimidating world. But that was her child the school officials were saying not to worry about, her child having the unexplained seizures and asthma attacks. And that made all the difference. Once they went into action, Lois Gibbs and the other citizens with whom she allied herself were able to meet and defeat bureaucratic indifference and every obstacle an unyielding system could put in their path. Their story, the Love Canal story, is an excellent example of what a small band of people with limited resources can do about a problem in which they have a huge personal stake.

Opinions vary as to the kind and amount of help the antiabortionists have had from powerful interests—the Catholic Church hierarchy, wealthy Protestant fundamentalists, and an array of right-wing demagogues and lobbyists. But much of the power of the antiabortion movement comes from the zeal of grassroots activists. Their singlemindedness and the belief that they are fighting what amounts to a holy war against Satan have given them tremendous power.

The pro-choice faction, while in many ways just as committed, has a broader agenda. For a few, freedom to abort a pregnancy has been central to the struggle for women's rights. Freedom to determine what happens to their bodies—especially freedom from control by the male-dominated medical profession—is the ultimate sign of deliverance. Unlike the antiabortion activists, however, many pro-choice advocates are unwilling to subordinate all other policy issues to this one.

The way people entered the two movements is instructive. Luker (1984) found that the typical antiabortion activist became incensed at the idea of "baby murder" and went looking for a movement to join. She had never been involved in politics before and tended to remain focused squarely on the abortion issue. The typical pro-choice activist, on the other hand, was recruited by those already active, and the message about abortion was linked to a broad spectrum of women's rights issues.

Strong personal commitment to a cause leads one to persist when it would be much easier to quit. The committed person will put in the extra time and effort that others are not ready to invest. It means going to meeting after meeting, being there at the beginning and staying through to the end, staying alert while other minds wander, always with that single agenda overriding all others. It means wading through page after boring page of legislative jargon and statistical tables. It means developing close working relationships with people one has little interest in, even some one personally dislikes.

Typically, it is a dedicated core of active leaders who keep an advocacy effort going. Sociologist Adeline Levine found that to be true in the case of the relative handful who led the successful two-year effort by Love Canal residents to get action on their demands. Most important, the workers gave of themselves. They provided a constant presence; they persisted; they were always there. They did all the tedious, laborious tasks familiar to anyone who has ever worked in a voluntary organization (Levine, 1982).

Many socially committed persons have a special liability: too many agendas. Their names appear on countless lists of supporters, on the assumption that if commitment to one cause is good, supporting three causes is three times as good. One trouble with that theory is that one can't invest the necessary time and effort to become a true expert—the kind that others turn to for information, the kind legislators learn to treat as a trusted resource—on more than one or two issues at a time. Another problem is that policymakers know that the advocate who tries to influence them on a wide range of issues can't hold them accountable on any one issue. If they see you as being hooked into every urgent cause that comes along, they will calculate—correctly, no doubt—that your readiness to stay the course for any particular cause is limited.

Multiple agendas can lead to paralyzing dilemmas. In Chapter 10, I discuss the involvement of the Pennsylvania Chapter of the National Association of Social Workers (NASW) in a lobbying campaign dealing with welfare reform. This was not the first time NASW had been urged to go to the mat on welfare reform. Several years earlier, the governor of Pennsylvania had sought to place new restrictions on general assistance, the catch-all welfare safety-net program. The trouble in that instance was that NASW was also desperately seeking passage of a social work licensing bill, and many of the legislators in favor of licensing were equally committed to the governor's welfare reform program. The NASW leadership tried to rally the membership behind both issues, but for the rank-and-file majority, licensing took precedence over anything else. The result was a divided chapter, with a few pro-welfare "generals" leading the charge with not enough troops.

The only reason a democratic form of government like ours actually works, actually gets things done, is that the majority of people have low commitment on the majority of issues. Were that not so, the country would be forever in one gigantic gridlock and would never achieve any results. Policymakers avoid offending anybody, so if everybody were intensively involved in everything, the interest groups would cancel each other out, and no public official would dare to do anything for fear of antagonizing someone. One factor that helped antiabortionists in the early days of the movement was that the issue held so little interest for other people. In a way they had the field to themselves. In time this changed, of course, as the pro-choice forces became aroused.

That lack of commitment by most people most of the time can be one of your biggest assets, because you, being strongly committed on your issues, get the attention of the policymakers. And that is more important than whether you agree with their biases or are considered an expert on the subject.

One piece of conventional wisdom in policy advocacy ought to be disposed of at the outset: the belief that people invest only in what has a personal, material payoff for them. It is a belief that politicians generally subscribe to. But many people work long and hard, at great personal sacrifice, for causes they believe in. For evidence of that statement, one need only consider the abortion issue.

The core of activists who have worked zealously over the years to outlaw abortion are not in it for personal gain. By definition they are driven by a concern for those who cannot even show their appreciation, the unborn. I am not referring here to politicians who use the abortion issue to make political gains, but to the people who give so generously of their time and money to pass petitions and travel to the state and national capitals to lobby and picket abortion clinics. One may criticize some of their tactics—just as one can find questionable tactics being used on behalf of most causes—but their sincerity is hard to question.

This is not to say that a self-interest stake in an issue is unimportant. There is no question that mental health professionals lobbying for better services are doing it for more than altruistic reasons. For many, their own jobs, maybe even their careers, are on the line. Good-hearted people concerned about the plight of this or that consumer population have a way of fading—or more typically being drawn into some other fight on behalf of some other consumer population. Any of us has only so much energy to devote to the common good. If professionals are driven by a concern for both the recipients of their services and their own careers, then they are likely to keep working longer and harder. Nor, when their jobs are on the line, should mental health advocates feel guilty or defensive about wanting to be able to continue in a career in the service of troubled human beings.

Acknowledging an element of self-interest in much advocacy work helps one empathize with the target of the advocacy, the public official. Do not judge too harshly the legislator who takes a particular position in order to get votes. That is, after all, how he or she stays in office. Elected officials are all keenly aware that they will do precious little good, as lawmakers at least, if they are voted out of office.

Commitment means little unless it is translated into action. The most obvious expression of one's commitment is the use of one's time.

## Time

Time is in many ways more valuable than money. In fact, a major use of money is to buy someone's time. That has advantages and disadvantages. The salaried employee is likely to be more dependable than the volunteer, in showing up when expected and adhering to the party line. Money can buy high-priced talent that is often unavailable to efforts dependent solely on volunteers. However, the salaried employee may not share the zeal of the committed volunteer.

When sociologist Kristen Luker (1984) wanted to identify a sample of antiabortion activists—the most committed—she used as a major criterion the amount of time they devoted to the movement. Her cutoff point was ten hours or more per week. She found that many activists devoted as much as forty hours a week. These were, by and large, homemakers, while the pro-choice activists tended to be tied to work schedules and had to fit their political work in around the job. One tangible advantage for the antiabortionists was that they worked out of their own homes, thus were available to get and relay phone messages at all hours. The pro-choice volunteers were more likely to be out when called. Voice mail is a useful tool, but it lacks the personal touch so necessary in lobbying and recruiting members.

The Love Canal Homeowners' Association (LCHA) relied almost entirely on unpaid volunteers, including a handful of lawyers and scientists. Their single-minded dedication made them a match for local and state public officials who had to juggle several issues at once and whose general orientation was to avoid damage to their agencies.

The activist core in the grassroots struggle at Love Canal, not surprisingly, was made up of homemakers, retirees, and workers on night shift. Lois Gibbs, a leader in this effort, had quit her job a few years earlier to raise a family, so she had flexibility in her schedule that full-time workers lacked.

Large corporations and entrenched political interest groups count on other people's lack of time as well as lack of commitment. By scheduling a public meeting in Albany, the state capital, hundreds of miles from Love Canal, officials hoped to cut sharply into the number of angry residents they would have to face.

The time investment exacts a price. Lois Gibbs describes how her work as an advocate kept preempting her time as a parent:

> It was Michael's birthday, and I didn't have a gift. No cake. Nothing. . . . I did manage a small birthday, however. I went out to Child World and bought a bunch of toys; but I didn't have time to wrap them. I bought a cake at the bakery and put some candles on it. The party had to be early, because I had an association meeting that night. (Gibbs, 1982:52)

To a great extent, the LCHA volunteers simply absorbed the costs. Physical and emotional health and some marriages suffered. The small core of activist leaders was up against public officials who had vast staff resources at their beck and call, and a corporation that could buy the time of experts on everything from engineering and toxicology to the finer points of the law.

This fact seems to have escaped the writer of one magazine article who chided Lois Gibbs for not spending time combing through old school board records (see Zuesse, 1981). But policy contests rarely take place on a level playing field. Rather than waste time and energy bemoaning that fact, advocates must pick their issues and do the best possible job with the time available. The only test in this business is results, as cruel as that may seem.

Because there are limits on the time any of us can devote to advocacy without running ourselves and our supporters into the ground, advocacy requires the help of a network of allies, all of whom have their own reasons for becoming involved.

## *Allies*

The image of the loner is deeply ingrained in the American psyche, whether it is wearing cowboy boots or a cape and a big *S* on the chest. The 1930s movie *Mr. Smith Goes to Washington* told of a young congressman who battled a big tycoon single-handedly, to protect the interests of the little people. The climax was a filibuster in which the young hero, exhausted from the ordeal, fainted amid a shower of supportive telegrams from around the country. The audience knew he had won the day. It was right out of the OK Corral. And just as realistic.

Policy advocacy is not a solo operation. Especially because you lack a big bankroll and blocs of votes, you will need to combine forces with people who share your concern. The lineup may change from issue to issue. Whatever the issue, there are sure to be advocacy organizations working on it—if not in your own locality, then in your state capital or Washington. If you have trouble locating them, call an agency that provides a related kind of service. Someone there will know.

An illustration of how disparate groups can work together to bring about change is provided by a welfare reform project in Delaware. An unlikely coalition of university-based researchers, social workers, antipoverty activists, and neighborhood leaders was able to get the state to withdraw a punitive measure that would have deprived some welfare families of food stamps. A critical factor was research data placed in the hands of community activists by the researchers (Curtis, 2001).

Some alliances are unintentional. Ordinarily, one might not think of welfare rights advocates and chamber of commerce leaders as having much in common. But when the Pennsylvania legislature was considering a punitive welfare reform measure, the Philadelphia

Chamber of Commerce leaders agreed with the attitude of the governor, who saw his reform bill as forcing able-bodied welfare recipients to go out and find a job. They also understood, however, that a sharp reduction in the welfare rolls could have a devastating effect on the city's retail trade. They had the potential for swinging critical votes of conservative legislators who tended to tune out any message coming from welfare rights advocates.

There is a potential downside to alliances: different priorities among the participants. If the abortion issue or welfare reform had suddenly intruded into the agenda of the Love Canal Homeowners' Association, the group would have become badly split. LCHA was made up of Caucasian, blue-collar workers and their families. They never succeeded in forming a close working alliance with African Americans in the area, who faced exactly the same threat to their health.

So it is particularly important to stay focused on one's goals in considering alliances. The groups one has least in common with may be the very ones with access to an unfriendly legislator. As a general rule, then, enemies are a luxury the advocate can ill afford.

Two important caveats must be balanced against the general rule of finding bedfellows wherever one can. The first is that it is essential to know as well as possible why the group or individual is supporting this particular cause. Is it with the expectation that the favor will be returned at some future time? It is good to avoid making long-term, binding commitments, especially to parties whose intentions are unclear. The second caveat concerns the network of allies. Will the advocate's involvement with one group alienate others, now or in the future? The solution is not necessarily to forgo the alliance in question but at least to try to reassure the others and help them see the necessity for it. In Chapter 9, I talk about the tricky terrain of collaboration between outsiders directly confronting the establishment and insiders negotiating with it.

Alliances between different groups that want the same thing for different reasons are common in policy advocacy. A bus caravan goes to the state capital carrying ex–mental patients, family members, and mental health professionals. All three constituencies want additional funding for mental health services. For the ex-patients, the services are not only valuable in their own right but could mean the difference between being able to stay in the community and ending up back in the hospital. Some parents may be along because of the disruption or threat their children pose at home when services are lacking. For the professionals, there is the dual commitment to the welfare of the mentally ill and their own careers.

As long as the coalition stays focused on the business at hand, the alliance will hold and the powerful combination can have an impact. If they get diverted to the subject of involuntary commitment to mental hospitals, the ex-patients (for many of whom hospitalization is a painful memory) and the parents (many of whom would feel safer with easier commitment procedures) may find themselves on opposite sides of the fence.

The right-to-life movement needed organizing ability, political sophistication, money, and the kind of computer hardware possessed by ultra-conservative lobbyists. The latter saw an opportunity to mobilize a huge, highly committed constituency to support their conservative agenda. Paige (1983) suggests that the antiabortionists allowed themselves to be used by the right-wing organizations. It is a theme echoed by Thomas Frank in his provocative 2004 work, *What's the Matter with Kansas?*

Mutual suspicion about who is using whom has been a chronic problem for those seeking humane welfare policies. Grassroots organizations of welfare recipients worry about the intentions of professors, lawyers, suburban church members, and other "do-gooders" who join their cause. Sometimes local leaders are suspected of harboring personal ambitions instead of the interests of the rank and file. The test of anyone's intentions is in the outcome. If a local leader aspiring to political office performs effectively for the movement, what does it matter that he or she also has a personal agenda? At the point that the leader ceases to work for the cause or begins doing things that undermine it, then it may be time to drop the connection.

Occasionally, there is a more insidious side to such second agendas. Those without the best interests of the group at heart may infiltrate to sabotage the effort. A troubled individual may play a divisive role out of personal need. Although it is necessary to be alert to such possibilities, the organizational paranoia thus generated can be far more destructive than any number of multiple agendas. Perhaps the time to be most suspicious of intentions is when an ally claims to have no special interest other than to do others a favor. Altruism in politics does exist, but it is typically mixed with other considerations, especially where organized groups are concerned.

This mutual aid principle presents a special problem to a group that has little to offer its allies. There are no free rides in politics, and this certainly applies to coalition politics. Groups must find a useful role to play or there will be little incentive for other constituencies to include them. That also applies, of course, to individuals who want to join an advocacy effort. They need to make themselves useful to the group effort or they become something of a liability. Usefulness can mean willingness to put in time on the dirty, boring little jobs as well as the more exciting tasks, being available when and where needed, not just when it is convenient, and informing oneself about the issues. It may also mean willingness to be a team player instead of trying to lead the march. If you are a potential leader, that will become apparent readily enough.

A specific kind of ally worth cultivating is news media staff. One should be aware that the first commitment for such professional communicators is getting the story. This typically takes precedence over helping your cause, a fact that has sometimes led to resentment when an activist felt "set up" by a reporter. Chapter 8 discusses using and being used by the mass media.

## Organization

The news media tend to cast elections in terms of money, candidates' personalities, and positions on headline issues, but not necessarily in that order. Not to deny the importance of any of these factors, but to a great extent elections are won or lost on the basis of effective organization. This is particularly true in state and local contests. The ability to raise large sums of money is one of the more obvious functions of good organization. Anyone who has worked in election campaigns knows how much time and energy go into updating voter lists, running phone banks, and keeping track of the candidate's schedule. What is true of election campaigns also applies to public policy campaigns. Keeping track of legislators' positions on a bill, alerting constituencies to where the bill is in the legislative process, getting mailings out on time, making sure to get feedback from individuals who lobby their representatives—these are all mind-numbing work but crucial to the outcome.

What confounded Luker (1984) about the early antiabortion activists was their apparent lack of the machinery ordinarily associated with political effectiveness. They rarely attended meetings yet were able to coordinate their activities down to the parish level. While the Catholic Church hierarchy surely helped in this, the activists themselves were the backbone of the effort. Along the way they learned how to stay in touch with one another. At a modest cost they were able to use telephone answering services with call forwarding, so if one advocate was not available, the call would automatically go to another. With the advent of personal computers it was possible to generate thousands of letters with relative ease. Using electronic banking, contributors could have donations automatically deducted from their bank accounts each month—an especially useful device for low-budget organizations whose constituency might balk at large annual donations. Such technical aids have been put within the reach of groups of modest means. But even without them, a well-organized constituency can multiply its effectiveness manyfold. It is more than worth the effort.

The Love Canal leaders had to invest a great deal of personal time in keeping their members informed and energized. As it turned out, one of their allies in this endeavor was the state department of health, an agency that in other ways proved to be an obstacle. The department provided the LCHA with an office and telephones. It may have seemed like an inexpensive goodwill gesture, but as anyone who has worked in campaigns knows, it was an invaluable asset to the residents.

The ability to maintain an effective organization—to keep good records and a constant flow of essential information to key constituencies—is not a universal attribute. In fact, some of the most creative and forceful advocates are terrible organizers. Good organization, however, is a must in any sustained advocacy effort, particularly where the work of several allied groups must be meshed. So if you are not a well-organized person, you need to team up with people who are.

## Information

We next consider the asset that transforms the others into an effective operation: information. That is what a major part of this book is about—determining what information is needed, where to find it, and how to make the most productive use of it. To a surprising degree, the information you need is easily accessible. Of course, that special expertise, funds to hire other people's expertise, computers, and years of accumulated experience will all make you much more efficient. Much critical information, however, is sitting in libraries and on the Web, free for the taking. You can also capitalize on other people's knowledge, including that of those who don't agree with you.

There are two necessary kinds of information: One is substantive policy information and the arguments with which to support or oppose a particular change. I call it *policy content*. The other is information regarding the process by which the change takes place, as well as the actors and forces that influence decisions. That I refer to as *strategic content*. Policy information can be found in books and other published materials, though not exclusively. Strategic information is more likely to come from people with hands-on experience.

### Policy Content

I used to teach a course to social work students in which the final assignment was to go out and be a policy advocate. In most cases that meant lobbying one or more legislators. Before they ventured out into the political arena they spent weeks preparing a "brief," which was anything but brief. It was an exhaustive summary of the arguments on the critical issues—both sides of the issues—with supporting evidence drawn from a variety of sources.

There was only a slim chance the students would use most of that content in their contact with legislators, but they were prepared, and they knew it. If they had any doubts about the value of all that research, they got over them quickly after realizing that in most cases they knew far more about the subject than the person they were talking to. And the person knew it, too. So the students were convincing advocates in the eyes of two parties: the target person and themselves. Especially as they continued to advocate for their chosen cause after the course was over, as I encouraged them to do, that depth of knowledge really paid off. They frequently became important sources of information for other advocates as well.

Lois Gibbs tells how she made an important discovery while sitting at her kitchen table charting on a map the locations of people in her area with health problems. This process led to the realization that toxic chemicals were traveling out of the Love Canal cavity along subterranean channels.

What struck me about this was the fact that I once made an important discovery while sitting at my kitchen table. The governor of my state, Pennsylvania—whose welfare reform proposal would virtually eliminate all able-bodied adults without dependents from general assistance—had recently made a speech in which he said jobs were easy to find if only one had a little initiative. Why, the newspapers were full of job ads. It was an argument for tough welfare rules that Ronald Reagan had also made.

So I sat at my kitchen table one Sunday morning with the employment section of the *Philadelphia Inquirer* and went through the job ads. Out of the first 1,000 ads, I found a total of twenty-seven for which the average general assistance recipient would meet minimal requirements, according to the state's own statistics. That discovery led to a letter to the editor, which got wide distribution by organizations opposing the governor's plan.

Critical evidence for policy arguments can be that easy to obtain. In both Lois Gibbs's case and mine, the advocate had been living with the issue for months and knew what to look for. But in both cases it required not special expertise, but rather just a little imagination and the time and patience to plow through detailed information.

Still, one often does need the help of experts and access to information that is not readily available. The data requirements vary with the policy question. Discoveries may occur regarding the medical side of abortion. There will certainly be new information on the social and psychological consequences of policies that make it harder or easier to obtain one. But, in large part, the arguments are couched in moral terms and by now are quite familiar. Many arguments regarding welfare reform are of this sort, although researchers and practitioners are continually turning up new evidence about poverty, the actual impact

of welfare on work motivation, methods of job training, and the economic side effects of public assistance payments.

Technical knowledge in the mental health field is necessary to
make a convincing case for spending tax money on community-based
programs. A standard question in legislative hearings on appropriations for such services is whether the services have been proven to do
any good. It is a tough question to answer because there is little solid
evidence of the success of mental health treatment. Often, the biggest
challenge for the mental health professional is not the need to be current on the research literature but having the ability to translate esoteric principles into common, understandable language.

The issue of toxic waste disposal is another one in which mastery
of technical content becomes important. The problem did not exist
until a few decades ago—at least not on the scale it does now. Not
only is there very little experience with policies in this area, but one
quickly gets into extremely technical content. That may seem to
make toxic waste an issue only for the professionals. But as Lois
Gibbs demonstrated, a young homemaker with no advanced education can learn to hold her own in this policy field, as in any other. She
doesn't do it on her own. This is where allies with the right expertise
become a critical asset.

*Strategic Content*

All the facts in the world will do you no good if you don't know
when, where, and how to use them. For this there is nothing like a
wealth of personal experience on which to draw. This book suggests
some principles for identifying key decision makers and who and
what influences them. These principles must be adapted to fit the particular case you are working on.

This is where good working relationships with other advocates
are beneficial. In particular, the people who do this sort of thing for
a living have to be conversant with the formal and informal policymaking system. When I want to lobby a legislator on a bill, I
frequently get on the telephone to a trusted friend who works the
corridors of the state capitol to find out what kind of reception I can
anticipate. My contact is also likely to know the best time and place
to act. The way to develop such ties is to be helpful in return when-

ever possible. For instance, if you are doing background research on an issue, you may have useful data to share with a lobbyist. There is one cardinal principle in this, which must never be broken: Be sure you know what you are talking about. Giving wrong information to a lobbyist or legislator is one sure way to end the relationship—permanently.

### Confidence

There is another asset that comes as a result of all the others: a belief in one's own abilities. In many ways it is a make-or-break factor. A sense of self-assurance is not something achieved entirely from a book or a course of study, though both may help. In a way, the best means of gaining confidence in lobbying is, as with so many things, to do a lot of it. As you discover for yourself that legislators are not ten feet tall, that you do know a great deal about an issue, and—perhaps most important—that you can survive a setback or two, your confidence will grow.

One of the most heartening parts of Lois Gibbs's story is what happened to this shy, retiring individual as a person. When she started out, she had a fairly shaky ego. She writes about her first attempt to interest her neighbors in taking action against the lethal dump underneath their homes:

> I went to 99th and Wheatfield and knocked on my first door. There was no answer. I just stood there, not knowing what to do. It was an unusually warm June day and I was perspiring. I thought: What am I doing here? I must be crazy. People are going to think I am. Go home, you fool! And that's just what I did. (Gibbs, 1982:13)

Within months this same woman was taking on highly placed officials in the U.S. Environmental Protection Agency and fielding questions on national television.

First-time advocates often assume that the legislator they are going to see will pepper them with difficult questions and generally make a fool of them. They are sometimes even a little disappointed when they are greeted by a warm, friendly, though usually noncommittal individual, who must be helped to understand the intricacies of the subject the advocate is so thoroughly steeped in.

A small, soft-spoken woman in one of my classes called the office of her state senator for an appointment. Expecting to get a secretary, she was surprised to find the senator himself on the other end of the line. He was obviously in no mood for small talk. When she stated her business, he suggested in a loud, unfriendly voice that there was no point in talking with him. Having come this far, she was not about to be turned away so easily. She waited for the tirade to subside, then asked quietly if she could come to see him. He finally gave her a few minutes the following week.

Back in the safety of the classroom she was still shaking from the ordeal and wondering if she should cancel the appointment. With the encouragement of the rest of the class, she agreed to carry through · with the task. When she did meet the senator, she was shocked to find him gracious and ready to give her an extended visit. She was not sure she had convinced him of her case, but her confidence in her ability to lobby had grown dramatically.

## *BEING REALISTIC ABOUT LIMITATIONS*

I am a little reluctant to talk about limitations because of my conviction that more people suffer from underconfidence than from overconfidence. However, it is necessary to acknowledge that one is up against formidable forces in the policy arena. When billions of dollars are at stake, as they are in the case of welfare policies and toxic waste disposal suits, for example, the interested parties are going to mobilize their resources accordingly.

We can take inspiration from the ability of a small group of Love Canal residents with very limited means to force concessions from the state of New York and very possibly from the Occidental Petroleum Company. To a significant extent, Lois Gibbs and her neighbors were lucky. They had an issue that seized the public's imagination and sympathy. Contrast this with the problem of the advocate for the welfare poor—stigmatized, viewed as hopeless, helpless, shiftless, or all three. If anything, public attention to the problem may make positive changes even more difficult.

At this point you may be prompted to ask, if it is so easy to have an impact, why doesn't it happen more often? You are right to be skeptical about the advocate's ability to make dramatic changes in a well-entrenched and powerful system. By being realistic about the limits of the feasible you can avoid the disillusionment that may follow exaggerated expectations.

Admittedly, we live in a political environment in which reactions to policy innovations often range from apathy to outright hostility. But people without the obvious trappings of power are able to make small changes that result in big improvements in people's lives—changes that warrant investing one's time and effort in policy advocacy.

This book will help you maximize your potential impact. That is different from saying the principles here are guaranteed to turn you into an effective advocate. At best, they can help you capitalize on the assets you already possess and will acquire as you go along. At some point, now or in the future, you will find that something you care very much about can be affected by a change in public policy. You will plunge in with intense commitment, take time away from other things if necessary, look for allies, organize your forces, and arm yourself with the necessary information. The willingness to invest yourself in this way cannot be manufactured, but your ability to translate the will into effective action can be cultivated.

## *POINTS TO REMEMBER*

1. Personal commitment to a cause is one of the most underestimated resources in advocacy. It is also entirely within your control.
2. Time, the availability of it and your use of it, is what translates your commitment into productive action.
3. Lobbying is not a solo activity. You must multiply your own strength by joining with kindred spirits. This may require balancing your agenda against items in someone else's.
4. Good organization and care in making sure the necessary supports are in place means maximum payoff for the investment. It enables relatively weak groups to have an impact on policy decisions.

5. A well-organized case, thoroughly grounded in solid information, is a critical element in successful lobbying. Another is knowledge of how and in what kind of environment decisions are made.

6. All of these elements are what give you confidence, perhaps the critical ingredient in lobbying.

# Chapter 2

# Setting the Action Agenda

Before one can map a course of action for change, it is necessary to answer the question, action for what? That sounds obvious, but too often advocacy groups neglect this important step. They are then vulnerable to divide-and-conquer strategies of a determined opponent. General goal statements, the kind that find their way into flyers and posters, are the easy part. It is much tougher to struggle with specific language that will ensure everyone is working in the same direction. The same principle applies to action by an individual advocate. Without a clear set of objectives, he or she is easily sidetracked or overwhelmed by the enormity of the task.

To avoid these problems, you should observe the four cardinal rules of agenda setting:

1. Know your agenda beforehand.
2. Decide between incremental and fundamental change goals.
3. Be clear about your priorities.
4. Develop fallback positions.

To see what can happen if you neglect these important rules, let us look at the plight of Betty and Brad Advocate: a tragedy in four acts.

*Act 1:* Betty and Brad corner Senator Artful in a corridor of the Capitol. They tell him they are very upset about the way women keep having babies and their boyfriends take no responsibility because they know single moms can always get welfare. "You have to do something about this mess," says Brad. He has been seeing on television and reading in the newspapers stories about families in urban America being destroyed by welfare. "What are you going to do

*Lobbying for Social Change*
© 2006 by The Haworth Press, Inc. All rights reserved
doi:10.1300/5782_03

about this?" they ask. "What do you want me to do?" asks Senator Artful. Betty and Brad look at each other. There is a lot of hemming and hawing, while the senator thanks them for coming by and walks away.

*Act II:* Brad tells Betty about a new bill in Congress, HR 13, that would provide funds to move mothers on welfare into mandatory job training. "We need to write to our congressman and get his support for HR 13," he says. Betty is appalled. "That's like putting a Band-Aid on a running sore," she says. "Job training without creating more jobs in the inner city is useless. We need a gigantic urban development program, one that will give hope to the people at the bottom. As long as that problem is neglected, a zillion job training programs are a waste of time." Brad disagrees, saying Betty's approach would take such a massive amount of money it would sink the economy. They finally decide the problem is so huge that there is little anybody can do about it.

*Act III:* A number of groups are now urging people to support HR 13 as a step in the right direction. Betty says they should support it. Brad says he is not so sure because he has seen one prediction that the program would cost billions in the coming years. "That is going to make the federal deficit worse," says Brad. "But if we can do something about the welfare problem, it is worth it," Betty replies. They get into an argument and end up not speaking to each other.

*Act IV:* To pick up the votes of several conservative senators, HR 13 has been changed from a comprehensive job training program to five demonstration projects running over the next two years. Brad says the original bill has been gutted, and it would be worse to pass HR 13 in its amended form than to take no action. "This will allow them to claim they've done something and kill any chance of a real attack on the welfare problem." "Are you kidding?" asks Betty. "If we give up now it will send the wrong signal. They'll figure we don't care about the problem, and if we don't, they won't." By the time Betty and Brad decide whether to support the watered-down HR 13, it has been voted down by the House.

Unlike Shakespeare, the drama of public policy has no final curtain, it just goes on and on. That is part of the frustration: One is never finished with the work of fighting for better policies.

Betty and Brad Advocate have failed to observe the four cardinal rules of agenda setting. Let's take them one at a time.

## RULE 1: KNOW YOUR AGENDA

Knowing what you want sounds simple, but it is a step that is all too frequently ignored in advocacy. In the first scenario, Betty and Brad never got beyond being angry over the welfare problem. They could tell the senator at length about the terrible conditions in America's inner cities. They were also keeping up on coverage of the issue in the mass media. Unfortunately, the media usually tell us what is wrong without saying much about what would improve things. The Advocates have to get beyond that point and define what they would like to see happen. Fumbling in the senator's office is not the only problem that can occur. Suppose someone else comes along with a family therapy program they claim will salvage inner-city families. Will Betty or Brad latch on to that "solution"? By knowing where you want to go, you are less likely to be talked into backing someone else's agenda, one that may have little to do with seriously attacking the problem you started with.

One advantage the antiabortion activists have is that they are crystal clear about their agenda: Stop abortion under any circumstances. Other interest groups, including many pro-choice activists, are much less certain about what would be a desirable policy. They have no trouble saying what they are against: the adamant position of the antiabortionists. But abortion on demand at any point during pregnancy? There are feminists who hold out for that, but many pro-choice activists have trouble with that position. Abortion on demand up to the point at which the fetus could survive outside the womb is a goal without wide support, but it can expand the support base.

Particularly as one enlists others to fight for a cause, it is essential to establish a common ground. The group must arrive at a position that all can live with comfortably. Otherwise, various members can send different messages, sowing the seeds of dissension within the group and confusion in the minds of those on the outside.

Spending proposals are always hard to sell. When the product is mental health services, the problems are compounded. Lawmakers

who will allocate billions for military hardware without blinking an
eye suddenly become very protective of the taxpayer's money when it
comes to human services. Not only do mental health programs smack
of a tax-and-spend welfare state mentality, but psychiatry is still a
mysterious realm to many members of the public. It is one thing to
feed the starving, house the homeless, and treat cancer patients, but
quite another to pay people high salaries to talk to other people about
their problems, prescribe exotic medications, organize therapy groups,
and create halfway houses.

So one must be clear about what is being sought—and be able to
explain this to others in plain English. The legislator asks, "What exactly do you propose to do with this money if we appropriate it? Why
does it take that much? Do you have any evidence that these programs
actually work?" These are legitimate questions that deserve good answers. The process starts with one's own clarity about what is being
sought.

In a society accustomed to thinking of poor people, especially
public assistance recipients, as lazy ne'er-do-wells, simplistic answers such as cutting people off the welfare rolls or assigning them
to menial jobs to work off their grants are especially appealing. Issues of race and class are usually involved. Champions of welfare
rights tend to be thrown on the defensive, so that they devote more
energy to answering the critics than to thinking through what sorts
of policies they favor.

"You don't approve of workfare? Just what do you propose to get
people off welfare—or do you favor making welfare a permanent
way of life?" Later we will consider ways of dealing with such questions. At this point we are looking at another issue: the need for the
pro-welfare forces to think the problem through and come up with a
clear agenda. Do they support the main thrust of a proposed work
and training program but propose safeguards against exploitation?
Do they favor a totally voluntary approach to participation by clients? Do they feel priority should be given to day care, transportation, and other support services? Do they favor an increase in welfare grants? Do they support a new program even if it leads to
automatic cuts in other means-tested programs such as housing and
food stamps?

The residents of Love Canal were angry and frightened—so angry and frightened that in the beginning they had trouble articulating specific goals. On one hand, it was tempting to want revenge on the villain, the Hooker Chemical Company, and its parent corporation, Occidental Petroleum. On the other hand, offers of a quick settlement on terms that were to the residents' disadvantage were also hard to resist. One of the main challenges for the leaders of the Love Canal Homeowners' Association was to figure out what they wanted. But without a clear conception of their goal they would have been an easy mark for other interests wanting to use the residents' plight for their own purposes.

By focusing on demands to be relocated and receive adequate compensation for their homes, the LCHA leaders could keep the members energized and united over the long haul. The specific objective was less important than the fact that they knew what they were after and were able to communicate this to others.

## RULE 2: DECIDE BETWEEN INCREMENTAL AND FUNDAMENTAL CHANGE GOALS

One may believe in the need for radical change in the long run yet work for improvements within the existing structure in the interim. In order to lobby effectively, one should be clear about which of these is being sought now, since some incremental and fundamental changes may work against each other. Making modest improvements in the status quo may simply create the illusion that real change has taken place. Conversely, by holding out for total victory, you may lose an opportunity to make tangible gains. On the surface this may seem similar to Rule 1. But whereas the previous problem was a matter of lack of clarity, this issue involves a dilemma between strategies for working toward the agreed-upon goal.

Betty and Brad Advocate are on the horns of a familiar dilemma. They know that their ultimate aim is saving the family in inner-city America, but they are unsure about how to approach the problem. Do they focus on job training programs, a stop gap approach according to Betty's way of thinking, or do they work for a massive economic development program? Either approach could be considered "right," in the sense that it has the potential for reducing the poverty of some families. The two strategies are not inherently incompatible; Betty and Brad could work on both levels simultaneously. They are aware that Congress is unlikely to invest large amounts of resources in both, so in effect it is an either/or situation. Unfortunately, the Advocates end up not making a choice—which is, in reality, a choice not to act.

*          *          *

In the mid-1960s, the pro-choice forces in California became split over the issue of abortion as a right versus liberalized abortion policies under the control of the medical profession. The proponents of repeal of the state's abortion law, the more "radical" faction, saw the issue in terms of the second-class status of women. As one put it, "When we talk about women's rights, we can get all the rights in the world—the right to vote, the right to go to school—and none of them means a doggone thing if we don't own the flesh we stand in. . . ." (Luker, 1984:97).

Those who favored reform of the law included members of the male-dominated medical and legal professions, who sought to ease what they considered to be archaic restrictions. The abortion reform act, passed in 1967, left intact the principle that abortion should be allowed only under circumstances considered harmful to the woman. Discretion was left in the hands of the doctor. Although this did not deal directly with the issue of women's status as rights-bearing citizens, what followed was, in effect, abortion on demand. Of the women who sought abortions, over 99 percent got them. The number of legal abortions in California escalated rapidly, and, says Luker, medical control of abortion became a legal fiction (1984:94).

Was the repeal faction wrong? One might argue that way if abortion is considered in isolation. But the repealers were part of a much larger movement, and undoubtedly their strong stand helped mobilize forces that might otherwise have lain dormant. During the abortion fight in California of the mid-1960s, they and the reformers needed to be clear about what they were after. Opposed to them was a powerful political force, the antiabortionists, who had no such dilemmas.

The tragedy at Love Canal helped speed the passage in 1980 of the Superfund legislation to clean up toxic waste sites around the country (see Zuesse, 1981; U.S. Senate, 1979). The act did not provide for compensating victims of pollution, such as members of the Love Canal Homeowners' Association. The Superfund was an example of incremental change, in the sense that it focused on cleaning up existing lethal dumps and offering industry incentives to stop polluting. It left untouched a market system under which government regulates privately run corporations, offers them incentives, and helps clean up their messes, but doesn't take outright control of the production process—to have changed this system would have represented fundamental change.

*       *       *

Who is to say which is better, incremental or fundamental change? There are arguments for each. As an advocate the important thing is that you know what kind of strategy you are following, because tactics that promote incremental change could be seen as undermining the potential for fundamental change. Or vice versa.

## RULE 3: BE CLEAR ABOUT YOUR PRIORITIES

Brad Advocate cares a lot about the inner-city family. He also cares about other issues, including the size of the federal deficit. Brad and Betty are treating the problem as an either/or proposition. In so doing they have created a false dilemma. Some economists say we cannot expand social programs, because to do so would simply add to the federal budget deficit. However, there are other ways of reducing the federal deficit than cutting back on social programs. We can reduce other expenditures, such as the amount we spend on weapons systems. Taxes can be raised, which many politicians agree to privately but not publicly. Further, some economists say the federal deficit is a phony issue (see Eisner, 1986). The real dilemma for Betty and Brad is that they have several priorities and can't agree on which comes first.

There are several ways in which confusion about priorities can get in the way of effective advocacy. Here we look at four common situations, which I shall call: "You Can't Have It Both Ways," "Getting Justice or Getting Results," "Trade-offs," and "Whose Agenda Are We Working On?"

## You Can't Have It Both Ways

Unlike the false dilemma that Brad and Betty have erected in their path, there are times when one must choose between alternative goals. One can't support greater freedom of choice for pregnant women wanting an abortion *and* restrictions designed to protect the fetus. For the antiabortion activists this presents no problem. "Protect the fetus at all costs," they say. Some people who identify with the feminist position on most issues have moral qualms about abortion. As long as they are unable to resolve this dilemma, they will be immobilized.

Some issues may pose either/or questions in practical terms, even though, strictly speaking, there are alternatives. For example, a large percentage of chronically mentally ill people live in nursing or boarding homes under very poor conditions. Most states have done an inadequate job of regulating these privately run operations, but one argument against cracking down on them is that this would reduce the supply of an urgently needed resource. Not surprisingly, the operators are often the ones who pose this concern. But it *is* a real problem, at least in the short run. Unless the state legislature is willing to spend large sums to develop alternative housing for the mentally ill, the supply may indeed go down as a result of strict enforcement of stringent rules. The lobbyist must think this issue through if he or she is not to be left fumbling when a state legislator asks, "What would you do if you were in my shoes?"

## Getting Justice or Getting Results

Justice is never retroactive, and the way to avoid injustice is to prevent it in the first place. Redressing wrongs through the courts, aside from the expensive, prolonged, and inefficient process involved, rarely ends up truly balancing the scales. Party A can sue Party B for a fatal accident that killed Party A's wife, but that will never restore her to life. The starting point in public policy is now, after damage may have already been done. The task of the advocate is to move on and reduce the likelihood of future damage.

The Love Canal residents' sense of outrage at the Hooker Chemical Company was understandable. Lawsuits against Hooker had a dual purpose: getting reimbursed for the costs—economic, physical, and mental—of the toxic waste dumping, and getting back at the company for what it had done. Having to pay punitive damages may act as a deterrent to future dumping, in which case something practical will have been achieved. But that can never really undo the damage.

Vengeance is a powerful motivator. The death penalty is presented as a deterrent to future crime, but it clearly has another function: satisfying the lust for revenge. Nations rally their populations to wage war by appealing to that same emotion.

The leaders of the Love Canal Homeowners' Association could have been drawn into an abortive contest with Hooker Chemical, trying to match their limited resources against those of a sprawling multinational corporation. They wisely kept their sights on something more practical: being compensated for the damage they had suffered and getting help toward making a new start in a new location. As they became big news in the national media, Lois Gibbs and her neighbors had an opportunity to make Hooker look bad in the public eye. It is doubtful that the company or its parent corporation, Occidental Petroleum, would have suffered greatly from this kind of campaign. Since Hooker sold its products to other industries, not to the public, it would have been hard to hurt the company through public pressure. And in time, the resident leaders would have had trouble keeping their followers involved if the only satisfaction they could offer was an outlet for anger.

The wish for revenge sometimes leads activists to make threats of reprisal at the polls against an unsympathetic lawmaker. Opponents of a punitive welfare reform bill vowed retaliation against a state senator who talked initially as if he would vote against the legislation, then appeared to betray the cause at the last minute. In so doing, they ran the risk of demonstrating their own weakness and his power by failing in their attempt to dump him in the next election. The threat of political reprisal is indeed a powerful weapon if one can deliver on the promise. But such threats should always be based on careful assessment of one's political resources and the legislator's, not on an angry reaction.

### Trade-offs

As they work their way through the legislative process, bills often pick up "sweeteners"—amendments designed to attract this or that pocket of votes. One state welfare reform proposal included a 5 percent across-the-board increase in public assistance grants *and* a limit of three months' aid per year for certain categories of needy. Pro-welfare advocates had to decide whether they were willing to accept the tightened eligibility as a necessary price of more adequate aid, or to lose the aid by getting legislators to vote down the entire bill. Later, this same proposal was packaged together with state support of child welfare services (urgently sought by certain pro-welfare groups) and an antiabortion rider (which would appeal to Catholics who had opposed the original bill).

A 1988 welfare reform bill in Congress included sections

1. making an optional provision for assistance to two-parent families mandatory throughout the country,
2. allowing states to force mothers with children as young as one year old to go into work and training programs,
3. requiring states to provide day care and other support services to working and training participants,
4. automatically ordering employers to withhold child support payments from their employees' paychecks, regardless of whether the worker was willing to make payments, and
5. requiring that minors live with a parent or guardian to be eligible for assistance.

The bill was clearly a mixed bag with some things the welfare advocates wanted and some things they opposed. It was necessary to decide what one was willing to trade off in one area in order to make gains elsewhere.

A Pennsylvania mental health reform bill would have made it easier to hospitalize the mentally ill against their will *and* expanded community-based services. Mental health consumers' organizations badly wanted the latter but were unwilling to accept the new rules making institutionalization easier. After trying unsuccessfully to convince the chief sponsor of the bill to separate the two components, they decided to oppose the total package.

There is no simple rule for deciding what to trade off for something else. One must look carefully at a piece of legislation, decide what is the most important priority, and decide what is an acceptable cost for obtaining the desired policy.

## Whose Agenda Are We Working On?

Coalitions multiply an individual's power many times over. To gain the benefits of coalition politics, it is necessary to serve other people's purposes as well as one's own. The original objectives must not be lost in this process. At one point, the New York State right-to-life movement joined forces with other groups whose main goal was opposition to school busing for racial integration (Shapiro, 1972). Each faction needed the support of the other. As long as each was clear as to how the alliance would further its own goals, the relationship could work effectively.

When ultra-conservatives adopted the right-to-life movement, according to Paige (1983), it was with the idea of exploiting this rich source of voting strength for its own conservative agenda. Both factions shared a conservative worldview, so were natural allies. For the right-to-lifers, with their single, specific goal, there was one major criterion in assessing the relationship: How did it affect progress toward the elimination of abortion? This involved more than simply the need not to be diverted to other right-wing concerns, to the neglect of the abortion issue. The right-to lifers also had to be mindful about the impact their romance with the political right would have on other potential allies in the abortion fight. Indeed, the Catholic bishops, with their broad social reform agenda including foreign policy and liberal social programs, became concerned about the ties to the far right.

Fear of being manipulated by others may threaten or prevent alliances. The Love Canal Homeowners' Association had trouble achieving a close working relationship with renters, who felt they were being used to protect their neighbors' investment in their homes. Similarly, mental health consumers may fear that they are being used by professionals to protect the latter's jobs. The welfare poor may come to view social work activists as being interested only in protecting their own jobs, researchers as wanting to exploit them as subjects, and liberal politicians as merely pandering for votes. However, as long as any such secondary aims are presented up front, the fact that people have more than one kind of motivation doesn't mean they can't be effective in pushing for a common goal.

The plight of the Love Canal residents was an appealing story, a natural for the national news media and a variety of advocacy groups, each with its own special set of concerns. There is a seductive quality to becoming an overnight celebrity. Lois Gibbs, who made good copy, not only had to keep her sights on her goal but also deal with the inevitable backbiting from others who saw the whole thing as an ego trip. Ralph Nader and Jane Fonda helped draw public attention to the Love Canal tragedy, but their primary purpose was putting the spotlight on a national scandal, not salvaging the lives of Gibbs and her neighbors. The Love Canal residents could have made the national issue of toxic waste their main agenda, saying in effect that what endangers people in Louisiana, Michigan, and California endangers everyone, and unless we deal with the national or even international problem of environmental pollution, we will never be safe. But once they had decided to focus on their own needs as a local community, that was where they had to devote their energies. They then had to gain whatever leverage they could from people such as Nader and Fonda without losing sight of their own purpose.

I am not saying that local interests should always trump national and international concerns. The Love Canal residents might have decided that they had the leverage to make significant inroads on the national problem of environmental pollution and serve their own personal interests simultaneously. The point is that they had to decide where to put their emphasis.

One should always be ready to support the interests of allies, when they are consistent with one's own values and priorities—but then it is doubly important to understand what is in it for everybody. An ally who appears to have no purpose other than being helpful should be viewed with a skeptical eye.

## RULE 4: DEVELOP FALLBACK POSITIONS

The first three rules concern one's initial position: what one would work toward under ideal conditions. But conditions are never ideal. No policy proposal ever comes out of the decision process the way it went in. One must be prepared to compromise. At what point is the original proposal so watered down as to be meaningless—or even worse than meaningless if the illusion of progress has been created, thereby lulling everybody back to sleep?

Our luckless lobbyists, Brad and Betty Advocate, can't decide whether to continue promoting HR 13, now pared down to a few pilot projects, or reject it as actually undermining efforts toward a real attack on the problem of poor families. Without any fallback positions, they stew over the issue until it is too late. It is not possible to anticipate exactly how an original proposal will be altered during deliberation, but it is possible to decide what kinds of changes would still retain enough of the original intent to make it worth fighting for.

The groups seeking to liberalize California's abortion law faced this kind of dilemma in 1967, when Governor Ronald Reagan threatened to veto their bill. The existing law stipulated that abortion could be allowed only when the woman's life was in danger. The reformers wanted to broaden this to include the condition of the fetus as grounds for an abortion. The reform campaign had been spurred on in part by a celebrated thalidomide case, in which a number of pregnant woman had unknowingly used a drug known to cause severe fetal deformities. Concern about the effects of rubella on the fetus had also gained wide attention. Reagan said he would veto the reform bill unless references to "fetal indications" were removed. The notion that one would destroy a fetus, not to save the mother but merely to produce a whole child, was the most offensive provision in the eyes of anti-abortionists (Luker, 1984:88-89).

After determining that Reagan meant what he said and there were not enough votes to override his veto, the pro-reform forces agreed to the modification. At this point the main movers were not militant feminists but doctors, lawyers, and even California's Young Republicans, so there was little danger that the compromise would cause a revolt in the ranks of the reformers. As it turned out, the concession had little impact on the main thrust of the new law. In effect, California had adopted something very close to abortion-on-demand.

Following the 1973 Supreme Court decision, the right-to-life movement campaigned for a constitutional amendment declaring that life begins at conception, thus fetuses at whatever stage of development have a right to life, liberty, etc. Amending the Constitution is a long, laborious, and expensive proposition. When it became clear that this strategy would cost more than it would gain, the right-to-lifers switched to adding antiabortion amendments to other legislation. They were able to limit Medicaid payments for abortions. In many states the antiabortion lobby sought obstructive measures, such as the requirement that the father participate in the abortion decision and that parental consent be obtained. None of these detracted from the main thrust, since all would make it harder to obtain an abortion. These were also ways of keeping the movement alive and providing political experience for antiabortion activists looking toward the day when more stringent rules against abortion could be enacted. On the other hand, by implicitly conceding that abortion was legitimate under certain circumstances, they might have alienated some of their bedrock supporters.

Legislation rarely specifies how its intent is to be carried out. That is left to regulations to be written by the department charged with implementing the law. The people who promoted the Community Mental Health Centers Act of 1963 wanted the federal government to subsidize professional salaries in the centers. The American Medical Association fought this provision, fearful of "socialized medicine," and that particular provision was dropped from the final bill (Brown, 1985:41).

The mental health advocates envisioned a bold departure from traditional practice in the centers, but as a concession to the psychiatric profession, the final version required that each center be headed by a psychiatrist. As spelled out by President John F. Kennedy, the intent was that a broad array of community mental health services would supplant state hospitals with community-based services. The language on this point was intentionally vague, averting potential resistance from the states (Chu and Trotter, 1974).

Were the proponents of change right in accepting these concessions, or should they have refused to go along, possibly leading to the defeat of the measure? Some observers feel too much was lost, implying that a firm stand for principle would have been wiser, even at the risk of having to start all over (see Brown, 1985). As it turned out, President Lyndon Johnson was able to add a provision for federal funding of professional salaries, so the particular concessions made little difference. But by placing psychiatrists firmly in control of center operations and leaving the state role vague, the Community Mental Health Centers Act resulted in a system markedly different from that which the reformers had originally envisioned.

In the fight over President Richard Nixon's Family Assistance Plan (FAP) in the early 1970s, welfare rights advocates came out against the bill because of the low level at which assistance grants were to be pegged. This would have been below existing levels in several northern states with high housing costs. However, passage of the bill, even with the very low assistance payments, would have accomplished much that the welfare rights forces were after by establishing a national plan with national standards and aid based on need, not on arbitrary categories. The law's effects in the Deep South could have been revolutionary in reducing the power of Caucasians over African Americans living in poverty.

After the defeat of the first FAP the administration came back with FAP II. When this bill faced almost certain defeat it was stripped of most of the provisions for reforming aid to young families in an effort to save other parts of the measure. Included in the law as enacted was a single national scheme, Supplemental Security Income (SSI), for all public assistance categories (with states having the option of supplementing the base amount) except Aid to Families with Dependent Children (AFDC). The latter remained a state-by-state program with different eligibility requirements and widely disparate levels of assistance. The revised bill also set up a series of demonstration projects to test the concept of a negative income tax (guaranteed minimum income) system. Note that welfare rights supporters could have stopped enactment of this watered-down measure, but should they have supported the changed bill, as a step forward? Conceivably, it may have been a step backward from the perspective of the welfare rights movement. By creating a national system for other assistance categories, including the blind, the disabled, and the elderly—dependent populations most likely to gain public sympathy—the act further isolated the highly stigmatized AFDC population. This is the program whose clients and their supporters made up the core of the welfare rights movement.

As for the negative income tax experiments, these yielded ambiguous results, which were then used to support arguments on all sides of the welfare question. Welfare rights proponents had little to gain, and maybe something to lose, from supporting the final revision of FAP II.

The residents of Love Canal faced a different dilemma in the offers by Occidental Petroleum to settle lawsuits out of court. By agreeing to this, the residents could save legal fees and be assured of getting partial redress without waiting for many years. But they would give up the possibility of being awarded higher amounts of money. And from a societal standpoint, out-of-court settlements don't set legal precedents, thus cannot serve as a legal standard in future lawsuits against toxic dumpers. Out-of-court settlements are also less likely to deter would-be dumpers.

These examples suggest a set of general principles for determining when a particular fallback position is warranted. Although each case will be different, and it is not possible to predict the specific modifications that will be introduced in the midst of the policymaking process, the following questions may help you in thinking about the matter.

1. *Is the essence of the original proposal retained, or does the new version undermine the original intent?* It can be argued that welfare rights supporters would have been further ahead by enacting FAP I, despite its stingy provisions and requirements, because of the structural changes that would have been enacted. Conversely, some observers argue that NIMH and other community mental health advocates gave up too much ground in seeking enactment of the Community Mental Health Centers Act of 1963. By acceding to President Reagan's veto threat, California abortion reformers managed to enact a bill which might have had tougher sledding a few years later; the modification did little to affect the widened access to abortion contained in the legislation.

2. *Does the new version set a precedent for future action toward the ultimate goal, or weaken the impetus for action by creating an*

*illusion of change?* Getting the federal government into the community mental health field paved the way for future expansion, despite the lack of federal support for professional staffing in the original bill. Conversely, a liberalized national welfare scheme for the blind, disabled, and elderly may have been a setback for AFDC recipients. The series of negative income tax experiments may have sounded to some welfare rights advocates like an exciting opportunity to promote such a plan, but they did little to advance their cause in the end.

3. *Will acceptance of "half a loaf" help to sustain momentum and morale in a movement, or alienate potential supporters by appearing to be a sellout?* The Love Canal community leaders were constantly under pressure from a variety of sources. Some neighbors wanted to get the matter settled and resented the idea of holding out for bigger gains. Others felt their needs were being neglected, for example, renters who were afraid the homeowners would look out only for their own interests. In accepting or rejecting offers from public officials and Hooker Chemical, the advocates had to weigh the impact on these factions.

Right-to-lifers saw the series of partial steps toward restriction of abortion in the 1970s and 1980s as a means of keeping the rank and file energized and the opposition on the defensive.

Sound pretty straightforward? "Just follow those four simple principles and your lobbying agenda will become clear." Except in real life, nothing goes according to script. Let's look at agenda setting in relation to an actual low-income urban public school system on the verge of collapse. You are coming in at a point when a lot of damage has already been done. You can't rewrite history or wish it away.

## AN EXERCISE IN AGENDA SETTING

The following exercise can be used by an individual or a group to try developing an action agenda. It is based on the experience of an actual urban school district. As of this writing, the issues are still very much up in the air.

### The School District

This district serves a city of 35,000 and two smaller communities adjacent to it. The city is not only the most poverty-stricken in the state but is one of the three poorest municipalities in the United States. Once a thriving manufacturing center, it has seen its industrial base shrink to a fraction of what it was only a few decades ago. The economic decline has been accompanied by an erosion of the basic infrastructure, in which its predominantly African-American population is beset by crime, drug abuse, family breakdown, poor housing, and so forth. The litany is all too familiar. Political corruption has also taken a toll.

In terms of educational achievement, this district ranks last among all the school districts in the state. Superintendents and high school principals have come and gone at the rate of about one a year. After years of mismanagement, corruption, and politicization, the state stepped in to run the schools. A three-member board of control was appointed to administer the system. Meanwhile, the elected school board has been left with virtually no function.

### Where Things Sit Now

The current board of control, the latest in a succession, was appointed for five-year terms by the outgoing state secretary of education, and the legislature locked things in by making it impossible to remove the board members except "for cause" (e.g., a flagrant ethical violation).

A number of charter schools have been created to fill the vacuum. Currently about one-fourth to one-third of the student population attends a charter school, a private or parochial school, or is home-schooled. The larger of the two remaining charter schools has an extensive operation on the city's east side and plans to expand to the west side of town. Its students have consistently performed better on standardized tests than those in district schools. The second charter school has trailed district schools in student performance.

Charter schools, unlike private or parochial schools, draw off district funds as well as students. The district is required to pay tuition to charters. Originally there was a cap on charter school enrollment, but that was removed two years ago by the board of control.

A few years ago, a private firm was brought in to run nine of the district's ten schools. That experiment ended this year, amid a lot of finger pointing on all sides.

Now the district faces the problem of taking over administration of the system. It does so with an added handicap: After years of deficit spending and a growing debt, the district is being required by the state to operate with a balanced budget. That has resulted in elimination of many supportive services and sharp reductions in others, class sizes averaging thirty-five, and loss of administrative staff.

The latest cuts will result in the loss of ninety positions, half of them classroom teachers. The teachers' union, far from being a militant force, has limited its role to helping determine the order in which staff would be dropped. Not surprisingly, teacher morale is low. Absenteeism has also been a problem.

As a way of coping with its financial problems, the board of control is planning to sell off its administrative building and two elementary schools. One of the schools was closed, due to its deteriorated condition, and its students transferred to another elementary school. The local university is seeking to purchase the other and run it as a charter school. That would, of course, increase the drain of funds as well as students from the school district.

I should point out that the board of control is not a monolith. One member has been a strong critic of the two-member majority who vote together on most issues.

The state education secretary, who has nominal jurisdiction over the board of control but little power to change things, has warned the board that sale of the buildings and failure to reinstitute limits on charter school enrollment could bring on the demise of the whole public school system. The acting school superintendent, who was appointed by the secretary of education, concurs with the secretary's judgment.

Meanwhile, community agencies, organizations, churches, and colleges and universities, both within the district and in nearby suburbs, have been trying to fill the gap in recent years by offering a variety of after-school and other support programs. Although these efforts have helped some students, overall they have had little impact on the situation.

Looming in the background is President George W. Bush's No Child Left Behind (NCLB) initiative. The urban school district we have been looking at is a prime example of a primary concern of NCLB: poor student academic performance in core curriculum areas, as measured by standardized test scores. Not surprisingly, this has resulted in primary emphasis on teaching to the test, and, in at least one case, charges of a school administrator's cheating on the tests by giving students the answers.

In the most recent testing for which data are available, a majority of students at all grade levels failed to pass math and reading tests. Because of its failure to make sufficient progress over recent years in this regard, the district, already under state control, has been placed on "restructuring" status. Restructuring status under NCLB calls for extreme action, up to and including transferring students to other districts, firing teachers and administrators, and turning schools into charter schools. So far, school districts in neighboring communities have refused to accept student transfers out of this district.

A major criticism of Bush's initiative has been the lack of sufficient federal funding to make the vision a reality. States have been reluctant to step in to fill the money gap. As it is, a deep and worsening financial crisis is a major handicap for the local school district we have been studying.

### Picking a Place to Focus

If the foregoing account is a little confusing, that's par for the course. Your first task, then, is to go back and sort out all those overlapping problems. You must decide which among these have priority.

Start by settling on your overall goals. Do you want to help the existing system (and the existing leadership) deal with the practical and immediate problems of finding more money and raising test scores, but leave things pretty much intact? Do you want to use this current crisis as an opportunity to press for more fundamental reforms? If so, should these be within the present structure (e.g., removing the current members of the board of control and replacing them with new blood), or should they involve a restructuring of the local district (e.g., getting rid of the board of control altogether and returning control to an elected school board)? You may instead decide to mobilize the community in a grassroots movement that would create an ongoing way of monitoring and pressuring whoever is running things. Or should your agenda include a combination of these approaches?

You may, of course, decide that you don't have enough information on which to base an agenda. In that case, think about what additional information you would need and how you would go about getting it. Once you've settled on an agenda, of course, you will be gathering more information as you plan your strategy. More on that in Chapters 4 and 5.

## POINTS TO REMEMBER

1. Be clear about what you want. Go beyond saying what you don't want, to deciding what you would like in its place.
2. Decide whether you are working for incremental change, which would leave in place the existing basic structure, or whether you feel drastic change of a fundamental sort is necessary. By opting for incremental steps you are not writing off fundamental change as an ultimate goal, but your energies will be devoted to working within the existing framework, at least for the time being.
3. Stay focused on your priorities. What are you willing to trade off on behalf of your goal? Avoid setting up an either/or choice when you don't have to, but keep your eyes on your own priorities in the process of working on other people's goals. Do not let yourself be distracted by the wish for revenge or personal distaste for a potential ally.
4. Think through the implications of making concessions: Will accepting half a loaf now help move your agenda ahead later, or make it harder to achieve in the end?

# Chapter 3

# Understanding Policymakers

Action agendas must be translated into decisions, so who can make the right decision and who can persuade that decision maker are critical questions. As the following true story reveals, the actual channels of influence are often not the obvious ones.

Senator Daniel Inouye of Hawaii was under intense pressure as he prepared to attend a meeting of the Senate Appropriations Committee one July morning in 1976. So he did what is standard practice under the circumstances: he turned to his legislative aide and asked her about the vote on the Condor missile program. It was a good plan and should be supported, she told him. Accordingly, he voted for approval of the controversial project, in which the Navy had already invested more than $300 million over a thirteen-year period.

What Senator Inouye didn't know was that the aide's recommendation was the result of months of intensive lobbying by a representative of Rockwell International, the nation's tenth largest defense contractor, in collaboration with Navy officers (Finney, 1976). Rockwell knew there was little point in working on the senator directly, since the liberal Democrat's state had virtually no defense industries. Instead, their representative focused his attention on the staff person who was relied on by the senator for defense information. There was no exchange of money, no promise of favors for the aide. The lobbyist simply made it a point to impress the aide with the merits of the project and provide her with language to insert in the final version of the appropriations bill. At strategic times, Navy personnel were enlisted to add their support. The Navy also had a stake in the matter.

The point of this story is not that lawmakers always rely on their aides for advice—in fact, the role of the congressional staff person

*Lobbying for Social Change*
© 2006 by The Haworth Press, Inc. All rights reserved.
doi:10.1300/5782_04

varies greatly. Rather, it is that advocates need to know whom to court when they are trying to influence decisions. Amateur advocates are sometimes disappointed that they "only" got to talk with an aide to their representative. The pros, like the Rockwell representative, know better. To whom should you direct your arguments? The answer is one you will find frequently in this book: It all depends.


## PICKING THE RIGHT TARGET

A first approximation in selecting targets is to think about who can have the greatest impact on policy decisions. Equally important for you as an advocate is your own access to policymakers. Fortunately for you, as the Inouye story shows so clearly, your potential influence doesn't depend solely on direct contact with policymakers.

### *Elected versus Appointed Officials*

We are most aware of the legislative phase of policymaking because it is most exposed to public scrutiny and lends high drama to the process. The president or the governor sends a message to the legislative branch outlining a new proposal, and a bill embracing the plan is submitted for consideration. The news media immediately seek legislative leaders of the two parties to get their reactions. Committee deliberations on the measure may be public, with various interests using the occasion to get their views across to the voters. Even when a bill has little general interest, it may be of intense concern to various factions. By their votes in committee and on the floor, representatives and senators establish their voting records, which may promote their political fortunes or come back to haunt them later. It can also be payback time, a chance to show one's appreciation for past support from well-heeled interests and assure more of the same in the future.

Committee assignments of lawmakers can be a critical factor in determining their influence on issues of concern to you. Universities have had to learn that. Researchers discovered that when a university is located in the home state of a member of the Senate Appropriations Committee, investing one dollar in lobbying for federal research grants pays off eleven- to seventeenfold. That means that the average "return on the investment" in such cases is $11-17 for every dollar spent on lobbying. In the House of Representatives, the payoff is twice as big. Having someone on the House Appropriations Committee results in $20-36 for every dollar spent. But if a university happens not to be located in one of these congressional districts, its return on the lobbying investment is zero, as far as federal research money is concerned (de Figueiredo and Silverman, 2002).

The bill is passed, always in modified form, the chief executive (governor or president) has his or her picture taken signing the measure into law, flanked by smiling legislative leaders, and the policymaking process is over. Or is it? Legislation is necessarily written in broad, general, and sometimes ambiguous language. The real policy, the sets of rules that will determine who gets what and under what conditions, is now hammered out by people no one elected and most never heard of. The writing of regulations is little understood by the public. But the officials responsible for doing the writing have the final say about what goes into the regulations. If this suggests to you that these appointed officials are important policymakers, it is an accurate perception.

If you are going to be an effective advocate, you must understand what makes elected representatives and appointed officials tick. Both are potential targets of your lobbying activity.

## Elected Officials

In general, you have the greatest access to policymakers who officially represent you. Not only is it the essence of democracy that they listen to what you have to say, but you are, directly or indirectly, the one they depend on for keeping their jobs. That is clearest with your state representative, who has two functions: to enact policies that benefit the majority of constituents, and to assist with personal needs of individual constituents. Thus, responsiveness is built into the relationship, at least in theory. As you become known to this and other policymakers as well informed and strongly committed, your access will grow.

It is good to learn the names, addresses, and telephone numbers—both in the local district and in the state or national capital—of each person who represents you: two U.S. senators and a U.S. representative, a state senator and representative, and local council members in whose district you reside. (Some local government lawmakers are elected at-large, and so represent all the citizens.)

Find out what committees or subcommittees your representatives chair or serve on. Do not be surprised if you find you are a constituent of some very powerful people. The president, your state's governor, and the local chief executive should be on your list.

I might be inclined to make less of a point of this if it had not been for an almost-tragedy in my own experience. I was visiting state legislative offices about an issue, very soon after I had moved from another state. I had seen frequent mention in the news media about a state senator in my county and jumped to the conclusion that I was in his district. I was lucky enough to find out the identity of my own senator from a friendly representative a short time before I was scheduled to visit the wrong senator's office. I would have felt ridiculous lobbying the wrong person—more important, I would have undermined my credibility as an advocate.

The nice thing about direct contact with your representative is that the more of it you have, the more significant you become to that person. It doesn't take too long for you to become known, usually on a first-name basis, not only to the representative but also to his or her staff. And never underestimate the importance of being on good terms with receptionists and other clerical staff.

It is not necessary to agree with the representative's political views, but you must treat everybody with respect—the way you would want to be treated by a constituent if you were in the other person's shoes. Regardless of your position on issues, at the very least you are part of the representative's reelection calculus. A well-informed visitor or letter writer, especially one who shows a persistent interest in a problem, is known to be the kind of person who will remember their representative on election day. In Chapter 6 we will look at direct lobbying in more detail.

### Working Through an Intermediary

As Senator Inouye's experience so clearly shows, there are times when a staff member is a better audience for your information than the legislator, in whose eyes you are less likely to be an information source than a vote in the next election. For this reason, I find it useful to talk about two kinds of targets: ultimate targets, whose decisions you are trying to influence, and intermediate targets, who transmit the message to the real quarry.

When reaching a decision maker through an intermediary, it is necessary to keep in mind that you are actually dealing with two audiences: the contact person and the ultimate target you may never speak to. What will make an impact on the aide and what will influence the policymaker are not the same. As you have contact with a representative and his or her staff over time, you will get to know what kinds of arguments are most effective with both.

Some legislative aides are very well informed about policy content. However, you may be talking with a person whose greatest expertise is in dealing with constituents' complaints or keeping local interest groups happy. The latter is most likely to be the case with state legislators' staffs and home district staffs of U.S. senators and representatives. It is not always easy to gauge how much a staff person or a representative actually knows because some feel impelled to present themselves as knowing everything—an impossibility, given the vast scope of legislative business.

## Subject Matter Specialists

Specialists in one area can typically be found on the staff of a committee chair, most likely at the federal level, particularly in the senate because of the staff resources available to those elected officials. Their purview is very narrowly focused. If you can locate such an individual, your task is to become a trusted source of information. That way your messages won't be tossed out without being read. In the best of all possible worlds, the staffer comes to rely on your information and judgment so fully that he or she calls you, instead of the other way around. Senator Inouye's aide, referred to at the beginning of this chapter, is a perfect example.

Later on we look at different kinds of communication. In general, e-mails are not the medium of choice when communicating with your representative or senator. But if you develop the kind of special relationship we're talking about here, the medium doesn't matter. Anything from you will get a careful reading, even published items you pass along. Warning: Don't just send along any old information. By being selective, you multiply the impact of any particular communication.

*Generalists*

Barbara Gleim, described in Chapter 6, is an example of a subject matter generalist. The advantage of working with one of these is that you can deal with a greater range of subject matter. And as with a specialist, once you have that trust relationship, whatever you send to the staffer will be thoroughly digested. In Chapter 10, I describe a grassroots campaign on welfare reform. Midway through the campaign the focus became child care. It helped to deal with staffers whose area of responsibility included both welfare eligibility and child care.

Occasionally an aide will question an advocate's stand, not because of personal doubts, but to force into the open the best arguments on the issue. Under such circumstances, it is important to keep in mind that your task is not to win a debate but to get across your message. Showing that you are well informed and thoroughly committed to your position is what will most impress the targets. Showing them that you are smarter than they are will impress them, to be sure, but not in the way you want to.

One group of advocates for community mental health services were disappointed to learn that they would not be talking to their state senator but instead his aide. The aide questioned them closely on their proposal for funding and also their views on the senator's own plan for involuntary hospitalization. It became clear to them that this aide was heavily involved in the issue and would report back to the senator in detail on what they said. By sending his aide instead of meeting with the group himself, the senator was able to avoid committing himself to a hard position or making promises he could not later keep.

Does it matter whether you get to talk to the big one or to his or her aide? Yes. A staff person is going to filter the message on the way to the boss, or even forget to transmit it. Filtering can be based on the aide's own agenda, or on assumptions about what his or her employer wants to hear. So there are definite advantages in talking directly with the elected official. You are most likely to be able to do that by scheduling your appointment in his or her district office. In the capital office you are more likely to be shunted off to an aide, even when there is a confirmed appointment with the boss (with apologies about having urgent business on the floor, of course).

In some cases you will be able to develop a good working relationship with a staff specialist dealing with your topic. This is most likely to happen if you and the representative have a common outlook. Then you may become a trusted source of information in the eyes of the staff person. In that case, there may be greater payoff in dealing with an expert on the staff instead of the elected official whose priorities are elsewhere and who has to be constantly brought up to speed on your issue.

## Appointed Officials As Targets

"Bureaucrat" was a dirty word until sociologists explained that a very large percentage of the workforce, private as well as public, consisted of bureaucrats, i.e., specialized employees of large organizations. The people I shall refer to in this section are more accurately civil servants. Not only do they turn legislated programs into rules for setting up and funding programs, but many legislative initiatives are first "thought up" by departmental employees who see firsthand what is wrong with existing policy.

Civil servants include everybody from senior administrators to mail carriers and schoolteachers. The civil servants we shall be concerned with here are the people in the upper echelons who have responsibility for translating legislation into regulations. This is a group responsibility and, depending on the political sensitivity of the subject matter, the drafting may involve substantial consultation with others within the department. The person may also discuss the work with professional colleagues and legislative committee staff.

Once the regulations have been written, they are published in an official document, and comments are invited from the public. In actuality, most of the public is unaware of all this; it is legislators, lobbyists, and interested organizations who know what is going on. The department may or may not rewrite the regulations on the basis of suggestions it receives. It can ignore them if it sees fit. After several weeks the final form of the regulations becomes official policy—that is, they now have the force of law. The courts can overturn them, but the only way the legislature can change them is by replacing or amending the law they are intended to carry out, or by eliminating from the budget the funds required to implement them.

Notice that unlike the elected representative, the appointed official is relatively free to ignore outside pressure. Because of technical expertise and available resources, this official may know more about the content of the policy than the people doing the lobbying. This is less likely to be true of legislators, whose special expertise is in getting elected. But that is not the advocate's only problem. It is also sometimes a challenge to find out which appointed official to lobby. The process of writing regulations goes on in small offices well insulated from public view.

Assuming you want to have an impact on this process, how do you proceed? You begin by turning to the people who do know their way around the bureaucracy. Professional lobbyists, including those who work for public interest organizations, make it their business to know this sort of thing, as do legislative staff aides, especially those employed by committee chairs and ranking minority party members of committees. This is one more reason to work closely with allies, as was discussed in Chapter 1.

The next task is to get access to the regulation writers. Some make themselves available, particularly if you are from the same professional community. Remember they are under intense time pressure and may not welcome visits from outside nonexperts while they are in the throes of writing. Needless to say, one must be thoroughly familiar with policy content, very focused and concise, and absolutely truthful. It may be wisest to attempt this kind of lobbying in the company of someone who knows the ropes. Later we shall look at the world through the eyes of appointed officialdom in order to understand the best strategy to employ.

In Chapter 10, I describe the experience of a grassroots lobbying group working on influencing state regulations regarding child care. Mid-course, the group learned of a little-known commission that had final say on state regulations of all kinds. Without this knowledge, the group would have passed up an opportunity to present its case to the commission and its staff.

### Interest Groups As Targets

Instead of a legislator or bureaucrat, your target may be an interest group representative. Your first task is to decide whether you are trying to convince the group that this is a cause it should work on, or stir the group into action, or arm it with information, or work with its members on lobbying strategy.

Social workers seeking to enlist their professional association in a fight over welfare reform had to get across to these colleagues— whose own practices were mainly in other fields—why the bill in question was relevant to them. This was also the challenge facing the leaders of the Love Canal Homeowners' Association, some of whose constituents had jobs in chemical companies and therefore were ambivalent about making too much of a stir regarding toxic waste disposal.

## Targeting Multiple Audiences

Often the problem is that one is dealing with different targets simultaneously, for example in a legislative hearing. On several occasions I have given testimony on welfare reform in public hearings before state legislative committees. Typically, I am dealing with three different targets: the committee members, who are of course different targets with different agendas; others in attendance, who tend to be the most partisan on the issue; and the news media. All three are intermediate as well as ultimate targets. The committee members are decision makers in their own right, but they also communicate with their colleagues. Allies in the audience are people I want to both inform and mobilize, by carrying the message to their wider constituencies. By providing information to the news media I help shape their perception of the issues and possibly their editorial position. Ultimately they are important insofar as they reach the public. Depending on which of these I have chosen as my primary focus, I have shaped my testimony accordingly.

Committee hearings are often a way to publicize an issue rather than inform the legislators. On one such occasion, I was testifying to a friendly committee regarding proposals to liberalize a harsh welfare policy. The state administration opposed the changes on the grounds that the state's economy was in trouble. I deliberately inserted into my testimony an analogy to a sinking ship which tries to deal with the problem by throwing half the crew overboard. The argument had nothing to do with welfare reform or state finances and did nothing to inform the committee members, all of whom were familiar with the subject. The reference to the sinking ship, however, was picked up by at least one major radio news program that evening.

When Lois Gibbs of the Love Canal Homeowners' Association made public statements, she had to keep in mind that several audiences were being addressed simultaneously. Unless she gave the news media a fresh angle or new information, they would not use her material. Unable to pay for advertising and lacking the natural platform that public office provides, LCHA was dependent on the news media to rally support, create a positive image in the public's mind, and most of all keep Love Canal from being forgotten as a critical issue. So Gibbs not only had to say something attention grabbing, she also had to do it so as to win public sympathy and not alienate the majority. Meanwhile, she had to respond to the frustrations of other residents and mollify factions eager for a more violent confrontation with the authorities.

The LCHA's campaign basically left alone what to many will appear to be the real villain of Love Canal: the Hooker Chemical Company. In fact, Hooker was the focus of a number of articles in the mass media that linked Love Canal with other toxic dumps the company had created in different parts of the country (see, for example, Nader and Brownstein, 1980; Tallmer, 1981). For its part, Hooker made it a point to avoid being a target. At first it kept a very low profile. Then, when public attention and a series of large lawsuits made it impossible to remain out of the limelight, the company tried to control media coverage of its role. To a great extent, it was able to let local and state public officials take the brunt of the residents' wrath.

Were the residents being naive in not going after Hooker? No, LCHA was simply focusing on its agenda: obtaining redress from governments with the power and clear obligation to help their citizens. The government agencies in turn went after Hooker and its parent corporation, Occidental Petroleum, in the courts. The state of New York and the U.S. Justice Department were in a better position to take on a $9 billion multinational corporation than was a local association of working-class families struggling to survive a massive economic, physical, and psychological threat. In addition, Hooker was in a good position to fend off a public assault. Aside from its huge resources, it was too far up the production chain to be easily embarrassed. In general, companies that sell their products directly to the public are the most vulnerable to media exposure. Chemical companies that sell to other companies are much less so.

In terms of precedents for the future, strategy was important: putting all governments on notice that they must assume the role of protector. There was undoubtedly another good reason for LCHA to focus on public officials rather than Hooker. The company was a major employer in Niagara Falls, and many potential supporters of LCHA would not have supported a direct attack on Hooker. In addition, everyone was aware that this corporation was in effect the surrogate for other employers in the area, and an attack on it could be interpreted as an attack on the chemical industry as a whole. In this way one important target group, employees of chemical companies who also had a stake in a safe environment, was kept from defecting.

All this may or may not have gone through the minds of the LCHA leadership. The case is nonetheless instructive in suggesting that identification of targets is a crucial step in planning one's lobbying strategy—not that one should never focus on the corporate sector. The real point is to stay focused on what will help you accomplish your objectives.

## WHAT MAKES POLICYMAKERS TICK?

What determines a policymaker's behavior is basically the same as what leads any of us to act in a certain way. This rather complex subject can be reduced to three basic factors: (1) the capacity to act (i.e., competence and opportunity), (2) the incentive or motivation to act, and (3) the justification for acting (see Compton and Galaway, 1989). For the advocate, it is the second and third of these that are the most important. Motivation is the more obvious factor. If one could tap into the existing motivations of a policymaker, that would seem to evoke the desired response. But it is not that simple. As is discussed later, the policymaker must also justify the action. The advocate may be able to modify the policymaker's behavior by challenging the justification.

### What Motivates Elected Officials?

If you think elected officials are preoccupied with being reelected, you are absolutely right. Put yourself in the legislator's place. If you, as this legislator, have chosen politics as a career (one in which you hope to serve your fellow human beings in addition to gaining whatever material and ego rewards may accrue to you), you are not about to throw it all away for someone else's pet cause. Even if this is only a temporary stage in one's career, a means to other opportunities, nobody likes to be fired. The problem is that every two or four years, someone, maybe many someones, want your job. They are not nice in the way they go about seeking it, either. If you, the legislator, lose your job, everybody will not only know about it, but most are likely to attribute your ouster to your failure to perform effectively and/or deliver on promises you made when you took the position. So you have a lot of pride wrapped up in keeping your job, as well as a livelihood now and economic security in the future. And if you do get "fired" from your legislative seat, your ability to use this position to improve the world will come to an abrupt halt.

Another thing to keep in mind about policymakers in government is the sheer range and volume of material they must handle. A legislator must address hundreds of issues during a typical session. It would be thousands of items if committees did not screen out many bills. Think of the junk mail that gets delivered to your door in the course of a week. Now add all the unsolicited e-mail and pop-up messages on your computer. You are on the mailing lists of many worthy and not-so-worthy endeavors, in addition to commercial enterprises that take advantage of the low cost of bulk mailings and spam on the Internet. If you study each and every piece of mail and each e-message carefully and try to weigh the merits of every one of them, you are the rare exception. Most of us take a quick look at the outside of the envelope, make a snap decision whether to open it, make another snap decision when we read the opening sentence, etc. As we scan the latest batch of e-mail messages, some of these urgent appeals are deleted before we even look to see what they say. For the lawmaker, multiply that experience severalfold. In addition to letters, legislators are constantly bombarded by faxes and e-mail messages and telephone calls and visits to their offices by people wanting something. Unlike Jack and Jill Citizen, they must act interested and at least minimally informed on everything from unemployment compensation rules to land-use policy. Because many persons with a personal stake in an issue try to cast it in terms of the public interest, lawmakers soon become skeptical about any person presenting himself or herself as concerned mainly with the public good.

How do legislators manage this awesome task? One way is to develop a kind of shorthand. To start with, there is a basic view of government and his or her role in it. This is typically the basis on which he or she ran for office. Having been successful, the legislator is likely to assume that what he or she stood for in the election is what the constituents want.

That general philosophy of government is the first screen with which the legislator tests a proposal (see Hurwitz, 1986). Many issues are not that simple. Opinion may be divided in the district, or the party leadership may push for one position and strong interest groups in the district for another. The president, governor, or the party whip in the legislature may be on the line asking you, the legislator, for your help—a flattering but also potentially threatening appeal. Lobbyists representing powerful interests let lawmakers know, sometimes not so subtly, that they can be helpful in the next election. Mail and telephone calls are flooding in. Or, conversely, the issue is ambiguous and the representative has no clear notion of which way to jump.

Under these circumstances, a common practice for lawmakers is to turn to one or more colleagues who share the same general philosophy and, because they sit on the relevant committees or are known to be well-informed, can be trusted. If the "cue-giver" is for the measure, it makes sense to be for it as well (Bibby, 1983). But, just as lobbyists can undermine their credibility with misleading or unfounded assertions, the cue-givers within the body must earn their colleagues' trust. They, in turn, may rely on other sources. A legislator may have several cue-givers of this kind, each looked to for guidance on a different policy area (Clausen, 1973).

Not surprisingly, political scientists have a lot of interest in what influences legislators' decisions. According to studies by Ray (1982), legislative colleagues and organized interest groups had the most influence, appeals from the executive branch and one's own research on the issues had the least, and in between were the party leadership, legislative committee reports, and communication from individual constituents. Songer et al.'s (1985) interviews with state legislators from

Kansas and Oklahoma gave this ordering: first, after the person's own value screen, was constituents; second, interest groups; third, fellow legislators; and last, party leaders.

How do legislators assess the will of their constituents? There is a tendency to generalize about the voters in one's district as being liberal or conservative and to act in terms of that general view. Especially on controversial issues, the legislator will make it a point to explain his or her vote. Just as there are cue-giving colleagues within the legislative body, there are key individuals in the district who will be consulted on problematic issues. Legislators have a dual function: deliberating on policy and providing services for constituents. Some see a responsive service operation as allowing them to be more liberal or conservative than the district voters.

You may be distressed to learn how little emphasis is given to personal reading in these studies. But remember the deluge of material the legislator faces. Kingdon (1973) has found that lawmakers rarely make an extended search for information. They will do more reading and talking to others when the issue is controversial or has high visibility in the news media. Their preference is for short summaries that evaluate as well as describe the policy and take political factors into consideration.

The greatest amount of background reading is normally done in the legislator's role as a committee member, where one is supposed to be something of an expert and very likely a cue-giver for fellow legislators. According to Whiteman (1985), the search for material by committee members is determined by how they define the problem. (The critical role of problem definition is discussed later in this chapter.) Members use such information in three ways: to gain substantive knowledge of the problem or policy in question, to extend and refine an existing position on the issues, and to justify one's position.

These are generalizations about elected officials. In Chapter 6 you will meet three former state legislators and find out how they arrived at conclusions on issues.

## What Motivates Appointed Officials?

Except for outright political appointees, whose fortunes rise and fall with those of their elected bosses, civil servants establish job rights as soon as they get past a short probationary period. Then, the only way to get rid of one of them is to get rid of his or her position. This job security may mean that this kind of work attracts people who by nature are not risk takers. One thing is for sure: The civil servant is keenly aware that his or her career prospects hinge directly on the continued flow of funds. Not surprisingly, then, avoiding reduction of one's budget is a high priority. According to one study, it is the first priority (Arnold, 1979).

That is not meant as a cynical comment. Just as legislators know they will cease to serve the public as elected officials if they are defeated at the polls, dedicated civil servants (of which there are many) will think twice before jeopardizing their opportunities to serve the public in the role for which they have been trained. Understandably, avoiding cutbacks in your agency's funding is a very high priority.

Aside from continued funding, the civil servant is dependent on positive evaluations by superiors and, even more important, effective working relationships with departmental colleagues. For this reason, there is a natural tendency to protect the people with whom one works and, more generally, the department itself. A byproduct of all this is resistance to outside interference, particularly by those who don't understand the agency's mission and technology (Gruber, 1987; see also Aberbach, Putnam, and Rockman, 1981).

Given all this, it is easy to stereotype civil servants as merely obsessed with hanging on to their jobs and unwilling to let any fresh air into the office. The reality is more complicated. Gruber (1987) has identified three kinds of civil servants: experts, workers, and administrators.

*Experts* are mainly interested in the challenge of the task, which fits in with their professional training. They share a commitment to excellence and public service with their professional colleagues, and they respect advice from people who are seen to have the same attributes. Competence ranks particularly high with them.

*Workers* come closest to fitting the popular stereotype of bureaucrats. They are mainly concerned with mastery of the workplace and, more than other kinds of public employees, are preoccupied with job security. They respect senior officials to whom they are officially accountable.

*Administrators* are mainly concerned with getting a job done effectively. They are more flexible and more ambitious, career-wise, than the other two. They are also more likely to respect the opinions of outsiders, whether elected officials or the public.

The would-be advocate should take the previous factors into consideration when planning to lobby appointed officials. It is less than useful to make too many assumptions about the particular official you are going to see. Each civil servant is a distinct individual, with gifts, feelings, and biases of his or her own, just like the rest of us. But these generalizations help in alerting one to the kinds of questions to ask, before meeting the person. Experienced advocates who have dealt with the department you are targeting are the best source of such background information.

## The Need to Justify

There are two things nobody wants to be: evil and stupid. People will go to tremendous lengths to convince themselves that they are neither. But in this competitive and moralizing world, we are continually exposed to signs that, yes, we are deficient in our competence, our goodness, or both. So each of us is engaged in a neverending process of reassuring ourselves, and others, that we are really all right. To be inconsistent is to violate this image: Either we don't know what we're about, or we're not abiding by our own rules of conduct (see Aronson, 1980; Festinger, 1957; Lecky, 1961).

One way to feel smart, moral, and consistent is to block out any signs to the contrary. One can do that by simply ignoring the signs or distorting the information, to bring it in line with good self-concept (Lecky, 1961). The problem is compounded when one is also trying to convince other people and has taken a public position. This is precisely what elected officials are faced with all the time.

In one experiment, householders agreed to reduce the use of their air conditioners to save energy. Those who did so only as a private vow were most likely to forget their promise, while those who declared their intent publicly tended to act accordingly (Pallack and Cummings, 1976). In the same way, legislators who publicly declare they will not compromise on an issue are less likely to do so than those who don't make such a declaration (Hurwitz, 1986; see also Deutsch and Gerard, 1955; Tedeschi, Schlenker, and Bonoma, 1971).

## Elected Officials and Justification

State Representative John Smith has to vote on a bill that would require pregnant teenagers to obtain parental consent in order to have an abortion. His attitudes on abortion and pregnant teenagers and parental consent have evolved over a lifetime of hearing what his own parents thought about such issues; reading newspapers, magazines, and textbooks; watching television; being married to a Roman Catholic; exchanging views with schoolmates and colleagues; and so forth. His sentiments are a tangle, some of which he is not consciously aware of. Most of the time he doesn't think about these questions and would prefer not to have to, especially since his district has both a substantial number of Roman Catholics who are in favor of the bill and many members of a well-organized feminist group that is just as strongly opposed.

Representative Smith is going to have to decide something: to vote in favor, to vote against, to abstain, or to be out of town when the vote is taken. There are potential costs, no matter what he does. But there is a prior task. First he has to decide what he thinks about parental consent, and he hasn't done that yet. Eventually, John comes to the conclusion that he personally is opposed to requiring parental consent. It may come about after his wife says something to him at breakfast, or he sees a particularly arresting story in the morning paper, or he has an argument with his independently minded teenage daughter. Whatever it is, this is the trigger, the small incident that shoves him over the brink of indecision. We know that it is not the sole reason for his position—that has come from the accumulation of his experiences.

Once John has taken the plunge, however, he begins to develop the explanation for his stance—initially to himself, then to his wife and other people around him. The explanation will have to "make sense" and be consistent with his values and his self-image. The more he repeats it and elaborates on it in subsequent conversations with himself and others, the more firmly committed to the position he will become. His self-persuasion, in other words, will take on a momentum all its own.

Being flexible by nature and buffeted by shifting political winds, Representative Smith may change his mind before the vote is taken. But if he does, he will have to rearrange his explanations. He can't simply talk one way and abruptly go off in a different direction. Aside from his credibility with other people, his own sense of personal consistency and integrity would be shaken.

Note the sequence of events. First came an evolving process of attitude development resulting in an amorphous set of biases that were not at the center of his attention. Then something brought this question to the fore, so he had to give thought to it. Then came the process of deciding why he felt that way. That is basically how all policy decisions come about, a fact which flies in the face of commonsense notions about policy decisions. I am talking about the point at which most policy issues surface in public debate. This says nothing about the kind of in-depth analysis that may go into formulating policies in the first place. A professional policy analyst arrives at answers as a result of painstaking analysis. Typically, elected officials do not do that. You should not conclude from this that analysis is only window dressing, designed to mask the true nature of policy. The analysis is vital and good policy requires it. That is because societies and interest groups must justify what they do—to themselves as well as others—and analysis that challenges initial assumptions can force people to revise their views.

Whether your name is Martin Luther King Jr. or Adolf Hitler, you have to convince yourself that what you are doing is right and makes sense. It is true whether you are deciding to invade another country or vote for a tax bill, pursue a career or buy a new raincoat. When the question is a public policy issue, something else is added: the need to convince others as well.

Let's begin with a nonpolicy problem for Representative Smith: the point at which he shares his decision with his wife. Her religious beliefs make abortion under any circumstances abhorrent to her. She sees the requirement that pregnant teenagers obtain parental consent as at least a limited deterrent to what to her is an immoral act. Her reason for supporting the proposal will also be a justification for a web of attitudes that lie deep in her psyche, as is true of her husband. During their years together, John and Mary Smith have not spent much time talking about abortion. Though he has not shared her strong feelings, he has accepted them. Now the public life of State Representative John Smith has intruded itself on the private life of John and Mary

Smith. A potentially divisive issue which they could once have ignored has become the focus of attention.

John must justify his opposition to parental consent in terms that are meaningful and acceptable to Mary. He won't, for instance, defend his choice on the grounds that abortion is good or that the mother's freedom of choice overshadows the extinction of an unborn child. Were he to do so, it would threaten their relationship and the foundations of their life as a family. Instead, he will seek a rationale that she can accept, for instance the possibility that some teenagers may resort to back alley abortions rather than face their parents.

Very much the same thing will happen when Representative John Smith is interviewed by reporters or reveals his position on the parental consent issue in his letter to the voters in his district. He will find grounds for his choice that will be acceptable to the majority. He must find some way of speaking to the concerns of his Roman Catholic constituents and the feminist activists at the same time. This is not an easy task, but it's typical of what makes life in the policymaking arena interesting. In this case, he is trying to keep both his job and his marriage intact.

Justification of policy choices has a function far more important than the career longevity of individual public servants. By grounding choices in arguments acceptable to effective majorities of the governed, regimes establish legitimacy and assure social stability. We espouse democratic decision-making because of deeply held values about the rights of the governed, and that is a value that few in this society would question. This democratic participation also helps to assure willing compliance with government decisions by the governed.

When Representative Smith's opponent chides him in a debate on his "flipflops" on key issues during his career, Smith must either give a plausible reason for the change in his position on an issue or focus attention elsewhere, for example on his challenger's questionable financial dealings.

## Appointed Officials and Justification

For appointed officials, justification is as important as it is for legislators, but the dynamics are somewhat different. First, regulations are supposed to reflect legislative intent — what the lawmakers had in mind when they passed the bill. Understand, of course, that the final version of the law is in all likelihood a conceptual nightmare, consisting of bits here and pieces there designed to corral a few more votes. So the people writing the regulations use a good deal of creativity in deciding what was intended. Many times there is also a lot of innovation, inclusion of things the legislators did not intend. This is a major reason for advocates to focus attention on this phase of the policymaking process.

The civil servants who write regulations are most likely to be professionally trained, either in law, economics, or a field related to the content of the policy itself. They will seek to justify their conclusions in terms consistent with the values and assumptions of their professional fields.

To whom must the decisions be justified? The most important audiences are senior officials in the department and legislative leaders. The writers must also deal with external interest groups that have a stake in the product. While adjustments can be made during the period of public review, before the regulations become final, it is less embarrassing to anticipate criticism than to have to accommodate it afterward.

Outweighing all other considerations is the belief among appointed officials that they are problem solvers, not politicians (Gruber, 1987). However much they may bend to political pressure, their system of justification requires that they deny it. Civil servants will acknowledge privately that, of course, they live in a real world and must learn to accommodate to it, but the public image is apolitical. Challenge that perception frontally and you run the risk of shutting off access to this aspect of policymaking. And remember, the bureaucracy is much freer to shut off access than elected officials are.

## CRITICAL FACTOR: HOW THE POLICYMAKER DEFINES THE PROBLEM

Think back to what was said about the basic need to see oneself and be seen by others as competent and moral. I must have a basis for assessing where I stand in regard to these qualities. This requires external standards by which to judge myself: my perception of the real world (a competent person acts in a way consistent with reality), and my value assumptions (a moral person acts in ways consistent with his or her values). This process of defining ourselves and the external world is so much a part of us that we are not even aware of it most of the time.

My approach to definition of the problem is very similar to what George Lakoff (2002) refers to as "worldview." I have found it helpful to break this global construct into the three components discussed here: focus, presumptions, and values.

Two critical components of definition, then, are our presumptions about the real world and our value assumptions. You are probably more familiar with the second of these terms than the first. One place you may have heard about presumption is in relation to courts.

John Doe is presumed innocent unless proven guilty beyond a reasonable doubt. He is certainly not assumed to be innocent; in fact, the public may be convinced he committed the crime even before he is brought to trial. The court, however, must start from the opposite end of things. If John Doe were presumed guilty, he would never be able to convince anybody that he was innocent. So a presumption can be thought of as an initial operating assumption, or expectation, one that can be overturned by sufficient evidence to the contrary. Theoretically, in public policy, one should always start from the presumption that changes are not needed. This is not because everything is great the way it is, but because otherwise we would have to prove beyond a reasonable doubt that every wild scheme that came along was wrong, or else we would have to accept it as valid. That is how it is in theory. In real life, the initial presumption is whatever an effective majority says it is. The attacks of 9/11 created a climate in this country in which the existing balance between the need for security and the need for civil liberties of individuals suddenly changed. Any member of Congress opposing the sweeping measures written into the Patriot Act would have had the burden of proving why these changes to the status quo should not be enacted.

The other critical component of definition is the focus of attention. Remember that one way of dealing with discrepancies between where one is and where one would like to be is to shift the focus to something else. Understanding the process of defining gives one a powerful tool for understanding policymakers, thus a powerful tool for influencing them. We should consider each of the three components—focus, presumptions, and values—in more detail.

## Focus

Your perceptions of the world are necessarily highly selective. When you enter a room your attention is focused on specific aspects of the environment and of your own reaction to it, while most of what is there is filtered out. As a student attending a course for the first time, you are likely to focus intently on the professor: Who is this person who will be teaching you? What will this person look for in your classroom performance and written assignments? What are his or her biases? Is he or she going to be boring? You may also check out your fellow students: Are they smarter than you? Depending on your age and current relationship, you may also see if there are any attractive people you would like to get to know better. As the syllabus is passed out, you quickly scan it to see what books you have to buy and, in particular, what is required for written reports and exams.

Psychologists refer to this process as selectivity, the universal phenomenon by which certain aspects of the environment are continually filtered out and others filtered in. By selective exposure, the person is insulated entirely from some content. Selective attention further filters the content. By selectively perceiving, we narrow the filter even more. And after exposure we recall selectively (see McCroskey, 1968).

These processes, necessary if you are to make any sense of your environment, are not random. They grow out of your attitudes and mind-set, which accumulate throughout your life, and, accordingly, your expectations for the future. If you have struggled in previous courses in this field, you become preoccupied with how others will judge you. If you have a physical disability, you may be on the lookout for signs of rejection or curiosity from the professor and other students. When you go around and introduce yourself, you may be so preoccupied with the impression you will make that you don't hear what other students say.

In the policy arena, the focus of attention is a critical factor in determining the agenda. It can make a crucial difference in the outcome of policy deliberations even before the deliberations take place. Political scientists Peter Bachrach and Morton Baratz (1970) have suggested the term "nonissue" to refer to a question that never makes it onto the agenda. Those with control over agenda setting may deliberately keep certain people and their concerns from getting a hearing, thereby shaping the decisions that can be considered. Think of a public official who got a lot of attention, say, at election time, got elected, and is now dwelling in relative obscurity. The reason may not be accident but instead a deliberate attempt to keep that person from gaining prominence.

Several years ago, in the days before welfare reform, work was not mandatory for welfare recipients. The governor of New Jersey proposed a workfare program under which recipients of aid would have to work off their grants in unpaid public service jobs. Here are excerpts from two news items about this policy:

> Governor Brendan Byrne said yesterday he would sign "as quickly as possible" legislation . . . that requires "able-bodied" welfare recipients to work for their relief check. . . .
>
> In his budget message last February, Byrne asked the Legislature to act on the bill, maintaining that no one who is capable of working should be allowed to "sit on his duff and draw a welfare check." (Lamendola, 1977)

> New Jersey's plan to put employable welfare recipients to work will cost the state more than it would to leave them on the dole . . . state officials said Thursday.
>
> Human Services Commissioner Ann Klein told the startled members of the Joint Appropriations Committee that the program Gov. Brendan Byrne announced in his annual message would operate under unforeseen restrictions. . . . (*Secaucus Home News*, 1977)

The supporters of the workfare bill focused on the issue of keeping able-bodied recipients from getting something for nothing. The human services commissioner focused on the net cost to the state of running the program. The difference in focus was not accidental. Legislators and the governor were keenly aware of the attitudes of voters toward "shiftless" welfare recipients. The commissioner knew that if her department ran in the red because of actual operation of the program, she would have to answer to those same voters later on.

### Presumptions

A presumption is what you already "know" before the evidence has been presented. It is the expectations with which you approach a situation. As a student on the first day of class, you "know" that you will do poorly in this course because you have consistently had trouble in similar courses. It may turn out that your presumption was wrong. (It would be presumptuous of you not to consider this possibility.) That initial expectation can dog you through the rest of the course, maybe keep you from performing up to your real potential.

As an advocate, you must size up the presumptions of the target, whether they are in favor of or against your cause. Suppose you are invited to take part in a debate on a new bill designed to outlaw all abortions. If the audience is mixed or predominantly pro-choice, you can claim that, since the new bill is a departure from the status quo, the burden is on your opponent to demonstrate the need for a change. Unless an effective case is made, you don't have to open your mouth. However, if the audience is full of antiabortion zealots, you'd better be prepared to take on the burden of proof.

### Values

Our values are so deeply imbedded in us that we are often not aware of them, and can articulate them only with great difficulty. In short, they are part of our very being. So any frontal assault on my values can feel like an attack on me as a person. Moreover, there is an implicit assumption that a person's values are his or her own business ("You have a right to feel the way you want to as long as you don't tread on my right to my own feelings"). Therefore, a direct challenge to a target's value orientation should always be avoided.

Assuming that people's values are basic to the choices they make, how can we ever hope to change things unless we do take on a target's negative attitudes? First, it is possible to modify values by presenting new evidence. Second, values are rarely totally integrated. A person may hold contradictory feelings about a subject, and it's possible to support the side that is more desirable for the dilemma.

A better strategy may be for the advocate to look for common ground, areas where his or her values are compatible with the target's, and build on that consensus. For example, a pro-choice advocate may be able to find common ground with an antiabortion activist on the value of life as it pertains to young children. Without either party giving up its views on the rights of the pregnant woman and the fetus, they may be able to collaborate on legislation to provide better nutrition for low-income families.

Care should be taken to keep value differences from degenerating into an out-and-out personal attack. The advocate should try to empathize with the target and convey respect for the sincerity of the target's beliefs.

In Chapter 4, we will look at how to go about making effective arguments for a policy position. It all starts with an assessment of how the target currently defines the situation: What is the focus of attention? What are the presumptions about reality? What is the value orientation?

The right-to-life movement has a highly integrated definition of the abortion question. Its members' focus is on the fetus and the moral as opposed to the social consequences of different actions. Their presumption, that life begins at conception, is consistent with their focus of preserving this person-to-be at all costs. Because the definition of the situation is so well integrated, it is hard to argue with this position once a person has bought any part of it. Only as the focus of attention shifts elsewhere can the right-to-lifer be unglued from intense commitment to antiabortion policies.

As a country, we have always had mixed feelings about poor people. When the poor seem to be getting something for nothing, the feelings are negative. Especially if they are males, able-bodied adults should work for a living instead of taking hand-outs from the government. Teenagers who become pregnant, apparently because they don't behave themselves or take precautions, are a source of much criticism in the mass media these days. Those who give birth and then turn to welfare to support them and their offspring are a particular target of public indignation.

But our attitudes toward poor people and pregnant teenagers are conflicted. If we see a television documentary on the homeless, especially if there seem to be mitigating circumstances, we may sympathize with their plight. Workers who become jobless because the local steel mill closed down may be more sympathetic toward other unemployed persons than they were when the plant was still operating.

One of the paradoxes of the welfare reform fight of the 1990s was the way it changed the image of welfare recipients, at least temporarily. The reform push was motivated in large part by the concern that welfare clients were getting something for nothing and were too lazy to work for a living. With the enactment of Temporary Assistance for Needy Families (TANF), the mass media began showing success stories of gallant women who were leaving the welfare rolls and making it on their own (see Chapter 10).

So new information can shake up our view of the real world of poverty and welfare. Americans are in a constant dilemma about what is right: Vulnerable people should not be neglected, but no one should get something for nothing. Because of the basic instability of the public definition of welfare, as contrasted with the stable views of the antiabortion activists, the same arguments keep coming up in slightly different clothing, and new information and changing political winds bring policy shifts.

## AN EXERCISE IN TARGETING

At the end of the previous chapter, we looked at alternative action agendas in the case of a problem-ridden urban school district. Let's now take that case example to the next step: picking targets for action. This can be done by an individual reader or a group. In the latter case, once you've identified a number of targets, you might try a simulation, with different members taking the parts of advocates and targets. You should begin by reviewing the material on agenda setting in this school system presented at the end of Chapter 2.

### Categorizing Potential Targets

Potential targets can be divided into a number of categories: those actively involved on behalf of the current thrust of district policy; the active opposition; and the less-involved (who may be inclined one way or the other).

Information on a number of major players in the school controversy follows. You have already met some of them in Chapter 2. Although there may be points at which people cross lines—i.e., favor existing policy in some areas and oppose it in others—for the most part, the parties now actively involved are pretty well polarized.

## Actively Supporting Current District Policy

*The chair of the three-member board of control.* An attorney who lives outside of the district and has close ties with the Republican party in the county. He has been the focus of much of the community's anger, for agreeing to unlimited expansion of charter schools, for taking the initiative in selling off district buildings, and for taking a hands-off approach to dealing with the private company that ran nine of the ten district schools. He has no special training or background in school administration. He was appointed by a former secretary of education for a five-year term, which he is now about halfway through. Board of control members cannot be removed from office except for egregious misconduct, e.g., unethical conduct. The fact that this man is Caucasian may be an issue for some community members.

*A second board of control member who typically votes with the chair.* A woman of color who came up through the public schools of this district but now lives in a suburban community outside of it. She was appointed at the same time as the chair. She is also active in Republican affairs, having run the election campaigns of a number of GOP candidates, including that of the state senator who was instrumental in appointment of the current board members (see following). She is currently employed as community relations director for the city that makes up the bulk of the school district. On a recent vote, relating to the selection of a new superintendent, she broke with the chair for the first time. This raises the possibility that, rather than a predictable member of the existing two-person majority, she will become a critical "swing vote."

*The state senator in whose senatorial district the school district is located.* Before being elected to the state senate, he was mayor of the city that makes up most of the school district. Last year he was easily elected to a second four-year term, but within the city where he was once the mayor, he lost badly to an unknown individual from outside the county. (Both he and that opponent are Caucasian.) He is a member of the senate education committee. He has remained in the background on school issues but is assumed to wield considerable influence within the district, in regard to education as well as other matters.

## The Active Opposition

*The third board of control member.* This man, who grew up in the school district, was something of a local hero, due to his prowess on the basketball court. When appointed to the board of control, he was operating the city's recreation program. Having been appointed by the former mayor and now state senator, he may have been assumed to be a loyal supporter on educational policy. But he has turned out to be a vocal critic.

Outvoted consistently, he has just as consistently used his position to publicly challenge the majority. Despite his position as city employee, potentially vulnerable to removal by the city council, he has refused to back down. At one point he was the center of a controversy over alleged conflict of interest, because his program stood to benefit from a federal grant on which he voted as a board of control member. As it was, other funds were found to replace the grant, and he remained on the board despite pressure to resign from either the board or the city recreation position.

*The teachers' union.* Union leadership has consistently voiced objections to board policy. It often criticized the private firm that ran many of the schools. It has spoken out against the expansion of charter schools. It has criticized the draconian cuts in the district's budget. But it took no action to fight the elimination of ninety positions, half of them teaching positions. It thus appears at this point not to be a major political force in the school district controversies.

*The state representative for this area.* A Democrat, he is also a product of the local community. He periodically attends board of control meetings to challenge the board majority on a variety of issues. His proposal to provide $12 million in additional state funds for the district has gone nowhere. He is head of the Black Caucus in the legislature, and is also chair of the local Democratic party organization.

*A militant group of parents, students, and their supporters.* Formed during the crisis last fall, when the high school came close to a total shutdown, this organization has led the fight against the current regime. Leaders of this group have attended and sometimes disrupted board of control meetings to demand the dismissal of the private company running nine schools, oppose the sale of district buildings, and call for limits on charter school enrollments. Among other things, they have cited overlarge class size, lack of textbooks and working computers, lack of security and discipline, and failure to handle student class scheduling properly. More generally, they have kept up a constant barrage of criticism about what they view as callous disregard of their children's educational needs.

The group, operating on a shoestring budget, has been struggling to define its agenda and fashion a coherent strategy. Although parents and students form the core of this group, there are several local clergy and other community members who have joined their ranks. They have also received support from groups based outside the district that advocate progressive educational policies.

*The local branch of NAACP.* This organization refers to itself as the primary civil rights organization locally. Over the years it has fulfilled this role by acting boldly on issues ranging from police brutality to housing to schools. It has run voter registration–education campaigns for many years. Its annual banquet can turn out hundreds of supporters. Politicians from both parties regularly "work the tables" at these affairs.

The NAACP branch defines education as one of its priorities. In recent years the couple who were longtime leaders of the organization made frequent appearances at board of control meetings as outspoken critics. Since their departure last year, NAACP has been less vocal on educational issues. In part this relates to the low-key personal style of the new president of the organization. But NAACP members are among the leaders of the militant parent-based organization and otherwise lend their support to that organization's work as individuals.

## Other Players

Beyond these most active participants are several groups and individuals with varying degrees of commitment to one side or the other and varying readiness to get involved.

*The state secretary of education.* A respected educator with years of experience in public school administration, he has become increasingly critical of the local board of control. During the tenure of the private firm operating nine schools, he expressed concern about alleged mismanagement and the failure of the parties to work together. Most recently, he spoke out strongly against the sale of school properties and allowing unlimited enrollment in charter schools.

On the other hand, he is limited in what he can do to control the board. And now, with his resignation impending, members of the board of control, with several years yet to go, can simply wait him out.

*The interim superintendent.* Appointed by the secretary of education and, like him, a seasoned educational administrator, he will continue only until the newly appointed superintendent assumes office. He has opposed unlimited enrollment in charter schools and the sale of school properties to balance the budget.

*The incoming superintendent.* A career educator with roots in the African-American community, this woman is something of an unknown quantity. She carefully avoided being drawn into the local controversies while she was under consideration for the post of superintendent. She won out over a candidate favored by the board of control majority, due to strong community pressure. The critical vote found the board of control member who usually votes with the chair switching sides. It was the first time community groups were able to influence board of control decisions.

*The elected school board.* The eight-member school board was effectively sidelined with the appointment of the board of control. At first the board of control dealt only with money matters, but it took over management of the entire educational enterprise a number of years ago. The elected board chair has a seat at board of control meetings but rarely attends.

*Parent teacher associations.* For the most part, the PTAs have been weak or nonexistent in this district. Two exceptions have been the high school PTA and that in one of the middle schools. But even these have had an ambiguous role when it came to affecting district policy.

*The local university.* After years of remaining aloof from local affairs and trying to wall itself off from its urban surroundings, the university, whose main campus is in the school district, is now seeking an active role in enhancing the quality of community life, particularly public education. Actively leading this effort is the man who was appointed president two years ago. He has brought with him the conception of a metropolitan university, lending its resources to the surrounding urban-suburban milieu.

University faculty and students are providing a range of educational support services, including counseling and after-school tutoring. In collaboration with other agencies, the university is working with residents of communities surrounding the campus to deal with a variety of neighborhood problems.

These developments have helped build a reservoir of good will toward the university. Now the reservoir is being tested as the university finds itself becoming more involved in the controversies impinging on the school district.

For several years the university has wanted to buy buildings owned by the school district, as part of its own expansion plans. Now that this becomes a tangible possibility, the university finds itself at odds with those who oppose selling off the district's assets. Another dream has been to operate an elementary school, enriching the education of local children while providing a living laboratory for faculty and students. The current plan is to seek authorization to open a charter school. The university sees this as a way of supporting public education, but in the eyes of some critics, it would exacerbate the problem by draining off students and money from the district to support the charter.

*City government officials.* The school district is a separate entity, and the city has no official say in its affairs, yet the city's fortunes are bound up with the ability of the schools to produce an educated work force.

The city government, completely under Republican control, is focused on efforts to jump-start the local economy in collaboration with private business interests. Current initiatives include development of a recreation complex along the riverfront, including a race track and slot-machine gambling; a technology center in the area between the university and a large health care complex that serves the entire area; a major housing development program that includes financial incentives to first-time home buyers and the building of new housing; and improvements in the blighted downtown commercial district.

Commercial and industrial concerns have begun to show an interest in this locality, and there has been some success in attracting private investment. But the city is still generally rated as an economic disaster zone.

To date, the city and the private sector have stayed out of the controversy surrounding the school district. If they see a connection between the economic viability of the community and the role of public education in developing a competent work force, they have done or said little to demonstrate it.

*The charter schools.* The charter schools have a proprietary interest in decisions being made by the board of control and others in the school district. The owner of the larger of these is politically well connected in the county. Supporting the owners themselves are charter school parents, who are increasingly vocal in support of this alternative to the district-run schools.

*The churches.* This city of 35,000 has more than 100 identifiable religious bodies, ranging from large, established churches in mainstream denominations to storefront operations led by pastors who have other full-time employment. Together they have the potential to be highly influential in community affairs, but with the exception of perhaps fifteen of them, they appear to have little interest in becoming active in community affairs. A few clergy are actively involved in groups seeking to affect educational policy.

*Other interest groups.* Beyond these players is a range of social agencies, community organizations, and individuals with an interest in what happens to the schools. They include suburban residents of communities outside of the district itself. A number of the social agencies receive grant money through the district, which affects their readiness to speak out on educational issues.

### Picking Targets

Here is a bewildering array of players and potential players. Whom do you want to energize and whom do you want to leave dormant? What is the potential power of these actors to impact educational policy? How do they appear to be defining the issues and how might you try to modify those definitions?

In Chapter 4 we shall see how arguments can be used to alter the policymaker's definition of the situation. That is the key to affecting policy decisions.

## *POINTS TO REMEMBER*

1. Who is the target, that is, the person or group who can make the critical decisions you are after? Know as much as you can about the target, the target's power to affect policy, and the likelihood that his or her power will be used the way you would like.
2. Keep in mind that when working through an intermediary, you have two targets: the person you are dealing with and the ultimate target of your message.
3. A high-priority concern for elected officials is getting reelected, and that helps to determine how an advocate should approach them.
4. Appointed officials' careers are closely related to continued funding for their agencies, so avoidance of budget cuts looms large in their thinking. They see themselves as problem solvers, not politicians. Other things being equal, it is harder to get to see an appointed official than someone who needs votes to stay in office.
5. When you are targeting an interest group, be clear as to whether you are out to persuade, educate, train for action, or a combination of all of these.
6. When your message is going to several audiences simultaneously, decide which of these have priority.
7. Be aware of the deluge of information and pressures with which the target is coping. Think of how you can get the attention of the target, a prerequisite to getting any action taken.
8. Who are the most important influences on the target's thinking on policy issues? To whom does he or she look for guidance on ambiguous or controversial issues?
9. How does the target define the situation? How do you want him or her to define it? Should you concentrate mainly on the focus of attention, the presumptions about reality, or the value orientation? (More on this question in Chapter 4.)

# Chapter 4

# Preparing the Case

The basic task of the advocate now becomes clear: to use information to create the conditions under which the target will modify his or her definition of the situation. Notice I did not say *change* the target's definition. The target is an active partner in the process. In effect, the advocate assists the target in finding the justification for the change. That is also what happens when an advocate shares information with which a policymaker can defend a decision to colleagues or constituents. The process by which all this takes place is referred to as "argument."

Are arguments just window dressing? It is tempting to believe that, but powerful interests would not spend huge sums to hire skilled arguers if it did not matter. In the political world, one is always trying to maximize support from a range of political constituencies. To justify expending political capital in this way, at least some of the constituencies must be convinced.

We tend to think of arguments only as disputes. However, some arguments involve no dispute, and some disputes—for example screaming matches between young children—are not arguments. An argument, as the term is used here, is a claim, with justification, that something is so, or else that some action should take place. Some writers say that, strictly speaking, any claim is an argument, since it is capable of being justified (see Rieke and Sillars, 1975). I find it more useful to limit the term to statements that include justification, through reasoning and/or evidence. "Drink Blotto!"—according to this definition—is not an argument unless some kind of support is added.

The approach to argument used in this book is audience centered; that is, the sole test of an argument is whether it persuades a particular

*Lobbying for Social Change*
© 2006 by The Haworth Press, Inc. All rights reserved.
doi:10.1300/5782_05

audience (see Perelman and Olbrechts-Tyteca, 1969). That is clearly what happens in policymaking. A decision maker or decision-making body must be persuaded in order for the argument to be successful. This is a far cry from classical argumentation, in which claims had to meet universal standards of proof.

This may seem to confirm your worst fears about the world of policymaking: no universal principles of justice or rightness, just interested parties trying to con the rest of us. There are some fundamental values on which this approach is based, though. One is free and unfettered expression. The danger of suppression of ideas is far greater than whatever mischief might be caused by the worst demagogue. Just as argument needs an open political system, such a system cannot survive for long without argument.

Every system of communication has its means of protecting its own integrity. The scholar exposes ideas to the community of scholars according to accepted rules of discourse; the clinician is trained in self-insight and professionally disciplined; the attorney abides by legal rules; and every set of interests, including the community itself, has its advocate, in theory at least. For the policy advocate, the integrity is built into the open exchange of views. The advocate for social policies aimed at advancing the common good has a special responsibility to give voice to those views in an arena of contending interests.

## MODIFYING THE AUDIENCE'S DEFINITION OF THE SITUATION

Chapter 3 enumerated three elements of definition: the focus of attention, presumptions about the real world, and values. These are the foundations on which an argument is based. The advocate asks these questions:

1. What is the target's present focus of attention, and what do I want it to be?
2. What are the target's presumptions about reality, and how might I modify these?
3. What are the target's value preferences regarding this question, and how can I connect my argument with these?

Note that these are different questions. The first asks where one wants to focus the target's attention, because that is the easiest aspect of definition to change. The second asks how one might change the existing presumptions; that is usually harder to do. The third asks how one can mesh the argument with the target's existing value set. That is because, of the three, values are the hardest to alter.

Let's see how different writers have sought to focus their audiences' attention on the subject of public welfare policy and the related problem of poverty. In this case, the target seems to be "everybody." But even here, the writers have specific kinds of readers in mind, just as this book does. This is how Charles Murray, a well-known writer on welfare reform, began his classic 1984 polemic, *Losing Ground:*

> Our topic is the poor and the discriminated-against as they have been affected by "social policy." We may narrow the focus: I shall be discussing the working-aged poor and discriminated-against, not the elderly, and federal social policy, not variations among states and localities. (Murray, 1984:13)

We may ask why Murray stakes out his territory in this way. Why not the elderly? And why not examine state and local variations? He wants to focus our attention on an age group that it is presumed should be working, because a major part of his argument will focus on why they are not working. "Working," incidentally, is an interesting term. By it Murray means being gainfully employed outside the home. A woman who has been separated from her husband and spends long hours raising several young children by herself is presumed not to be "working."

By excluding state and local variations from the discussion, Murray keeps off the agenda the fact that welfare recipients in some states receive grants that are a fraction of the allowances in other states. These tend to be states that underspend on education and other public programs. Actually, a discussion of federal policy should deal with interstate variations, because the federal public assistance laws are set up to allow for those differences. Some social policy analysts believe the rates should be standardized across the country.

An additional point to notice about Murray's beginning is his reference to the "discriminated-against." He is defining not only the topic but himself as well. "I am not against the welfare poor, in fact

I sympathize with their plight," he seems to be saying. Here is how another book on welfare reform, written around the same time, began:

> Over the last decade, the welfare state has become the target of a concerted ideological attack. From the expanding network of conservative think tanks and foundations on up to the president himself, the same themes are reiterated: that social welfare measures are a drag on the economy, an incentive to immorality, and a cruel hoax on the needy themselves. (Block et al., 1987:ix)

A leading figure in this "concerted ideological attack" was none other than Charles Murray. Just as Murray sought to focus our attention and mold our view of the problem well in advance of any substantive arguments, the authors of the latter volume wanted to prepare us to be receptive to their evidence before it was delivered. Note also that, whereas Murray wanted to narrow the audience's focus by excluding certain aspects of welfare from consideration, Block and his colleagues sought to broaden it. "Don't look at welfare reform in isolation," they were saying, "or you will miss its true significance."

The titles of the two books above were designed to lay the groundwork for their respective messages. *Losing Ground* conveyed a sense of hopelessness about federal welfare programs, as well as identification with the plight of their supposed beneficiaries. The title of the second book, *The Mean Season*, carried with it the Scrooge-like qualities attributed to the conservative critics of the welfare state. In effect, say the authors of this book, the foes of welfare have already scored an important victory by defining the issues for the public. According to the authors of *The Mean Season*,

> It is their charges that have set the research agenda and dominated ensuing public debate. Researchers who defend the welfare state are reduced to claiming that the charges are not true, that the receipt of welfare benefits does not produce most of the deleterious consequences attributed to it. . . . That the main body of empirical evidence provides scant support for the critics is important, to be sure. But it is much more important that the charges have come to frame public discussion. (Block et al., 1987:72)

Environmental protection is a subject of great controversy in this country. Part of the intensity of the debate comes from the monumental and in some cases irreversible effects of one policy or another. It is also the majority who are the direct objects of policy actions, not a stigmatized "they." Proponents of strong governmental action emphasize the long-term effects of environmental pollution, the hazard to the health of people from all walks of life, the world our grandchildren will inherit, and the problem of corporate greed. Opponents stress the need for jobs, the elitist nature of the proponents who are said to care more about some species of hop toad than honest, working men and women, and the need to defend local control against interference by the federal government.

Presidential news conferences offer an interesting lesson in how to mold the definition of the situation to suit one's agenda. Once upon a time, the public learned of the contents of these meetings between the president and reporters by reading about them in the next morning's paper. The president had to rely on the news media to handle his comments as he wanted them to get to the people. The reporters were thus an intermediate target.

All that changed with the arrival of the televised news conference. The reporters have become bit players in a staged presentation. Although they are free to ask any questions they wish, presidents are able to shape the dialogue to a great extent by presenting an introductory statement, picking the questioners and then, after giving an answer which might or might not bear on the question, going on to the next reporter. By avoiding a reputation as a hostile questioner, a newsperson is likely to be picked more often. Reporters have regained a bit of the initiative by asking follow-up questions or simply posing a two-part query. But an insidious aspect of the whole performance is the fact that the reporters, like the president, can now come into American homes in living color.

Presidents exert a great deal of control over news conferences and can have the primary role in defining the situation. What to me is still the all-time classic is an exchange that took place during one of President Richard Nixon's news conferences in 1972. The Watergate break-in had been discovered and there were widespread reports of corruption at high levels, but the administration's image had not yet reached its lowest point, Nixon, knowing what he did, wanted to keep the focus off these problems.

Q: Mr. President, what are you planning to do to defend yourself against the charges of corruption in your administration?

A: Well, I have noted such charges; as a matter of fact, I have noted that this Administration has been charged with being the most corrupt in history, and I have been charged with being the most deceitful president in history. The President of the United States has been compared in his policies with Adolf Hitler. The policies of the U.S. Government to prevent a Communist takeover by force in South Vietnam have been called the worst crime since the Nazi extermination of the Jews in Germany. And the president who went to China and to Moscow, and who has brought 500,000 home from Vietnam, has been called the number-one warmaker in the world.

　　Needless to say, some of my more partisan advisers feel that I should respond in kind. I shall not do so—not now, not throughout this campaign. I am not going to dignify such comments.

　　In view of the fact that one of the very few Members of Congress [Representative Jerome R. Waldie of California] who is publicly and actively supporting the opposition ticket in this campaign has very vigorously, yesterday, criticized these kind of tactics, it seems to me it makes it not necessary for me to respond.

　　I think the responsible members of the Democratic Party will be turned off by this kind of campaigning, and I would suggest that responsible members of the press, following the single standard to which they are deeply devoted, will also be turned off by it.

Q: Mr. President, do you feel, as Vice President Agnew said the other day, that Senator McGovern [Nixon's Democratic opponent] is waging a smear campaign against you? Would you characterize it as that?

A: I am not going to characterize the senator's campaign. As a matter of fact, I don't question his motives. . . . Incidentally, I have no complaint when he raises doubts about mine. That is his choice. (Nixon, 1974:952-954)

　　And on to the next question, which was on the subject of the possibilities of a peace settlement in Vietnam before the elections. You may have a little difficulty recalling what the original question was about. Apparently the reporters did.

Fast-forward to March 2005. Congressman and House Majority Leader Tom DeLay (R-Texas) is embroiled in a nasty series of ethics scandals that threaten to, and eventually do, topple him from power. His critics sit on both sides of the aisle, adding to the seriousness of his plight. Then comes the high drama over the fate of the comatose Terri Schiavo. DeLay becomes her champion, threatening reprisals against the many judges at all levels who have consistently sided with those who would allow her to die. Alas, when Schiavo does die, the news media frenzy over her also expires, and DeLay is once again faced with the problem of having to defend himself on the ethics charges. Translation: Shifting attention away from an issue generally works for only a limited time. Moral of the story: Don't be diverted; stay on message, and be ready to bring other people's attention back to it.

## STRATEGIES OF ARGUMENT
## WITH FOUR KINDS OF AUDIENCES

### The Active Ally

It may seem at first that argument has no place with an ally. Certainly the target shares the advocate's focus, presumptions, and values. One purpose of sharing arguments with supporters is to give them ammunition with which to promote the cause. They are constantly in need of fresh material. But a potentially more serious problem with active allies is the risk that they will become less active or shift their interest to another problem. So the advocate must keep attention on the mutual concern and emphasize its importance, relative to other issues.

Any group of activists loses momentum from time to time. An issue drops out of the headlines, maybe moves from the legislative arena to the courts. In court, obscure, protracted arguments and long stretches when nothing seems to be happening are guaranteed to sap the energy of even the hardiest among us. One of the most draining experiences is to feel that one is fighting a losing battle—all this time and effort going for naught. Opponents sometimes deliberately create that impression. So information about small successes, support from new quarters, and the like can have an important role in rousing the troops to renewed enthusiasm. Allies are also in constant need of updated information to support their position and answer questions from others.

The leaders of the Love Canal Homeowners' Association had to work constantly to keep their members actively involved. As long as the national news media were interested, the leadership of LCHA had a built-in way of keeping up morale. Seeing oneself on the evening news or in the pages of a news magazine was stimulus enough to keep many residents going.

Inevitably, the news media lost interest. Reports of early research that supported LCHA's position were criticized for methodological flaws, seeming to undermine the residents' case. Some people, including the mayor of Niagara Falls, accused the Association of hurting the tourist trade. Conflicting research findings sowed confusion within the group. The Hooker Chemical Company eventually abandoned its low profile and placed ads in the newspapers. Seeing the well-heeled opposition presenting its case in this way was demoralizing to the residents with their meager resources. Then there were the reactions of neighbors who did not feel threatened by the chemical waste as much they felt their jobs threatened by too much criticism of their employers. One way of countering flagging morale among the convinced was to continually find new angles with which to interest the news media. When there were no new angles, the advocates made it a point to remind the public that the problem was still there.

When their drive to enact a constitutional amendment failed, antiabortion activists changed their agenda to seeking to limit federal aid for abortions. One purpose was to keep the movement alive in the face of apparent defeat. However, such fallback strategies carry with them a degree of risk, as committed followers may interpret the scaled-back tactics as betrayal of the original mission.

### *The Committed Opponent*

The first thing to understand is that your active opponent is rarely the audience you are interested in reaching, unless you are engaged in direct negotiations, as in collective bargaining. Most of the time your real target will be allies or potential allies. So when you are locked in a debate with an antagonist, remember that this is not the party you are trying to persuade. Your task is to compete for the support of those outside of the battle. Strategies for dealing with two such nonpartici-pants, the uninvolved and the ambivalent, are presented below.

When you want to have impact on the opponent, your task is the opposite of the active ally's. Instead of energizing the opposition, the advocate seeks to neutralize it. In most instances, the best way not to achieve that end is to engage in acrimonious debate. Unless you be-lieve that the other side's case is weak and can be disposed of easily, a frontal attack may simply rally the opposition. They will then mobi-lize themselves to defend their position all the more vigorously and stimulate even more active involvement in the cause you are against.

Occasionally, an advocate wants to find ways of collaborating with an opponent. For example, the parties to the conflict are wasting time and resources in an impasse, or the fight is creating a dangerous schism. It may be that both antagonists have a common foe and should combine forces against it. Suppose that Caucasian and African-American parents in a low-income neighborhood are locked in a struggle over school policies. In time, they discover that their real problems emanate from a school system that is failing to provide enough resources overall, so the two parties are reduced to fighting over crumbs.

This suggests an argumentative strategy of shifting the focus of at-tention away from the original fight. The groups can collaborate only when they are able to empathize with each other and view the former opponent as an earnest and dedicated advocate of a point of view. The less defensive the person feels, the easier it will be to work together toward shared goals.

## The Uninvolved

In some ways the outright opponent is easier to deal with than the person or group who is not interested in the question. But by using the right argumentative strategy, it is possible to involve people who ini-tially have no interest. The goal here is to get some commitment, however limited, on which to build a larger commitment. Shills on the boardwalk at Atlantic City used to employ the "buy-in" principle. Get the customers to put up a dollar in hopes of winning a big prize. Once in the game they are likely to stay because they don't want to lose that first dollar. Countries sometimes follow the same principle, turning a small investment of military resources into a bigger and bigger war.

Focus is used initially to get the attention of the uninvolved. The public and policymakers are constantly bombarded with various appeals. So advocates must come up with new and interesting ways to catch people's eyes. The trouble is that everyone soon learns the latest trick and starts using it. Direct mail works until everybody is using direct-mail appeals. Then first-class mail gets opened while letters sent at the bulk rate are thrown in the waste basket. Famous names add interest until they simply become a signal that there is a request for funds inside. The word "free" on the outside of the envelope may entice people to take the next step of looking inside. Time was when individually addressed envelopes, as opposed to address labels, rated special attention—until computers made it easy to do mass mailings that looked individualized. The same is true of the insertion of the addressee's name in the letter itself.

There are hundreds of gimmicks for getting attention. You are familiar with many of them because you are frequently the recipient. Our focus here is on the intrinsic interest of the content rather than devices for delivering it. By understanding the value orientation of the target it is possible to tap strong sentiments, tying them to the advocate's agenda.

Joe Public loves children. He is shocked at the idea that very young children have to live in homeless shelters and go to bed hungry at night. But Joe lives in a comfortable suburb where, as far as he knows, such problems don't exist. He rides the commuter train through a poverty-stricken area on his way downtown every weekday morning. He has long since blanked out the scene moving past the train window. Of course, chances are he never did associate the abandoned refrigerators and peeling paint with blighted young lives. The children playing in the vacant lots seemed happy enough.

A television documentary on the plight of poor children may get a temporary reaction from Joe Public, but that soon fades into the background; there are more pressing problems such as payments on the new car and what to do about Jane's mother now that she is living alone. It will take more exposure to the reality of poverty, possibly a firsthand look at the problem, to jar Joe out of his apathy. This is only a first step in moving him to actively support legislation to alleviate the problem. Joe may simply become angry at the parents who allow their children to suffer in ways that he is sure he never would. This is at least a starting point on the way to getting his support for positive programs. Better that he be involved and misguided—temporarily, at least—than that he continue ignoring the problem.

We also have to deal with Joe's presumptions. Two kinds are evident: the belief that things are generally all right, so there is no need to be involved in changing them; and the belief that the problem is the behavior of the parents. Maybe more aid from the government would only make things worse, thinks Joe, by making the adults more dependent.

As we provide information to correct these misconceptions we need to do it in a way that doesn't tell Joe he is stupid or unfeeling. He is neither. As we tap into his basic humanity and credit him for it, he is free to respond. Once we have begun to involve Joe, it is important to keep going. Otherwise, he may simply be reminded of his antagonism toward the poor. Better that he be left asleep than that he be roused and then ignored.

Advocates of more enlightened mental health policies have sometimes tried to scare the public into supporting their cause. At points, graphic depictions of life in the snake pit can grab one's attention, but they can also lead people to tune out, particularly if the problem seems insoluble. One sure way to induce apathy is to create a feeling of hopelessness. So, in addition to focusing attention on the problems of the mentally ill and dispelling the illusion that everything is all right, advocates for the funding of community–mental health programs must show what can be done if adequate support is forthcoming.

The same problem exists in relation to poverty-impacted urban communities. Too often, people who are truly distressed by what they see figure it's never going to change. Know what? If enough people assume that, then, indeed, it's much less likely to happen.

### The Ambivalent

Ambivalence is not always easy to evaluate because it can look like apathy or opposition. One way a person resolves inner conflict is to deny that a problem exists. Joe Public has never thought much about poverty. Jane, his wife, has thought almost too much about it—her thoughts move in circles. As a young college graduate, she was strongly committed to ridding the world of the ravages of poverty. She took a job in a public assistance office. Suddenly, she discovered that poor people were not all paragons of virtue. In fact, the stresses of their existence led many of them into very unadmirable behavior. Unable to adopt the cynical attitudes of some of her co-workers, she "resolved" her dilemma by running away from it. Underneath that apparent apathy lies an uneasy conscience.

Fred Mobile knows what it is to be poor because he was once there himself. He managed to escape the alcoholic father, the defeated mother, and the siblings who began to repeat these patterns. Now having made it to a job in Joe Public's engineering firm and a comfortable apartment in the suburbs, Fred is clear on what to do about poor people: Let them pull themselves up by their own bootstraps, just as he did.

This nice, neat analysis breaks down periodically, for example when Fred's sister is deserted by her husband and left to bring up three children on her own. Having dropped out of high school when she became pregnant the first time, she has few skills with which to get a stable job. Fred is willing to help his sister, but the conflicting feelings simply harden his attitude toward poor people and programs designed to assist them.

The first task of the advocate is to understand, as well as possible, what sorts of feelings lie under the surface. Joe Public, his wife, Jane, and his assistant Fred each present a different picture requiring a different argumentative strategy.

Simply focusing Jane's and Fred's attention on the problem of childhood poverty will do little to move them to support positive programs. Nor is it very productive to try to win debates with them when they raise objections to helping "those people." In both cases, their ambivalence and underlying guilt will drive them to fight harder to resist your message.

Instead of trying to beat them into submission, you should act as if there is no debate. Focus their attention on your side of their dilemma, for instance by citing concrete situations that have come to your attention involving the plight of poor children.

The same goes for dealing with presumptions. Avoid trying to win a debate. When they present their arguments to justify their position, accept these as sincere and let them know you are aware that it is possible to have mixed feelings about poverty. You may even acknowledge that what they are saying may be true. At no point should you say you share their view that there is no problem or that it's all the parents' fault. You can simply agree to disagree. But then keep bringing the focus back to the conditions you have seen or heard of. The more concrete the better.

As you introduce information, you are helping Jane and Fred find justification for resolving their dilemma. In the last analysis, the only person who will convince Jane Public is Jane Public. Ditto for Fred Mobile. You are merely assisting them in that process.

How do we help Jane and Fred get beyond their dilemma? The advocate gets them, in effect, to put themselves on record. As with the apathetic target whose small commitments are used to build larger ones, each time Jane or Fred publicly takes a stand it becomes harder to renege. Fred and Jane can't afford to repudiate their own position. The more public it is, the harder it is to switch sides. If they acknowledge to you in private that they agree with your stance, that is better than no agreement. But if they do so in the presence of others, the commitment is stronger. If they are led to sign a petition, lobby their representatives, or make a statement at a public meeting, it is even better.

It should be clear from what has been said that it is not always possible to tell what kind of audience you are dealing with. An active ally in your campaign for mental health funding may show up on the other side when the issue is welfare reform.

This suggests some presumptions for you. Presume that the target is sincere, shares your concern for people, and is open to change. As with all presumptions, this one may have to be revised in the face of evidence to the contrary. But this positive approach is the place to start. If you presume the best, you have not lost anything except possibly some time wasted on a lost cause. If you start by presuming the worst, you are likely to miss opportunities to gain allies and may provoke unnecessary antagonism.

## THE POLICY BRIEF

A policy brief is a detailed set of arguments on both sides of a question, with supporting evidence. It is organized around a set of issues designed to cover all bases regarding a policy proposal. By preparing two cases, your own and your adversaries', you are in a position both to present forceful arguments and to answer questions that might be thrown at you. It is not fail-safe—nothing is in lobbying—but it greatly increases your effectiveness and your confidence. Think of the brief as a resource paper rather than a document to circulate to policymakers. Occasionally, however, you may want to share your brief with a friendly legislator, as a resource to him or her. "Brief" is something of a misnomer; some run thirty or forty pages. How long should a brief be? Long enough to answer all the major issues and rebut some or all of the answers.

### Issues

Issues are critical "questions at issue," which is another way of saying potential points of contention in an argument. Think of the issues as the bones that make up the skeleton of the argument. Like a skeleton, they fit together to become one piece. And like a skeleton, if they were missing, the argument would collapse. The person proposing a new policy must have good answers to all the issues, while an opponent can overturn the entire case by rebutting the proponent's argument on one major issue. That may seem like an unfair advantage for the opponent, but the logic of it will be clear as we look at how an argument works. In any actual case, the issues may vary but there are standard questions that must always be answered by the proponent.

### Arguments Based on Definition

This is the simplest kind of argument. It states that something is so. John Doe, it is charged, is guilty of murder. There are two basic issues: (1) What is the definition of murder? (2) Has John Doe done something that fits this definition? If the accuser can't define murder satisfactorily, the case against John collapses. If the accuser gives a satisfactory definition but can't apply it to what John has done, the case also collapses. The legal system has a well-defined definition of murder, so court cases are more likely to focus on the second issue: Does this apply to John Doe?

Some arguments by definition are more complicated. For example: Are mental health services a good investment? The first issue—what is meant by a good investment—will be a major point of contention, as will the second—whether one can apply that designation to mental health services.

## Cause-Effect Arguments

Showing that something causes something else is more involved. To start with, the line between cause and effect in social matters is complex, not the unidirectional and unidimensional link that is often portrayed. There can be multiple causes and effects of a phenomenon. Sometimes cause and effect work in a cycle, so effect is also cause. So the question is not whether A is the cause of B but whether A is a significant factor contributing to B. The implication is that, if one reduces A, then B will also be reduced to a significant degree.

What are the basic issues in a cause-effect argument? (1) Are the alleged cause and effect accurately defined? (2) Is there a plausible connection between them? (3) Can one rule out other explanations, or at least show that the alleged cause is more important than the others?

Suppose someone says, "Toxic chemicals in the soil have caused the recent upsurge in cancer cases in this area." Issue number one is: Are the terms accurately portrayed? How are you defining "toxic" chemicals? And has there in fact been an upsurge in cancer? Are we talking about the number of cancer cases or the rate?

That first issue—the accuracy of the description of the alleged cause and effect—is often overlooked. A welfare critic says "the rise" in the welfare caseload is a result of "the epidemic" of teenage pregnancy. There is a tendency for an opponent to accept these alleged trends and go on to argue the causal relationship. That is a mistake, because there may be neither a rise in welfare cases nor in the rate of teenage pregnancy. One has, therefore, made an unnecessary concession to the welfare critic.

The second issue regarding toxic chemicals and cancer is whether it is a plausible connection, that is, does it "make sense?" Yes, it stands to reason that toxic chemicals might cause cancer. Contrast that with the argument that, since cancer rates and medical technology have both been advancing at the same period in history, the latter is the cause of the former. We would reject that kind of argument as preposterous.

Many arguments end right there. Once a believable case has been made, a person may not push on to the third issue: Can other explanations be ruled out? That is a mistake. Toxic chemicals may indeed be the villain, but, the lawyer for the chemical company says, a new retirement home was opened at this site, bringing many elderly people—some terminally ill—into the area. That may be a better explanation for the increased cancer, he says. He may be wrong, but it is the proponent's task to demonstrate that.

This last example points out an important lesson for the advocate, and one of the major values of analyzing the issues. In order to make one's case, it is necessary to cover all the bases and make sure the arguments are solid on all major issues. Otherwise, it is easy to be caught off guard by an opponent.

## Arguments Calling for Action

The kind of argument involved in advocating a policy change is the most complex of all. It is really made up of a series of arguments by definition and cause-effect arguments. Here are four basic questions the proponent must always be able to answer:

1. Is there a need for change? (If not, there is no point in presenting a plan for change.)
2. Will the proposed plan meet the need? (If not, the argument need go no further. It is not necessary to show that the problem will be solved entirely, just that the situation will be materially improved.)
3. Is the plan feasible? (A plan may be great in theory, but if implementing it will cost too much, is unconstitutional, or is too complex to administer, then it should be rejected.)
4. Would the benefits of the plan outweigh any harmful consequences? (A plan may be relevant to the initial problem and feasible, but it might produce side effects so devastating as to make it worse than no action at all.)

Remember that the advocate for change must make a convincing case regarding every one of the previous points. The opponent can overturn the whole case by knocking out one point. Strictly speaking, it is up to the opponent to decide whether to offer a counter-proposal, but to be a naysayer without offering an alternative plan can place the opponent in a vulnerable position.

## WRITING A BRIEF ABOUT ABORTION

To show you what goes into a brief, I will lay out the basic design of a brief calling for a total ban on abortions. Then I will do a 180-degree turn and argue for total discretion in abortions. These are not simply opposite sides of the same coin. In each case, the definition of the problem will be different, so the issues that flow from that definition will be different. In the first case, that of the antiabortion proposal, the advocate will focus on the immorality of abortion, the definition of the beginning of life, and the potential harm to the fetus. In the second, the focus will be on the rights of the pregnant woman. At points the issues will overlap.

### The Antiabortion Brief

"The U.S. Constitution should be amended to prohibit abortions under any circumstances."

The advocate must show that abortions are inherently wrong and that it is a legitimate role of the government to ban them. The Need for a Change section of the brief will therefore focus on what is wrong with abortion. The strategy will be to show that abortions are wrong legally, morally, and socially.

### Need for a Change

1. When does life begin? The advocate must show that from conception onward a human life is at stake in order to argue on the grounds of legal rights, morality, and the social consequences for the fetus. Evidence for this part of the argument will be sought in philosophical and theological as well as scientific literature.

2. Is a fetus a "person" in a legal sense? This is a different question. It could be argued that human life at its earliest stages lacks the legal definition of a rights-bearing person. Unless the personhood of the fetus is established, it will be difficult to claim constitutional rights for it. The evidence for this part of the argument may be found in treatises on constitutional law. However, the advocate will not base his or her case solely on constitutional grounds. The advocate will also argue that abortion is morally wrong, regardless of how the constitution is interpreted by the courts.

3. Does abortion deprive the fetus of its constitutional rights? If the advocate has established that the fetus is legally a person in its own right, it follows that it cannot be deprived of life without due process of law. It is absurd to think that the fetus can have done anything to justify killing it.

4. Is abortion morally wrong? Here the advocate must establish some moral criterion acceptable to the audience. If the audience shares the same religious beliefs, the argument can be grounded in these religious tenets. Or the advocate may cite statements from leaders of diverse religious communities or respected philosophers. Most likely, the appeal will be to broadly shared beliefs in the value of human life.

5. What are the consequences of abortion for the fetus? Not content to rely on constitutional and moral grounds, the advocate now tries to show that abortion is cruel and inhumane. We don't base the humane treatment of animals on their being humans. So the advocate will seek evidence showing that fetuses not only die but suffer in the process. Antiabortion organizations are the most likely to know where such evidence is. The advocate will seek data from objective scientific studies, rather than relying solely on dramatic material from interested parties. In the next chapter, we consider kinds of evidence and how to obtain them.

6. What are the consequences of abortion for the mother? (The opposition may question the use of the term "mother.") Here the advocate will focus on trauma, stress, guilt, and conflict over the decision connected with abortions. There is also some evidence (mixed) regarding the effects on future pregnancies. Evidence on this will be sought in psychological research and clinical data from psychiatry, social work, and other supporting professions.

7. What are the consequences of abortion for society? One line of argument here is the loss of human potential for society. There are the unknown contributions of the unborn to art, literature, and science. Abortion cheapens the value of human life, thus generally cheapening values in society. By focusing on abortion as a solution to the world's problems, we fail to focus on the real problems of hunger, want, and maldistribution of resources. This line of argument relies heavily on interpretation of evidence, which might be drawn from a wide range of sources.

8. Is the problem urgent? The advocate pulls together statistics on the number of abortions being performed and any projections of future trends. Standard statistical sources are the most likely place to find evidence.

## The Plan

9. What action is proposed? The advocate must state the plan clearly. Examples of the same or similar kinds of proposed constitutional amendments could be offered. This also helps lay the groundwork for feasibility. Books on the abortion issue are the most likely place to learn about precedents of this kind. Previous bills in Congress proposing such an amendment could be appended to the end of the brief.

10. Will the amendment remedy the problem? The advocate demonstrates how the plan deals specifically with the nature of the problem as described in the earlier section, Need for a Change. Each issue raised in that section should be restated and the case made that the plan will address that particular concern. If similar actions have been shown to be effective in curbing abortions, that evidence should be included here. Evidence is most likely to be found in books on the abortion issue. Antiabortion organizations can give leads on where to find this information.

## Feasibility

11. Is such a plan economically feasible? Such an amendment would automatically preclude expenditure of state funds for abortions, and thus reduce, not increase, direct costs. However,

the advocate will have to deal with the question of paying for the care of additional children, many of whom will undoubtedly be at high risk, since so-called unwanted babies figure prominently in the aborted pregnancies. Bringing some fetuses to term could mean astronomical medical costs over a lifetime. It is important to get as accurate figures as possible on the costs of any proposal, so as not to give a misleading impression. Figures of this kind are going to be a combination of the scientific and the speculative.

12. Is the plan politically feasible? The advocate should try to show support for such a bill in Congress, in state legislatures, and among voters. Evidence can be found in Congressional Quarterly Almanac and in public opinion poll data. Books on the history of the abortion issue are a good source.

13. Is the plan vulnerable to challenge on constitutional grounds? It might seem at first blush that by definition the total ban would be constitutional because it would be in the form of a constitutional amendment. New amendments have sometimes reversed older ones (as in the case of prohibition), but for all practical purposes, an amendment on abortion would need to be grounded in some way on constitutional precedent. More to the point, having argued that abortion violates the constitutional rights of the unborn, the advocate cannot now turn around and ignore the same guarantees for the living. There may be articles in law journals dealing with this question. Books on constitutional law might also be consulted.

## Consequences

14. What are the potential benefits of a total ban on abortions? The advocate summarizes positive effects of such a step. Some of these may have been covered previously but would be reiterated here.

15. What are the potentially harmful effects of such a ban? At this point the advocate must consider likely objections to be raised by an opponent. Would the ban interfere with the rights of the pregnant woman, or what is sometimes called the right of a child to be wanted? What about the specter of overpopulation? Does a total ban on abortions discriminate against women too poor to

travel to other countries for the operation? In response, the advocate might take on the relative priority between the burden to the woman of giving birth and the very life of the unborn child, the unlikelihood that any child would prefer being dead to being unwanted and alive.
16. Do the potential benefits outweigh the potential harm? The advocate must obviously be able to answer this in the affirmative.

## Rebuttal

Wearing the other hat, advocates now attack their own case. They may elaborate on negative consequences cited in item 15, but they will also go back and raise questions about the definition of the problem and whether the proposed solution will really do the job. They may propose an alternative solution. They will attack at any and all points where they think a real opponent might. Finally, they will say how they would deal with these attacks on their case.

## The Pro-Choice Brief

"The state should make no restrictions on abortion beyond those that apply in any medical procedure."

Our focus shifts sharply now to the pregnant woman and her rights. The alleged immorality and other issues raised in the previous Need for a Change section will have to be dealt with at the point that this brief engages the potentially harmful effects.

## Need for a Change

1. What are constitutional rights? The advocate wants to define these as applying to the living. This will lay the groundwork for distinguishing between the legal claims of people and those of fetuses. Evidence might be found in books on constitutional law and articles in law journals.
2. Are women being denied their constitutional rights by current restrictions on abortion? The advocate wants to place the right to control one's body in the context of equal rights of men and

women. The argument will be made that restrictions on abortion are part of overall oppression of women.

3. Should decisions regarding abortion be based on medical opinion? You may recall that in California in the 1960s, abortion restrictions were liberalized to give doctors wide discretion in determining whether abortion was appropriate. Under this reform, over 90 percent of women seeking abortions got them. But the advocate will reject this benign domination by the medical profession and argue instead for abortion as a right. As long as women do not have absolute discretion, they are not treated equally. One can think of many analogies, such as employees who are treated in a humane fashion but are denied the right to form a union. This issue can be placed in the historical context of sex discrimination. Evidence could be found in the literature on civil rights and equal protection before the law, and history of female oppression.

4. What are the consequences of abortion restrictions for women? Consequences include greater risk of illegal abortion under unsafe conditions, with hazards to women's lives and health. In addition to continuing with the equal-rights-for-women line of argument, the advocate focuses on poor and minority women, linking denial of reproductive rights to race and class discrimination and feminization of poverty. Teenage pregnancies that cannot be terminated lead to school drop-outs and aborted career aspirations. Affluent women will still be able to get abortions outside of the country. Social science literature, especially material used in women's studies courses, may be helpful here. Also, substantial information can be found in popular books and magazines. When studies are cited, see if you can get back to the original.

5. What are the consequences of abortion restrictions for society? Abortion restrictions bring births of unwanted children and overpopulation. Teenage parents have high risks of health problems (for both mother and child) and welfare dependency. A teenager's potential contribution to society is lessened if she drops out of school and doesn't get career training. Pro-choice groups may be helpful in steering the advocate to sources of evidence. There is a larger threat to freedom in the antiabortion crusade: the attempt of one religious group to impose its values on

society. This raises question about the basic principle of separation of church and state. Evidence may be found in some books tracing the history of abortion.

6. What are the consequences of abortion restrictions for the fetus? The chances are greater of babies being born deformed or otherwise impaired and vulnerable to abuse and rejection. Antiabortionists play on the abortion-as-cruel theme; it helps to show that the suffering is not restricted to the aborted. Again, prochoice groups are likely to know about supportive evidence.

7. Is action urgent? The advocate focuses on estimated risk of maternal injury and death due to illegal abortions and the continued discrimination against women. Again, the advocate starts with pro-choice groups to find evidence but doesn't stop there. The advocate wants objective information sources.

*Plan*

8. What is the proposed remedy? The advocate can simply call for enactment of a statute and not take on the more difficult process of amending the Constitution (two-thirds majorities in both houses and ratification by three-fourths of the state legislatures). The reason for this is the rule of presumption: Unless a restriction is enacted, there is no restriction. Until states enacted antiabortion laws in the nineteenth century, abortions were not prohibited except for mild and limited common-law sanctions. (It did not even take the involvement of a licensed physician.) What the Supreme Court did in 1973 was to overturn these statutes. It said states may prohibit abortions in the third trimester, and under certain circumstances in the second, but it did not declare that fetuses were protected. Therefore, new legislation guaranteeing women the right to have an abortion would challenge existing state laws but not the Court's interpretation of the Constitution.

We can be sure, of course, that such a law, assuming it could get through Congress, would be challenged in the courts by antiabortion groups. The advocate could go for a constitutional amendment, a more limited version of the Equal Rights Amendment that failed for lack of ratification by enough states. Pro-choice groups may be aware of model legislation of both the statutory and constitutional amendment kind.

9. Will the proposal remedy the problem? The advocate takes each issue of need and shows how such a law would help to correct it. Establishing reproductive rights in law will not erase sex discrimination, nor oppression of low-income minority women. It is necessary, however, that the proposal improve the situation significantly, especially as one considers potential negative consequences later on. For a bill to risk causing problems without simultaneously remedying those it was intended to deal with would make it a harmful bill.

## Feasibility

10. Is the plan economically feasible? It is hard to see how cost would loom as a major factor in enactment of such a law. It may actually reduce costs of law enforcement. It may also reduce indirect costs of caring for additional high-risk children, birth trauma to women, and women less able to contribute to the economy, although these cost factors might better go in the section on positive benefits. One might try to get evidence of these costs. The Alan Guttmacher Institute of New York has issued reports summarizing some of this evidence. Start by checking the Internet or a university library for these items.

11. Is the plan politically feasible? A bill making abortions totally discretionary on the part of the woman is probably not feasible at this point but might become so in the future. A case can be made for introducing the idea now, in order to set the political debate in motion. It is not unusual for new proposals to take ten years or more to move to the point of enactment—usually in a form different from the original. National health insurance legislation, discussed as a possible part of the 1935 Social Security Act, was enacted in limited form (Medicare) thirty years later. Evidence on political feasibility can be found in previous votes and opinion polls. (See the Feasibility section of the preceding brief.)

12. Is the plan vulnerable to challenge on constitutional grounds? The ambiguity of the Supreme Court's *Roe v. Wade* decision, one that was itself highly controversial, raises a serious potential

problem for a law as sweeping as that proposed. For evidence, the advocate should review those court decisions and discussions of the issue in law journals.

## Consequences

13. What are the potential benefits of the plan? The advocate summarizes the positive consequences anticipated, including any not covered previously.
14. What are the potential negative consequences? The advocate must take each of the grounds on which antiabortionists base their case and answer it. (See the Need for Change section in the preceding brief.) Are the legal "rights" of the fetus compromised? The status of the fetus as a rights-bearing citizen is challenged.

    Is abortion morally wrong? The Roman Catholic Church, one of the main proponents of that view, did not always ban abortion. There is disagreement among different Protestant denominations. The original state laws were enacted mainly on medical grounds, at the urging of the medical profession, which was then seeking professional recognition and wanted to retain control over this sector of health care. Many of the people performing abortions at that time were quacks. If abortions are restricted, it will drive young women into the arms of quacks and undercut the original rationale for abortion statutes. Books on the history of abortion are good sources of evidence on this. As far as the lost contribution to society is concerned, there is a much greater loss in terms of the suffering and disadvantage that many of these high-risk children will experience. The alleged trauma of the aborting woman must be weighed against the trauma of unwanted births and back-alley abortions. (See preceding brief for sources.)
15. Do potential benefits outweigh potentially negative consequences? Again, the advocate must show that they do.

## Rebuttal

Play devil's advocate against the case, as in the previous brief, and say how you would answer the challenge.

## NOW YOU TRY PLANNING A BRIEF

Having seen what a brief looks like and how one goes about developing one, you are ready for the next step: engaging in the process yourself. I am not suggesting that you undertake to complete a brief at this point but that you go through the steps required in planning one. Basically, this will be a brief minus the evidence. Below are two suggested issues: one involving the funding of community mental health centers; the other dealing with the kind of troubled urban school district described in Chapters 2 and 3.

### *Mental Health Funding*

The proposition: "Federal funding of mental health services should be expanded."

In the Need for a Change section of the brief, you should ask what was the intent of the current policy. Then ask if current funding allows for the full implementation of that intent. What are the effects of the gap between intent and implementation on (1) the mentally ill, (2) the maintenance of professional services, and (3) the community at large? Finally, why is the need for a change urgent?

In the section on the Plan, what is it that is proposed and what specifically would be done with the money? (You need to avoid being accused of wanting to "throw money at problems.") Does the past track record of such services give us reason to believe that spending more money will actually remedy the problems laid out in the needs section?

A major feasibility issue, of course, will be economic. Can the country afford the extra expenditure? Do you propose reducing other expenditures? Or would you raise taxes or increase the federal deficit? Do not fudge on the cost of what you are proposing. The figures in the full brief would have to be real figures. Closely related to the economic feasibility question is political feasibility. What leads you to think Congress and the administration would buy your plan?

What are the potential negative consequences of your proposal? Is this plan a way to help the mentally ill, or a donation to the welfare of mental health professionals? Do we get full value out of dollars spent this way? Will this take political and economic support away from other pressing social needs?

In your rebuttal, you may need to take issue with the way the opposition has interpreted the question itself. You will also probably want to go back and see what was intended by Congress in the first place. Also, pay attention to the time that has elapsed since enactment of the original legislation and the present. In the same way, scrutinize how the opponent has responded to each issue.

### Low-Performing Schools

In this case, rather than provide you with a proposition, I'll let you come up with your own. For example, should there be a massive infusion of federal funds to jump-start school districts with low test scores? Should troubled school districts be converted to publicly funded charter school operations that are free to experiment with minimum interference from the public school system? Should compulsory education for all be abandoned, with some sort of trade training or apprenticeship system being devised for those children manifestly unable to profit from public school? Or can you come up with a different approach to the problem of troubled school systems?

Whatever your plan, you will need to demonstrate a need for change and propose a plan that will meet the need, one that is feasible, with positive effects that outweigh the negative consequences. And, of course, you will have to work out a rebuttal against your plan and how you would answer the rebuttal.

### POINTS TO REMEMBER

1. Preparation of the argument begins with an assessment of the target's definition of the situation: focus, presumptions, and values.
2. The task is to create the conditions for the target to change his or her definition by shifting the focus, modifying presumptions, and tapping into shared values.
3. Active allies must be kept engaged and provided with supportive information.

4. With active opponents, the task is to direct one's arguments to the real target, who is usually not the opponent. It is sometimes possible to collaborate with opponents on other agendas.

5. With apathetic targets, the task is to get small commitments as a basis for larger commitments. Focus is used to gain attention. Information is used to dispel the illusion that there is no need for change.

6. Ambivalent targets are harder to assess than others because their reactions may be similar to those of apathetic targets or antagonists. The task is to get public agreement—the more public and irreversible the better. Focus and information are used to provide the justification for taking the desired position and abandoning the unwanted one.

7. The advocate should presume that targets are sincere, share one's concern for people, and are open to change. Above all, one should neither concede the argument nor provoke unnecessary opposition.

8. A brief is a resource for the advocate's own use, not a document to share with targets. Occasionally, however, advocates find it useful to give a copy of the brief to a friendly policymaker or advocacy group.

9. The brief is a presentation of the evidence, with documentation, organized around the set of issues that structure the argument. This makes it maximally useful in preparing a presentation or finding answers with which to respond to questions from others.

10. The advocate first puts together as complete and airtight a case as possible, then seeks to attack his or her own case in a rebuttal. Finally, the advocate indicates his or her strategy for dealing with the issues raised in the rebuttal.

# Chapter 5

# Gathering Evidence

In Chapter 1, I stressed the importance of information as an asset to bring to the lobbying task. One kind of information (strategic) has to do with knowing where, when, and by whom the critical decisions will be made. The other type of information (policy) concerns the content of policy itself, the kinds of data that would support your arguments. This chapter is about the latter kind of information.

This chapter goes hand-in-hand with Chapter 4, "Preparing the Case." The formulation of your case will determine what kinds of data you need. Without the structure of the argument, you could go on amassing facts forever without knowing how to use them.

We will start with the different kinds of evidence and their potential strengths and weaknesses. Following that are some pointers on assessing how good the evidence is. Finally, we look at different sources of evidence and how to use them effectively.

## KINDS OF EVIDENCE

### Cases in Point

These are examples of policy in action, generally personal narratives to show how a particular policy impacts real people's lives. Even when atypical, cases in point, stories about individuals, are among the most powerful kinds of evidence in the world of politics. To demonstrate this I'll use—what else?—a case in point.

In mid-March 2005, the nation was locked in a debate about social security that could have huge implications for current retirees, future

*Lobbying for Social Change*
© 2006 by The Haworth Press, Inc. All rights reserved.
doi:10.1300/5782_06

retirees, and the generations of children and grandchildren yet unborn. Social Security aside, Congress was contemplating actions that
would balloon the federal debt out of sight. Meanwhile, young Americans were dying daily in Iraq, and the slaughter of thousands of innocent women and children in the Darfur region of Sudan went on.

In the midst of these portentous events, Congress and the president
and the national news media suddenly put all that aside and turned
their attention to one woman who had been lying in a vegetative state
in Florida for fifteen years. What had started out as a family dispute
about Terry Schiavo's fate became a national cause célèbre. For a
brief time, the question of whether to stop life supports for this
woman, then whether to reconnect them, simply took over the national psyche—midnight debates in Congress, a president flying back
to Washington at a moment's notice, prayer vigils involving thousands, media pundits discussing the issue at length. If there was ever
any question about the power of the individual case to dominate the
political process, this wholesale diversion of the nation's attention
from matters that might arguably be considered more important from
a national policy standpoint should provide a clear answer.

The most powerful images are indeed those of real people and
places. Chances are that long after you have forgotten some of the
major principles in this book, you will still remember how Senator
Inouye's legislative aide gave him advice based on information fed to
her by a defense contractor. We are by nature curious about people,
and our minds find it easiest to place events in actual locations, graph-
ically described. Good storytellers will put their listeners right in the
story, so they can "see" what happened, not just hear about it.

Sit in a legislative hearing on homelessness. Watch the body language of the representatives as they listen to a learned recitation of
facts about the problem of homelessness. The numbers are truly stag-
gering, even numbing, as can be seen by the glazed expressions on the
legislators' faces. Now see what happens when seventy-year-old
Jenny Sidewalk tells what happened to her last week. The committee
members sit up and pay attention. One individual versus banks of statistics? Obviously a single case tells us nothing about the extent of the
problem; find a home for Jenny and her immediate problem is solved.
The purpose of her testimony is policy change, not personal rescue.
That single case will stay with the legislators when they have to vote

on a bill to finance shelters. The story will be passed along to colleagues over lunch.

This is not to say that statistics have no place, but without a concrete example or two to bring them to life they tend to be forgotten quickly. The most effective testimony will include both, so we can see the extent of the problem overall and how it affects real people.

Jenny has two things going for her: the arresting reality of the tangible example and the fact that she is speaking from her own experience. People whose work brings them in close contact with the victims on a daily basis can be nearly as persuasive. They are actually in a better position to show that this is not one older woman's idiosyncratic problem, but something happening to many persons with whom the advocate works.

Another way of using real-life examples to get a point across to an audience is to get each person to imagine himself or herself in the situation. You are huddling on that street corner as the temperature plunges. You turn down the opportunity to come into the city shelter because it is actually safer out in the open. You refuse to live with your son and daughter-in-law because they abuse you.

Notice that in order to get across my point about real people, I used an example of one. I put you in the hearing room and told you about Jenny Sidewalk rather than speaking in generalities.

Now if I were arranging firsthand testimony in a hearing on a homeless shelter bill, I would want to include more examples than just Jenny. Maybe a young mother and a young man just out of a mental hospital. It would be important to have my concrete examples represent the range of situations the bill is supposed to address. Two cases are more than twice as good as one. Three are more than three times as good. Beyond a certain point, of course, I run the danger of overkill.

In giving examples, I want to avoid giving my target any excuses for justifying inaction. Several years ago, a group of welfare mothers visited the Ohio state capitol to plead for an increase in benefits. At that time assistance grants were running at less than 70 percent of the state's own standard of need, so an improvement was clearly needed. The lawmakers appeared to be impressed until one of the mothers lit up a cigarette. That was all some conservative legislators needed. "They get enough to spend on cigarettes instead of food for their kids," one snorted. That image fit in with existing stereotypes about welfare clients drinking up the taxpayers' money while their children went hungry.

Because of their appealing quality and the fact that they involve small numbers of situations, concrete examples are open to misuse. When an opponent trots out a "typical" case, be ready to ask how typical it is. Can he or she back it up with any figures? Even more to the point, is this an actual situation or a hypothetical one? If the former, how does the person know that?

Ronald Reagan used to tell a story about a woman who drove up to the supermarket in her white Cadillac to use her food stamps. Implication: She didn't need them, since she was obviously a lot better off than the hard-working taxpayers who were treating her to this buying binge. Welfare advocates used to comment that this woman sure got around. They had heard about the same woman in Boston, Phoenix, Chicago, St. Louis, and Denver. Implication: The woman was a figment of someone's imagination.

Reagan was able to cite a concrete instance of a person who seemed to be getting thousands of dollars illegally through welfare fraud. Critics responded by showing the small percentage of cases of fraud in the welfare rolls, but the image of the fraudulent individual was likely to stick in people's minds better than the statistics. Rather than persist in arguing about the accuracy of the case example, which merely rivets it more firmly into people's minds, it is probably wiser to make a brief rebuttal and shift the focus to the plight of the people who are suffering because of punitive and restrictive policies.

### *Official Policy Actions*

Official documents giving legislative decisions, court rulings, and administrative regulations speak with special authority, since once the decision is made it sets a new precedent. Policymakers tend to follow precedent unless there is a powerful argument to the contrary. Is the current mental health center's program fulfilling congressional intent? Is a law requiring welfare recipients to allow caseworkers into their homes constitutional? Is a chemical company liable for damages caused by its previous deposit of toxic waste if the local school district agreed to assume responsibility for all damages when it took possession of the waste site? "Let the record speak for itself," as they say.

The degree of authority varies. Legislative intent itself carries a great deal of weight, but someone's interpretation of that intent can be challenged. The intent is stated in general and sometimes vague terms, so the adherence to it is at best ambiguous. The second example, the requirement that welfare recipients open their doors to caseworkers, was the subject of a Supreme Court decision in 1971; a majority opinion written by Justice Blackmun ruled that welfare recipients could be required to admit caseworkers to their homes (*Wyman v. James,* 1971). This might be overturned in the future, but until then it is a rule that must be obeyed. Once a ruling has been made it tends to be respected by subsequent courts.

In the case of toxic waste damage liability, the United States District Court for the Western District of New York declared that the Hooker Chemical Company was not absolved of liability for damages caused by toxic chemicals in Love Canal, even though the Niagara Falls Board of Education signed an agreement at the time it purchased the site from Hooker (*United States et al. v. Hooker,* 1988). Since the company and its parent corporation had billions of dollars at stake in potential judgments against them elsewhere, they were sure to appeal this ruling. The U.S. Supreme Court could overturn the judgment.

In general, administrative rulings are most subject to later reversal and judicial decisions are least. Legislative actions are somewhere in between. Decisions by lower courts can be reversed by a higher court. In short, official actions are authoritative but not gospel, and some are more "official" than others.

The *Congressional Record* is supposedly a faithful account of everything that happens in sessions of Congress, and it's not supposed to include anything that doesn't happen there. But, not only do members include such extraneous material as editorials from hometown newspapers, they can also "clean up" the record after the fact. Some people cite statements in the *Congressional Record,* implying that they therefore must be true. I recall seeing one forgettable book in which the author cited the *Record* to back up several outlandish claims but did not bother to identify the specific location of the material. Of course it was impossible to check any of his citations for accuracy.

Relying on secondary sources for information about official actions is risky. When possible, check the original source. In one debate on facilitating school desegregation, a student made an impassioned appeal for mandatory busing, citing what he said was the law of the land as interpreted by the Supreme Court. His eloquence was moving and one wondered what the opponent could say in rebuttal. The opponent pointed out that if one read the Court's decision in full, it was possible to come to a very different conclusion. By showing that she had done her homework, she successfully undercut the first student's argument. In the review of the debate afterward, the first student acknowledged that he had not read the original decision but had relied on a popular book on the subject.

Because official acts are subject to legal challenge, they are written in exact but difficult language. To avoid misinterpreting the record, check it out in a number of secondary sources. If *The New York Times,* the *National Journal,* and *Congressional Quarterly Almanac* (standard sources available in most college and university libraries and many large city public libraries) all agree in their interpretation, it is reasonable to go with their reading of policy. However, there are times when consensus among these "giants" is wrong. Lacking such means of corroboration, you might ask a lawyer about court decisions and a knowledgeable (and friendly) lobbyist or public official about legislative action and intent.

Precedents are especially persuasive with legislators. These are successful implementations of the same kind of program elsewhere. As is pointed out later, the comparability of the two programs and the respective jurisdictions is a critical test for the relevance of precedents. A program that worked in New York might or might not be appropriate for North Dakota.

### Statistical Data

Some people love numbers. They enjoy plowing through census tables and columns of budget figures. I am not one of them. Like many advocates, I have an aversion to wading through endless pages of numerical data. I would rather have a juicy case history or sharply worded polemic any time. But I am aware that in order to know what I am talking about and get a respectful hearing, I must do my homework. So you should develop a healthy respect for statistical data.

Respect it, but do not be infatuated. Cool-headed skepticism works best. We are warned repeatedly that it is possible to lie with statistics and that one can use numbers to prove anything. Still, there is something very convincing about numerical data. There is a natural tendency to trust anything with numbers attached to it. But while figures don't lie, people do, and it is easy enough to distort facts with statistics. More often than outright distortion of the facts, a selected set of figures may be designed to cast circumstances in a particularly good or bad light.

A policy analyst opposed to raising the minimum wage was making a point about part-time versus full-time employment:

> Most of the recent job growth has occurred in the full-time permanent job category. Between December 1983 and December 1987, part-time employment rose by only 1 million, or 5.3 percent, while full-time employment shot up by 9.9 million, or 11.8 percent. (Meyer, 1988)

Of course "only 1 million" and "shot up" are ways of helping the reader define things the way the writer wants her to. Moreover, the selection of 1983 is not accidental. Another analyst commented that it was misleading to use 1983 as a benchmark to examine job creation. In 1982 we had just come out of a deep recession. There is a lag between the end of a recession and the creation of new jobs. Because of that recession, 1983 had the highest rate of unemployment since World War II.

But if one used 1979 as the benchmark, then the picture changed somewhat. Over the long haul, part-time employment grew at a faster rate than full-time employment (*The New York Times,* 1988).

Bob Votegetter, a candidate for governor in the State of Confusion, announces at a news conference that since the incumbent, Gary Gladhand, has been in office, the number of auto thefts in the state has risen 25 percent. "That is a lie," says Gary. "Anybody knows that when Bob's party was last in power the rate of auto thefts was actually higher than it is today." It will take some research to see who, if anybody, is lying. It turns out that neither man is. When Bob talks about an increase in the number of auto thefts, he neglects to add that when Gary came into office there were fewer vehicles on the road because of a severe fuel shortage. The number of thefts could increase merely because there are more cars to steal. Gary talks rates because that helps his case. What he fails to mention is that the age group that is most likely to commit auto thefts—adolescents and young adults—has been steadily declining in the state over the years. So there are fewer potential auto thieves than there once were. Also, Bob has referred to the year Gary came into office. Gary speaks of the last time Bob's party held the governorship. Those are two different times, because Gary succeeded a member of his own party.

Of course, one could ask other questions, such as what auto thefts have to do with being a good governor. It might be possible to show that the governor presided over an improving economy, which reduced (or increased) the likelihood of auto thefts, or that he urged the legislature to raise or lower the amount of money for law enforcement. But it sounds as if Bob is stuck for good issues to run on and is trying to focus voters' attention on secondary concerns.

We have uncovered a few caveats in relation to statistical information:

1. Always be clear about what is being measured, particularly the difference between frequency (total number) and rate (the ratio between actual cases and possible cases).
2. Note the time period being selected and ask why that particular time.
3. What is the geographical area being discussed? For example, the rate of auto thefts in the state capital may be going up, while the rate for the state as a whole is going down.

Then there are the statistical comparisons. "Did you know," says Bob, "that there were more auto thefts in the State of Confusion last year than in the whole country of Bangladesh?" No doubt. Also more automobiles. So it goes. Whenever someone starts quoting statistics, be on guard. Back during the Korean War, I was told that more people died in auto accidents on America's highways in the previous year than all the U.S. Navy personnel killed in the war that same year. I forget now whether the conclusion was that we should worry less about battle casualties or more about highway fatalities. But without knowing the potential numbers of each, one would have a hard time knowing what to make of that statement.

Statistics can be intimidating, but as Lois Gibbs demonstrated, advanced degrees in the subject are not necessary to make effective use of numerical data. She had a high school education and a strong motivation to get answers to questions. She knew little about either statistics or toxic chemicals, so she set out to learn about both. Rather than try to master these arcane subjects on her own, she turned to people who were experts and whom she could trust. The credentials of her allies helped, especially when the chemical company and the state bureaucrats tried to discredit their work as "just housewives' research."

When she started, Lois Gibbs had the same problem with experts that she had with politicians: She was both too trusting and too timid to take them on. That changed in time, as she learned how to question their wisdom. After all, it is a basic rule of science that one's assertions are always open to challenge. This brings us to the final kind of evidence: testimony.

### Testimony, Expert and Otherwise

I am talking here not just about witnesses in court, but any kind of assertion of fact or opinion, written or spoken. When a person takes a position, a point of view on a controversial subject, one tends to raise one's guard . But when material is presented as factual it is easy to relax one's vigilance. Knowing that, most people pushing a point of view clothe their claims in a mantle of objectivity.

There are two basic questions to ask about any testimony: How much does the person know, and what are his or her biases? These questions establish source credibility.

#### How Much Does the Person Know?

Firsthand experience is a very impressive kind of credential. The residents of Love Canal who could not pronounce half the names of the toxic chemicals under their backyards, to say nothing of understanding their derivation, knew what it was like to have their children come home with the bottoms of their feet scorched. They could speak convincingly of the psychological toll the incident was exacting. That impressed the news media a lot more than the technical bulletins from the state department of health. Ex–mental patients and psychiatrists each speak with their own authority about what it feels like to be penned up in a mental hospital.

This is not meant to minimize the expertise of people trained in a relevant field. The closer to hands-on work the person is, the more convincing the testimony. On the other hand, researchers can provide a kind of information the practitioner may be unaware of.

The first point to understand about experts is that they are just people who have devoted more time to learning about a special area of knowledge than other people. Reasonably, they therefore know more. However, they should be treated with the same skepticism with which one approaches any source. Useful questions to ask about all experts are: (1) What exactly are their areas of expertise, and how are they viewed by their colleagues? (2) Do their professional communities agree with what they are saying, or are their views a matter of controversy within their fields? (See Gilbert, 1979:76-84.) Before taking on an expert, you might do well to get a second opinion on the subject to be discussed.

Written opinion has a credibility in the eyes of the public that spoken opinion lacks. This trust may be misplaced, however. As is discussed later, being published is less important than the kind of publication the item appears in. Still, one sure advantage of the print media over television and radio is the existence of a record that can be referred to.

## What Are the Source's Biases?

It is rare to find a completely unbiased source of information. Researchers are expected to meet a high standard of objectivity, but even here bias creeps in. This is particularly true in relation to social policy, which by nature is of intense interest to many people and less precise than other kinds of scholarly work. For example, two studies of the economic progress of African Americans, one by a U.S. government commission and the other by a highly respected private consulting firm, were found to reflect a conservative bias against government equal opportunity and welfare programs. It turned out that the same individual oversaw both studies. This was not publicly acknowledged in the study reports (Richan, 1987).

News reports are notorious for being influenced by everything from intentional selection and choice of color words to stereotyping and plain ignorance. This is not necessarily the result of a conspiracy at the top, although that has been known to happen. Reporters, editors, headline writers, and graphic designers continually have to make quick judgments against press deadlines and with limited information. It matters a lot, in terms of public perception, whether an item is in the top right-hand corner of page one or at the bottom of page sixteen, whether its headline covers one column or three, and how the reporter begins the story.

Now, of course, we are having to deal with non-news by non-newspersons who present themselves as reporters, as well as with reporters who fabricate "news." Moral of this story: Be skeptical of everything, no matter how trusted the publication in which it appears. Can you trust anything you read in the print media? The fact is, you will have to, unless you simply abandon the effort to back up your opinion about policy with evidence altogether. But at least check your sources and seek more than one source for everything.

Although radio and television news are more restricted than newspapers in explicitly editorializing, their reporting is more open to bias than the print media because of time pressure and the fact that some on-the-spot accounts are ad-libbed. Use of the mass media in advocacy is discussed in Chapter 8.

## The Reluctant Witness

One way to deal with the problem of bias is to use a source that seems to be speaking against its own interests or prejudices. In court, the reluctant witness is forced to testify when he or she would prefer not to. The presumption is that if this witness gives damaging testimony it should be believed, because it is against his or her own interests to do so.

Lefty is a longtime friend and confidant of Spike. Lefty testifies that Spike was in the vicinity of the liquor store on the night of the robbery. If anything, it is reasoned, he would want to shield his friend, so he must be telling the truth.

A member of Bob Votegetter's own party acknowledges that Bob has a less than pristine record as district attorney. This is far more damaging than for one of Gary Gladhand's henchmen (from the other party) to say the same thing. A retired general speaks at a peace rally with an image of authenticity that an avowed pacifist lacks. Statements by Roman Catholics for a liberalized abortion policy or by feminists against abortion would have the same kind of impact.

Reluctant witnesses must be approached with the same skepticism as one uses in other cases. Especially if such testimony is being circulated by those with an axe to grind, try to determine why the witness is doing the unexpected. We now look more specifically at ways of testing the validity of evidence.

## THE QUALITY OF EVIDENCE: WHOM AND WHAT CAN YOU TRUST?

### Reducing the Risk of Error: General Rules

1. When possible, use more than one source of information. If the sources are in disagreement, try to get a third opinion and figure out who is more likely to be correct.
2. Test source credibility. Is the source knowledgeable? Is the source free from bias?
3. Is the information original or secondhand? If the latter, get as close to the original source as possible.
4. How current is the information? If related to an earlier time period, is the time relevant to the issue? Be especially alert to time discrepancies in secondhand information. When was the original article written? When were the data gathered? There can be lapses of as much as ten years between an original research project and the point at which findings are printed in a book or article.
5. When a comparison is made, is the comparison relevant? If you are looking at crime statistics in California, is a comparison with Utah appropriate? These are literal comparisons between parallel situations; the presumption is that what happens in one state

has at least some relevance for another. A figurative analogy—say, using a face off at the OK Corral to make a point about a legislative issue—is purely symbolic, and strictly speaking is not evidence of anything.

When the supporters of the Equal Rights Amendment were trying to get the last few states to ratify it, they sought an extension of the seven-year time period for ratification. One opponent likened the maneuver to the losing side's asking for an extra quarter in a football game in order to have a chance to improve its score. The argument had a certain popular appeal (fair play and a popular all-American sport), but in reality football games have nothing to do with constitutional amendments. National defense policy is sometimes translated into terms of police officers walking around with or without guns. Same problem.

## CONDUCTING THE SEARCH

### What Do You Know (Or Think You Know) Already?

Let's say the issue is something you have strong feelings about. In fact, let's say you're mad as hell. Good. That's the kind of zeal you need to see you through the hours and days and weeks of humdrum work when you have to wonder if anything will come of it. Not to mention the pages and pages of boring legalese and statistical tables you'll have to plow through.

Suppose the Christian conservatives in your state legislature are trying to get an amendment to the state constitution banning abortion under any circumstances. Suppose you are thoroughly opposed to their position. Being strongly pro-choice, you are ready to go on the warpath over this issue. You need good information to fight the battle in the legislature, in the newspapers, and on call-in radio talk shows.

It wouldn't be bad to start by putting down on paper everything you know (or think you know) about the subject. That means both facts and opinions, your own and other people's.

Add the files and newspaper clippings that are gathering dust somewhere in your office or bedroom or garage. Save all that material. You will eventually heave more than half of it into the dustbin. The rest you will organize into a usable store of information.

What you are doing is immersing yourself in the topic. As you proceed, bits and pieces of information, recalled from the dim past or newly acquired, will take on new relevance.

There are major hazards in researching an issue you feel strongly about. You know this territory so well, you may not feel the need to research it further. Is it enough to check over the handouts you've been getting from NARAL and Planned Parenthood all these months and years? Plenty of talking points there.

Nothing could be further from the truth. You must constantly update that file of friendly evidence. Don't glance at the op-ed column whose author you agree with and move on. That op-ed column is almost certain to contain added case material or statistics that can strengthen your case. Even more important, you must read all the evidence you can find on the other side. Get past your anger and really absorb what the opposition is saying and the evidence it is bringing to bear. You're going to have to become your own devil's advocate, deliberately take the side you love to hate, in order to be prepared to deal with hostile questions, as was discussed in Chapter 4.

Suppose instead you have come to this topic late in the game and haven't really had a chance to develop a definite position. Let's say that you are a social worker in a mental health clinic with no real interest in politics. One day you learn that the funds for your agency and others like it are going to be slashed in half if the governor's proposed budget goes through. All of a sudden, you are thrust into the middle of a policy issue. You accept your supervisor's invitation to work on an interagency committee trying to restore mental health funding to the state budget. You know virtually nil about state finance, but you are very clear about the devastating effects a reduction would have on the ex–hospital patients you work with. From colleagues in and out of the agency and through your professional training, you know the problems that a sharp cutback in state support would cause. That is where you start in building your store of information.

### Organizing the Data

Before you go any further, you need to develop a system for cataloging the information, so you can retrieve what you need, when you need it. Write down a list of categories under which you can assemble the data. Don't worry if later you need to change the system as new information comes in. Keep the master list handy and up-to-date so you can find things quickly.

For physical pieces of evidence, like newspaper clippings, I like to use manila file folders—the more the merrier. Categories can be collapsed or expanded into subcategories as you go.

In all likelihood, sooner or later you will be storing information on your computer. The urge to make a hard copy of anything and everything plus save the document in the computer itself can be irresistible. I won't try to dissuade you from that kind of duplication of effort. Who knows, your house may burn to the ground or, more likely, your computer may die. The most important thing is to have everything cataloged by the same system. The other rule, which may be impossible to follow with old clippings you've dredged up, is to put a date and a source on everything.

## Expanding the Search

One of the best sources of information is people who have been there and done that. They are likely to know the critical issues and the most common talking points regarding them. In every state there are advocacy organizations whose functions include trying to influence policies. They get a large amount of material from national lobbying groups and professional associations. Depending on the problem, newspapers will have additional useful information. Once you have an interest in a topic, you will discover a great deal of information you had been ignoring up to that point. Advocacy organizations will love to add you to their mailing lists. Needless to say, you should be prepared to be inundated. You can survive the onslaught by sticking with that filing system and being ruthless about throwing out the junk.

The Internet is of course a marvelous source of all kinds of solid information—sometimes too much to digest—but it is also where you are likely to get junk, squared. So, not surprisingly, the Net is where issues of credibility are paramount, as is discussed in the following.

### Credibility of Different Sources

You must weigh carefully how credible any source of information is. Your own credibility is at stake here. As is discussed elsewhere in the book: Pass along a piece of bogus information to a legislator and let it blow up in his or her face, and you can forget about future contact with that individual. So here are some suggestions.

First of all, I wish I could list the Internet as a credible source of information, because it's a quick way to pick up a huge amount of information, and it's free. Free, that is, after you or your family or your employer or your university has laid out the monthly subscription fee to connect with a server. The problem is that it's hard to tell how trustworthy a particular bit of information is. The sources range from official documents and respected institutions to often anonymous (and sometimes outlandish) opinions floated right along with the good stuff. Also, the information may have no date, so you won't know how current it is. A general caveat: Whatever you pick up off the Net, unless it's fully documented and dated, check it out with other sources.

This is my list of favorite sources, in order of presumed credibility:

1. *Your own experience or direct observation of someone else's.* For the reasons discussed earlier, knowing a situation firsthand gives you a special kind of authority.
2. *Official documents.* As was said, you need to weigh the credibility of the specific document and its source. But overall, these are particularly trustworthy.
3. *Articles in juried academic and professional journals, based on empirical research.* Juried publications are those in which other professionals—a jury of the author's peers—have reviewed the article and recommended publication. The credibility test has thus been administered by people with expertise equal to or greater than that of the writer of the article. These publications require footnotes or other means of identifying source material. The article should include a section on methodology and tables to allow the reader to determine whether the findings support the conclusions. If you have trouble understanding some of the technical jargon and statistical notations, consult a person in the relevant field.

4. *Theoretical and other nonempirical papers in juried academic or professional journals.* These are of essentially the same caliber as reports of empirical research but are less rigorous and are likely to be based on conclusions drawn from other people's research.

5. *Scholarly books.* These presumably abide by the same scientific standards as the above categories of scientific work, but the standards vary more. All a scholar need do is convince a publisher there is money to be made (or a payoff in terms of image). There are also some not-so-scholarly books whose reach exceeds their grasp. You have to be careful in assessing source credibility. One way to do that is to look up reviews of such books in juried journals. But because reviewers can be even more biased and unscientific than authors, it is well to check more than one review.

6. *Newspapers, popular magazines, and popular books.* Standards vary greatly. Some books are carefully researched, others are not. Some newspapers are more careful than others to avoid bias in their news columns. Magazine articles are written over a longer period than newspaper items, allowing them to go into greater depth. Some newspaper series, on the other hand, are exhaustively researched. Unlike scholarly books and journals, these publications for general readership rarely require documentation, so you don't know what a writer is basing his or her ideas on unless such information is incorporated into the body of the article. Newspapers are famous for quoting unidentified sources.

   In newspapers, straight news and news features are most likely to strive for objectivity, or at least make a pretense of same. Columns and op-ed items usually have a very marked bias but may be written as if neutral. Editors often look for controversy in these pages, so diverse views are encouraged. Editorials, avowedly biased, are sometimes good sources of information possibly missed in the news columns. Least to be trusted, of course, are letters to the editor, although sometimes authoritative writers use this method to get their message out. Use these as leads for further investigation, unless what you are looking for is an example of a viewpoint rather than valid information about the subject.

7. *Television and radio.* The biggest problem with these sources is that there is no permanent record, unless the program is taped or is a documentary or discussion program and transcripts are available. Many broadcasters now offer added information about the program content on the Internet. If the content is on your topic, you may want to take them up on the offer. You forget much of what you see and even more of what you hear, so the dangers of distorting what you have been exposed to are great. Still, the broadcast media are valuable sources of information, especially when they do in-depth analyses. A second problem with these sources is the pressure they're under to be brief and go for attention-grabbing material over thoughtful analysis. This is a highly competitive business—the consumer can turn off a message simply by pushing a button. A third problem is that television and radio depend by and large on the print media for their information. Not to say they never do serious journalism, but the evening news is selected at least partly for the spectacular photography it allows; the person reading the news is chosen primarily for physical appearance and on-camera charisma. "Ah," you say, "PBS isn't like that." Maybe not, but then again. . . .

8. *Electronic media.* In addition to Web pages sponsored by news organizations, there are several independent news sources you can tap via the Internet. But you have to be ready to separate the wheat from the chaff. You'll find plenty of both on pages like Buzz Flash and the Drudge Report.

9. *Public meetings.* These can be extremely valuable—and variable as to accuracy of what you are exposed to. Most such meetings include a question-and-answer period which helps to keep them honest, but platform speakers learn to anticipate and have ready answers for the three or four standard questions about the topic. Here again, you have to watch the accuracy of your own interpretation of what you hear, since your attention may wander during the presentation. Take notes; your selective recall will trip you up otherwise. Keep in mind, it is not the lecturer but contending political interest groups that will be administering the final exam.

Much depends on the particular public meeting. Is this a learned discourse at a professional conference or a stump speech by Bob Votegetter? Again, the question-and-answer process is a great safeguard. If you are prevented from asking a question in the meeting, either because of lack of time or shyness, you can usually corner the speaker afterward, or give him or her a call the next day.

As you consult people, you must apply the source credibility test discussed earlier. Do your sources have an axe to grind? How current is their information? Do they know it firsthand? If not, how trustworthy are their sources? Don't be shy about asking people how they came by their information.

## Some Standard Sources

You can do a blind search by using a standard search engine such as Google or Yahoo. Using that route, you may get more or less than you bargained for. For books on your subject, the library book catalog is the best place to start. For anything else—e.g., journal articles and government data—you are better off narrowing the search to a few basic source materials, such as the following list. They can all be found in most college or university libraries and/or on the Internet.

### In Print

*Statistical Abstract of the United States.* Annually updated (with a time lag) compendium of everything from demographic data to economic statistics. Many of these items are broken down for states and metropolitan areas, making this an exceptionally useful source.

*Vital Statistics of the United States.* Annual data on births, deaths, morbidity, broken down for states and municipalities.

*Public Affairs Information Service.* Allows you to access journal articles, books, government documents, and other source material on a wide range of public policy issues.

*Social Work Abstracts Plus.* Abstracts of journal articles and book reviews, and not just from social work publications.

*Education Resources Information Center (ERIC).* Abstracts of journal articles on education issues going well beyond the classroom.

*Congressional Quarterly Almanac.* Covers action on federal legislation and committee assignments as well as voting records of members of Congress.

*National Journal.* Less comprehensive than the previous source cited but more in-depth on specific issues.

*Catalog of U.S. Government Publications.* This includes all U.S. government reports, including those from administrative agencies, where much of the real policymaking takes place.

## Online

All states have a "portal" (think "port of entry") to government information, ranging from status of bills before the legislature to how to get a driver's license. Type in: www.state.(two-letter abbreviation for the state's name).us. For example, in New York you would type in www.state.ny.us.

For federal government information in general: www.firstgov.gov

For federal legislative information: www.thomas.loc.gov (The Thomas is for Thomas Jefferson, incidentally.)

For federal statistics: www.fedstats.gov

Other online sources include Center on Budget and Policy Priorities (www.cbpp.org) and, for health information, The Kaiser Family Foundation (www.kff.org).

You can also sign up for various LISTSERV mailing lists that will regularly send you information on specified subject matter. Pick your topic, go to a search engine and type in LISTSERV and the topic, and you will get the names of several such sources.

Does this sound like an impossible job? It would be if you pursued everything to its sources, and every source to its sources, ad infinitum. But you won't. By the way, being part of a team of searchers saves you time and energy and multiplies your effectiveness in the search process.

At some point you will decide enough is enough and stop the frantic search for evidence. That doesn't preclude being on the alert for fresh additions to your collection. But long before you reach that point, you will have started on the next step: putting together your case and your opponent's, as we saw in Chapter 4. It will give the necessary structure to all this information you have been amassing.

# PART II:
# PRACTICAL APPLICATIONS

The emphasis here is on practical. The second part of this book translates the basic principles discussed in Part I into tactical guidelines for engaging in advocacy in five different contexts:

1. direct contact with a policymaker, the most basic meaning of the term "lobbying";
2. presentations to groups in a variety of settings;
3. testimony before a legislative committee, a special kind of public presentation with its own rules;
4. what is becoming increasingly important in all facets of political action, the mass media; and
5. direct action designed to dramatize an issue or sometimes to provoke those in authority into reacting in ways that actually enhance the power of the advocates.

This material is more than simple "helpful hints for the aspiring advocate." The specific tactics proposed are at times very explicit: how to practice in front of the mirror before going to testify at a committee hearing, how to write a press release. The more general guidelines set forth in Part I always serve as the basis for the tactical decisions.

Chapter 6 discusses the kinds of people you will be lobbying and how the process looks from their side of the desk. It takes you step-by-step from preliminary planning to the follow-up letter after your visit. Exhaustive planning and preparation of every step is essential.

Chapter 7 deals with a subject that will terrify some readers: getting up in front of a group of legislators, presenting one's views, and, worst of all, fielding their questions. As you proceed through the steps, you should find that much of your initial anxiety melts away. Not that it is any less of a challenge, but it is one for which you can muster your best efforts instead of being paralyzed by fear.

The mass media, the subject of Chapter 8, surround us every waking minute of our lives. Their power to influence decisions is obvious. You will find access to this strategic realm is easier than you might at first think. There are many messengers competing for attention, so skill in presenting your message effectively will be a crucial factor in whether the media work for your cause. Thanks to the wizardry of the electronic industry, you can now, in effect, become your own mass medium of communication, with the potential (and pitfalls) of the Internet.

Chapter 9 addresses direct action as a political tool. Such an approach is not intended to win the hearts and minds of policymakers. Rather, it seeks to raise the consciousness of potential allies, raise the awareness of the general public, and, often, to goad the opposition into reacting in order to expose its true nature. Confrontation of this sort is full of risks and can even be self-defeating if not thought through fully, but there may be times when the advocate finds it is the only way to bring about change.

# Chapter 6

# Lobbying One-on-One

The ultimate target of policy advocacy is the person who casts a vote for or against a bill, helps draft or revise legislation, submits a new measure, writes regulations, or vetoes any or all of the above actions. The most direct way of influencing that person is by talking with him or her in person. Face-to-face advocacy in any context is far and away the most effective approach, whether you are a lobbyist, a used-car salesman, or a missionary (Hayes, 2005). There are other ways of communicating with policymakers, through letters and phone calls for example, although they have less impact. Sometimes you communicate through someone else, for instance a staff aide to the policymaker. All these activities go under the rubric of lobbying one-on-one. We will consider what the process looks like through the eyes of the person being lobbied as well as the person doing the lobbying.

Chances are you have lobbied for or against something at one time or another, although you may not have thought of it as lobbying. A large part of lobbying can be classified as special pleading, making a request for a response to one's personal or corporate needs. In this book we are talking about a different kind of lobbying; the kind directed toward changing public policy that affects many people. However, much policy lobbying grows out of the self-interest of various parties. The industrialist who pays huge sums to a professional lobbyist to get a clause inserted into a tax bill is trying to protect his or her firm's interests. But it is a policy change, nevertheless, affecting everybody if only by shifting a certain amount of the tax burden to other people.

I shall assume you are not interested in lobbying in order to tell your friends, "Today, I lobbied," nor to demonstrate that, yes, democ-

*Lobbying for Social Change*
© 2006 by The Haworth Press, Inc. All rights reserved.
doi:10.1300/5782_07

racy lives. I am going on the assumption that you have a commitment to specific kinds of policy goals, enough of a commitment to become actively involved in promoting them. That strong investment in the substance of policy is the driving force that can make you effective as a lobbyist. Whatever satisfaction you may find in keeping the democratic process alive, whatever ego gratification in rubbing elbows with power, these you should consider fringe benefits, the frosting on the cake, perhaps, but not what we are concerned with here.

## LOBBYING AN ELECTED REPRESENTATIVE

### Lobbying As an Exchange

When people think of lobbying, they usually have in mind the kind that is directed to a senator or representative. Implicit in this kind of one-on-one activity is an exchange relationship between the advocate and the person being lobbied. The former wants action on a bill, let's say. The latter wants support in the next election. Neither party will likely state this exchange openly, but both know it is the basis for the relationship.

Several years ago, when "message" posters (i.e., those trying to make a point regarding large issues) were in vogue, one of the favorites had a picture of a series of fish, each about to be gobbled up by a larger one. The message was, "There's no free lunch." The real point was that life is a series of exchanges and everyone pays something for what he or she gets.

Being clear about what you want from the target helps you avoid becoming distracted from your real goal. Recall the plight of Betty and Brad Advocate, whom we met in Chapter 2. They never could decide on their priorities nor what they were willing to settle for. Confusion about that can set you up for failure. If lawmakers can buy you off cheaply, without making any real changes, that leaves them more elbow room for dealing with other interests who know what they are after. If you and your allies can't arrive at a common agenda, the alliance is doomed, and with it your chances of having an impact. If what you are really after is to show how corrupt or futile the whole policymaking business is, that will yield little in the way of satisfaction in the long run. What it won't yield is policy change.

The lawmaker's agenda may not be obvious. It may seem that he or she doesn't need anything from you. After all, this legislator got elected, maybe several times in a row. Especially if you are a member of the other party or you backed the opponent last time, the legislator must have written off your support by now, right? Don't believe it. Aside from the fact that, as a constituent, you have the right to a serious hearing, the smart politician will never write anyone off. Besides, your support in elections is not the only thing he or she needs from you. You can play a key role in supplying him or her with arguments for doing what you want done, especially if you come armed with good information. And, regardless of a lawmaker's private sentiments or those of the majority of his or her constituents, those arguments are important.

A friend of mine used to work in the election campaigns of a U.S. senator. He described what happened when any advocates approached this senator asking him to support a particular bill. He would immediately express skepticism about the bill, no matter what he really thought about it. In that way, he found out if the advocates knew what they were talking about. Even more important, it was a way of getting the best arguments possible on behalf of the measure. Then when the senator lobbied one of his colleagues on the bill, or was asked by reporters why he took the stand he did, he was prepared for them.

Remember that politics is not a solo operation. When you lobby your representative you are not just after that one vote. You want him or her to urge other representatives to support the same measure. In order to do that, he or she must have a good rationale for taking the action. Remember State Representative John Smith, who had to take a stand on the bill requiring parental consent for abortions. A critical task for him was to develop a strong case, once he had decided which way he was going to vote. You can help your representative justify the action you are after. For a lawmaker to say he or she is backing a bill because of pressure to do so doesn't sound very good. A legislator has to be able to put it in terms of public interest and the needs of his or her district.

Regardless of how compelling the case for action, without maximizing your power base you won't get very far. So you need to attend to both aspects: the political leverage and the means of justifying the position. We will start with the power base.

### Establishing a Power Base

"Negotiators or lobbyists who forget the power of their supporters and the thrust of their goals cannot be effective," writes Maryann Mahaffey (1982:70), long-time elected official and social work leader. "They can even sell out their constituents." It should be added that a lobbyist who sells out his or her constituents is soon a lobbyist without a constituency.

Policymakers are very astute at sizing up your power base. If you approach them as a lone individual, let us say a resident of their district, that will count for something. You may represent more than one voter, because they know you talk to other people, and you had to have more than average interest in the issue or you would not have bothered to come see them. But if you are seriously interested in influencing social policy, you need a bigger power base than that.

So your first task as a would-be lobbyist is to locate a constituency, a power base. Naturally, you need allies who share your policy goals. Suppose that in your preliminary research you have come across the names of various local, state, or national groups that are working on the same set of issues as you are. As you explore different possible alliances, you should try to get a sense of what they can do to help you and what you may have to contribute to their work: for example, professional expertise or strategic information on the topic. When you mesh all your lobbying activity closely with this organization, you multiply your effectiveness. By keeping its members informed of what you are doing, you demonstrate your value to them, thus increasing your leverage with this group.

Two critical questions to ask yourself: Do you and they have the same priorities? And how much political muscle do they bring to the bargain? These may be in conflict; an organization with which you are in total agreement may have little political clout, while a major power broker would demand too many concessions on your part. You must strike some sort of balance between these two factors.

There are definite advantages in becoming an active member of a group. You then have an identity beyond your own, you get the regular newsletter and other materials sent to members, and it may be possible to influence the actions of the total group. In effect, you become one of the regular players. It also helps your morale to know you're not alone. On the other hand, there may be factors which preclude it: ineligibility, high membership fees, inadvisability due to your position, or unwillingness to go along with the overall goals of the organization. Conversely, there may be advantages in joining more than one advocacy group. The important thing is to combine forces in working toward a common objective.

### Carving Out a Specific Action Agenda

Organizations often work on several related concerns. You can be most helpful to them and to yourself if you can define a specific role in relation to one policy area. You then become identified with that issue, and as you bone up on it, you enhance your value to the group and to your own concerns. The more involved you are in the group, the more your agenda will be part of what the body as a whole sees as a priority.

Let's say you have settled on a bill currently in committee, one which is likely to be acted upon in the coming months. As you study the bill and do preliminary background research on the topic, you come up with a clearer idea of where you want to go. What would you consider the optimal outcome? What would be a significant change for the better, short of the ideal? What are your fallback positions? What would you consider so limited that it would be better not to support it?

It is best, of course, to do this in collaboration with an advocacy group so that you and they are working together, thus maximizing your collective impact.

### Targets

The next question to ask yourself is, whom should I lobby? And how does that person define the situation? Your approach should be focused on a specific individual, and you must tailor your arguments accordingly. To help you understand what makes legislators tick and how lobbying looks from the other side of the desk, I shall introduce you to three former members of the Pennsylvania General Assembly (state legislature). Together they represented a wide range of individuals and constituencies. One was a liberal Democratic house member representing a blue-collar district in the southwestern part of the state. The second was a conservative Republican senator from a mostly rural district in the northwestern section of Pennsylvania. The third was the state's first African-American woman senator, a Democrat representing an inner-city district in Philadelphia.

I'm not claiming that these three represent the full range of lawmakers you may come in contact with. There were no out-and-out scoundrels here, though indeed there are plenty of those among elected officials. These three had a well-earned reputation for taking their legislative responsibilities seriously. The political context in which they operated—Pennsylvania state government in the 1990s—could be described as moderately conservative. A relative balance in party strength in the General Assembly (legislature) created a highly partisan atmosphere. You may be from a state dominated by one party, or generally more progressive or conservative in orientation. Your representative may be thoroughly unprincipled or under the thumb of powerful moneyed interests. (Don't rely too much on the campaign rhetoric of the opposition in making that assessment, incidentally.) Yet the dynamics driving these three individuals are similar to what you are likely to find, no matter where you live, in whatever year. And the implications for planning your lobbying strategy will be the same.

Here are the three, as I interviewed them and others who knew them a number of years ago, while they were still serving in the General Assembly.

## Representative Allen G. Kukovich

Representative Kukovich, a Democrat, has been in the Pennsylvania House of Representatives for thirteen years. He is an attorney by profession. Kukovich represents Westmoreland County, which is a "bedroom" for Pittsburgh and contains several large electronics, steel, and glass manufacturing plants. The district is 60 percent Democratic, but it consistently supported GOP President Ronald Reagan. The southern segregationist George Wallace once won here in a presidential primary. The extreme right-wing John Birch Society has been active in the area in the past.

There is a large Italian Catholic population, a majority of which is strongly. antiabortion. Kukovich, a Lutheran (the name is Yugoslavian) and an avowed feminist, says his opponents can count on 2,000 votes on the abortion issue alone in any election. The ultraconservative newspaper in his district has published more than 100 editorials that were critical of him, but he has the support of the Philadelphia and Pittsburgh papers. Among media people based in Harrisburg, the representative has a reputation for being available, willing to talk, and honest.

How does Kukovich manage to buck the odds and keep on being returned to office? He says it is because he is a no-nonsense legislator who works hard for his constituents. He has demonstrated that he will go to bat for them on issues of special concern to them. Senior citizens, unions, and feminists have all been supportive. In addition, he has high name recognition.

In 1988, Representative Kukovich's power in the Pennsylvania House took a big leap upward when he was elected by his Democratic colleagues as chairperson of the Majority Policy Committee for the 1989-1990 session of the legislature. Not only did this give him a key position in the formulation of the party's agenda, but it put him in line for further moves up the ladder of house leadership in the future.

Prior to this, he was a member of the following house committees: Consumer Affairs, where he chaired the Subcommittee on Public Utilities; Health and Welfare, as chair of the Subcommittee on Youth and Aging; Appropriations; and Judiciary. When he first came to the house, his main interest was in reform of public utilities and government, but when the support for human services eroded during the Reagan years, that became his priority concern.

Representative Kukovich denies future aspirations beyond continuing to serve in the house. A few years ago he gave serious thought to making a run for governor, traveled around the state, and developed a wide network of local support. He had statewide name recognition of 10 percent, high for a state representative. But a combination of poor relations with the state's powerful insurance industry and a realization of what he would have to do in order to garner enough financial support led him to drop the idea. The aborted campaign was not without its impact, however. The representative believes his activity had a significant impact on the administration of Democratic governor Robert Casey.

Kukovich has the support of a number of public interest groups at election time. His biggest contributions come from the National Organization for Women. He gets substantial support from organized labor, the Pennsylvania Trial Lawyers Association, and the Pennsylvania State Education Association. He also holds special fund-raising events. Major campaign expenses include radio advertising and direct mailings. He divides legislators into five categories in their dealings with lobbyists: devil's advocates, ingratiating, rude, fence-sitters, and listeners. Which is he? A listener, he says; he tries to decide based on what he hears. If that sounds like a standard politician's answer, in Kukovich's case it appears to be an authentic statement of how he views himself.

*Lobbying Allen Kukovich.* How do we translate this profile into a lobbying strategy? It is clear that Representative Kukovich is an issues person, drawn to the political scene because of a burning interest in several policy concerns. In approaching him, one should be prepared for some searching questioning. If you are talking about one of his pet topics—consumer protection, women's issues, or children and youth, for example—you will have his attention. Demonstrate that you and he are on common ground on an issue that interests him or that you are speaking for a significant part of his district and you can get his active support. If you can't show one or the other, chances are you will get a respectful hearing, maybe some practice with your debating skills, but little more.

Representative Kukovich likes to meet with lobbyists personally so there is an opportunity for give and take. He will sometimes play devil's advocate to smoke out the strongest arguments from the lobbyist. Handwritten letters from constituents—but not form letters or petitions—get his attention.

How does Representative Kukovich assess lobbyists he doesn't know? Much depends on how these people present themselves, how cogently they make their cases, and whether they are straightforward.

The fact that people take the time to come to see him personally counts for something.

## Senator John E. Peterson

The 25th senatorial district, located in the northwestern part of the state, is the largest rural district in Pennsylvania and the third largest, geographically, in the United States—a fact that John Peterson, a Republican, and his staff often cite to people they are dealing with. This says a lot about Senator Peterson and the way he sees his mandate. He takes very seriously the task of representing the constituency that has been sending him to Harrisburg since 1977, first as a state representative, and since 1984 as a senator. The district, which covers all of five counties and parts of three others, is roughly 55 percent Republican, a clear margin but close enough to keep any elected official mindful of the need to be attentive to the range of interests he or she represents.

Senator Peterson's roots in the district run deep. He lives in the same area where he grew up and for many years ran a grocery business. He is past president of the local borough council, the chamber of commerce, and the Lions Club, a former trustee of the Titusville Hospital, member of the Venango County Industrial Board, and active in the Pleasantville United Methodist Church.

For John Peterson, politics was one more challenge, not unlike that of building a small business into a successful, profitable operation. He ran unopposed in the last election. He relies on his many regional ties to know the sentiments of his constituents. Although at one time he gave some thought to running for Congress, Senator Peterson has been content to focus on the job at hand and not nurse larger political ambitions. (Note: He later ran successfully for a congressional seat.)

Frequent appearances at meetings in the district offer the senator another way to tap local views. The geography of his district—5,000 square miles with a scattered population—is reflected in the fact that he has three district offices.

Were one to conclude from this that John Peterson has a narrow, provincial outlook, it would be an erroneous conclusion. The fact that his district includes a portion of Erie County, whose center is an industrial lake port of 280,000, keeps him attuned to urban as well as rural issues. However, it is Senator Peterson's role as chair of the Public Health and Welfare Committee that has done much to broaden his perspective. Its area of concern—health and human services—is the · largest segment of the state budget. It involves the senator heavily in urban problems far removed from the place he grew up. He has also taken increasing interest in the substantive issues involved in health and welfare policy. But his greatest commitment is to be the outspoken advocate for a constituency which he feels tends to be overlooked amid the claims of competing factions: farmers, whom he calls "constituents without a voice."

In addition to Public Health and Welfare, he serves on the Senate Committees on Agriculture and Rural Affairs, Game and Fisheries, Community and Economic Development, and Consumer Protection and Professional Licensure. These all suggest areas where he can be expected to have an interest and more than average influence.

*Lobbying John Peterson.* For Senator Peterson, it is not broad social issues as much as service to his district that is his main driving force. One has to keep this in mind when trying to promote a cause with him. How will it affect the 25th Senate District and, more generally, rural Pennsylvania? This is not all that concerns him, but it is a first hurdle to get past. Peterson takes seriously his responsibilities as head of the Public Health and Welfare Committee, and his mind is open to compelling arguments regarding the questions that come before this body.

When approached by lobbyists for the first time, Senator Peterson wants to know who these persons are, where they are from, and why they want to talk with him. Are these people interested in finding out his views or merely wanting to sell their own? Most important, there has to be some point to the meeting. The senator doesn't like to waste time on idle conversation, so the would-be lobbyists had better be able to make clear why their meetings are worth his time. The one exception to this insistence that the time be productive is where his own constituents are concerned. They have a right to expect a hearing, he says.

· We can imagine Allen Kukovich using a lawyer's principles of tight logic and solid evidence with which to assess people and their ideas. To a much greater extent, John Peterson relies on his knowledge of the person. Over time he gets to know who is most competent, who is to be trusted. He constantly tries to determine what is driving the other person. In considering lobbyists and their appeals, he draws upon his years of experience in retailing. They are selling themselves and their ideas. He must be a thoughtful consumer.

There is one important additional thing to understand about Senator Peterson: the extent to which he looks to the expertise of his staff for guidance regarding human services issues. In addition to being knowledgeable about substantive policy questions, they are familiar with the region the senator represents. When lobbyists want to discuss the details of policy, they are as apt to talk with a staff member as with the senator himself—most likely Barbara J. Gleim.

*Barbara J. Gleim.* When John Peterson took over as chair of the Public Health and Welfare Committee, he brought Barbara Gleim along with him. Her official title is Executive Director of that committee. Finding her is your first challenge. She works in a small cubicle physically removed from Senator Peterson's office suite, and the clerical staff is a buffer between her and the many people who want her ear.

One quickly gets the idea that Barbara Gleim is not a person impressed by the trappings of high office. The best way to describe her work area is "spartan clutter." The walls and files are gray-on-gray and, except for a news clipping whose headline reminds us that health and welfare are at the top of the budget priorities, the walls are bare of decoration. Her desk is piled high with an assortment of documents. She grabs a quick snack at her desk (lunch) and puffs on a cigarette while telling her visitor about the work she did in helping to put together an antismoking bill. The apparent incongruity tells us that Barbara Gleim is interested in the process of legislating as much as in the substance of what is produced.

Just as Allen Kukovich thinks issues and John Peterson thinks district, Barbara Gleim thinks workable consensus. In the case of the antismoking bill, she called each person known to have an interest in the legislation—ranging from the Tobacco Institute and the tavern owners to the American Cancer Society—and asked, "What can't you tolerate?" Over a two-week period she gradually mediated the conflicting views down to the point where she felt a common stance could be crafted. Meanwhile, she was in contact with staff aides to key senators from both parties.

She sees as one of her chief functions that of acting as the lightning rod for the various factions on a controversial issue. Concerning the antismoking bill, she says, "If people got angry, they'd get angry at me, not each other." When it looked as if a compromise was possible, she brought together the various interests, including legislative staff, to hammer out the final version of the bill.

What does she do when some person(s) won't budge and the rest are ready to act? She keeps the tone diplomatic, but lets them know that if they can't go along she is sorry, but the action will go ahead without them. That is often enough to bring the adamant ones around. Underneath the mild manner is a tough operator when toughness is necessary.

Health and welfare is a sprawling area. How does she get up to speed on an issue with which she has had little previous experience? As soon as she senses that the problem will eventually hit her desk, Gleim begins collecting everything she can lay her hands on. When AIDS first began to get national attention, she alerted the news clipping service to send her everything they could find on the subject, talked to people she felt would be knowledgeable about it, and attended AIDS conferences. She was thus able to write a report on the topic for the GOP caucus. Based on her knowledge of the subject, general attitudes toward it, and the typical response of localities to issues of this sort, she recommended that educational efforts be focused at the local level—for example, through a series of town meetings. She was convinced that the public needed to get its information from personal contact with someone who was known and could be trusted.

*Lobbying Barbara Gleim.* In working lobbyists into her busy schedule, Barbara Gleim is guided by three considerations: (1) Is this an authentic source of information, preferably from firsthand experience rather than from theory? (2) Is this a voice that will need to be included in a future working consensus? (3) Does Senator Peterson want her to meet with the person? As for the third consideration, Gleim understands the first law of politics: loyalty. She would never cross or upstage her boss. He knows he can entrust major responsibility to her. But it goes beyond that. One way to close the door forever on any further access to a person such as Barbara Gleim is to embarrass her or the senator or others involved in the legislative process.

You don't start dealing with her and then go hunt up her opposite number on the Democratic side and share information with that person.

Letters, typed or handwritten, are useful ways to get your views to senior staff aides like Barbara Gleim. They can easily spot canned arguments and will quickly write them off as an orchestrated attempt at manipulation. She needs more than just the fact that you are for or against a bill. She also wants to know the reasoning behind your position.

## Senator Roxanne H. Jones

On one occasion when I was scheduled to meet Senator Jones, she suggested it be at her home, a second-floor walk-up over a fabric shop on a congested street in North Philadelphia. When I arrived she was busy mopping the floor of the shop, because a carton of frozen chickens the shop owner had agreed to hold for her had thawed and made a puddle. She was about to cook the chickens for a supper at her church. She once surprised fellow legislators by inviting them to an African-American dinner—prepared in part by none other than the senator herself. Senator Jones treats her staff as "family." The atmosphere is egalitarian, with a sharing of work roles among the members. She has sought to avoid losing touch with the world she once inhabited: that of a welfare recipient struggling to raise a family.

These homespun images should not mislead you. Roxanne H. Jones, a Democrat, is a very savvy politician. She probably has her senate district locked up for as long as her health holds up. (Sadly, this ended with Senator Jones's untimely death in 1996.) Though she was elected to her first political office in 1984, she has been in politics for more than two decades—as an outsider. In 1967, as a recipient of Aid to Families with Dependent Children (AFDC) (the precurser to TANF), she organized a local unit of the National Welfare Rights Organization. The following year she became president of the Philadelphia Welfare Rights Organization.

Roxanne Jones defies other stereotypes. While deeply committed to the needs of the people of her district, and African-American and low-income people more generally, she can just as readily relate to Caucasian legislators from rural Pennsylvania.

What is the main moving force for this state senator? First, she is a people-oriented legislator. Her natural warmth pervades everything she does. That personal touch and readiness to respond to human needs freely and openly is a must in the third senatorial district. There, one's value is measured less by espousal of esoteric policy issues than by willingness to answer urgent calls for help and act as an intermediary with an often hostile public bureaucracy.

Roxanne Jones is a living demonstration of the possibilities in people in the meanest of circumstances. She has received numerous awards and is in demand as a speaker at schools and youth group meetings. Her legislative priorities are housing and drug abuse, urgent concerns in her district. When interviewed, she was getting ready to resubmit a bill that would set up rehabilitation centers throughout the state for drug-dependent mothers and their children.

The one-time provocateur who led many a noisy demonstration of welfare recipients in the Capitol rotunda now rubs elbows with some of the same senators who used to be offended by her tactics. She is the ranking Democrat on the powerful Senate Public Health and Welfare Committee.

*Lobbying Roxanne H. Jones.* As might be expected in a rather informal operation where roles overlap, lobbyists are equally likely to deal with the senator herself as with one of her legislative aides.

When approached by a lobbyist, Senator Jones starts with the assumption that this person has a job to do for his or her employer, be it an insurance company or a public-interest organization, and will try to make the best case possible. Rather than get into a debate with the person, the senator will listen to the presentation and then present her own views. Always uppermost in her mind is the impact on her constituents. She then goes into extensive consultations with people she trusts, to get their assessments of the issue: ward leaders and other key informants in her district, other legislators, members of the Philadelphia City Council, maybe the mayor. Her staff shares in this survey of friendly sources. Jones often pleads ignorance, on substantive issues as well as legislative protocol, an approach that can be flattering to others and ensure that she will get maximum information.

If one wants to interest the senator in a cause, it is clear that, above all, it must have meaning to the lives of the kinds of people she represents. Demonstrating an understanding of her world increases the advocate's ability to get a sympathetic hearing. But one should be aware that soon after the interview, the senator will be on the phone, seeing if what has been told her is corroborated by the people she trusts.

Unlike many of her senate colleagues, Senator Jones sets up few barriers between herself and those seeking her attention. This ready accessibility is one of the reasons for her popularity and growing influence in Harrisburg. The calls keep coming in at all hours concerning public policy issues and personal crises in the lives of constituents. No matter to Roxanne Jones—they are equally what being a state senator is all about.

*         *         *

We have seen three very different legislators, each with a distinctive style and sense of mission, but for each of whom the interests of his or her district had top priority. To each, then, the would-be lobbyist had to be able to say, convincingly, "This will help your constituents."

There are state legislators who lack the dedication and energy of these three. Some have given up trying to make a difference but somehow can't leave their posts. Some can be bought if the price is right. But it has been my experience that the Allen Kukoviches, John Petersons, and Roxanne Joneses have been more the rule than the exception.

How a lawmaker sees the world in general, his or her role in it, and people like you will help to decide how your pitch will be received. More specifically, when a representative thinks about, say, mental health services or welfare reform, what does he or she focus on? What presumptions from experience come into play? How do his or her deep-seated values and those of his or her constituents color the way the person will receive an advocate's message, even before the advocate has a chance to present arguments? If the subject is abortion, we know that a substantial number of Representative Kukovich's constituents started with a different definition of the situation from his.

A John Peterson's focus, presumptions, and values will be different. Because this is a complex individual with a mixture of definitions, it is important to try to understand how he or she defines the specific problem one wants to discuss.

A Roxanne H. Jones will have still another definition of the situation. You can be sure that if you approach this kind of elected official about welfare reform, you will have his or her attention from the beginning. Right from the start, a Roxanne Jones will hear something different from what a John Peterson will hear when you say "welfare reform." That is because their respective frames of reference, their focus, presumptions, and values, will be different.

Once you have a sense of how your target defines the situation, you can then prepare your case to move that definition where you want it. What follows is the sequence of steps you must engage in, in order to do that.

## FACE-TO-FACE MEETINGS

Suppose you have received an action alert from an advocacy group with which you have been working. It says:

> Members of Congress will be on spring recess next week! Now is our chance to tell them what we think about HR 213. Call your congressperson's office tomorrow and make an appointment. His local address and telephone numbers are on the attached sheet. Below are the points we want to make about HR 213.

The moment of truth has arrived. You are going to have to put all that research to work and meet your U.S. representative face-to-face. Actually, it may be a staff member with whom you will talk, but you are still a little nervous about the meeting. What do you do now?

### Preparing for the Visit

I shall assume that you have already laid the groundwork by thoroughly researching your subject, including having written a brief, and have done an equally careful job of sizing up the representative and his or her likely definition of the situation. The next step is to call the office and try to get an appointment with the representative. The person on the other end of the line will want to know what it is you would like to discuss with the representative. "HR 213? Could you tell me what that is in relation to? Services for the chronically mentally ill? Oh, yes. Let me see. He's going to be pretty tied up next week. Would you want to write to the congressman about it? That way he could probably be most helpful to you." No, you are anxious to talk with him in person. Your schedule is fairly flexible. "Well, it looks as if he will have a little time next Wednesday afternoon, say about 1:30?" Yes, that would be fine.

As soon as you hang up, write a letter to the congressman thanking him for his willingness to see you regarding HR 213 on services for the chronically mentally ill. Specify the date and time of the appointment and include where you can be reached by phone and e-mail. Don't be surprised if you get a call Tuesday morning asking if you can switch to a different time. Be willing to change the time but stick to your request for a face-to-face meeting.

In writing the letter you are already lobbying. You are beginning to create in the minds of the representative and his staff the association between you and HR 213. You are demonstrating flexibility, appreciation for his responsiveness, and determination to be heard on the issue. You are already not someone to be stroked a couple of times and forgotten.

The next step is to go back and review your brief and other material. If you can do a dry run with a friend, do it. Does this sound like excessive preparation for a visit to your representative? Advocates would do well to take a leaf from the book of one James Baker, when he was scheduled to appear before the Senate Foreign Relations Committee in confirmation hearings for the post of Secretary of State. Baker was a very seasoned political operative, and it was generally assumed that the Senate would unanimously confirm his appointment to the cabinet position. But he took nothing for granted, even though he was down with the flu a few days before he was to appear before the committee. Here is one newspaper account of the preparations:

> Mr. Baker, who has been ill with the flu over the last several days and studying his briefing papers at home, has prepared a 10-to-15-minute opening statement for the hearings. . .

Mr. Baker, a master of stage-managing political events, sent an advance team to the hearing room on Friday to check acoustics, camera angles and the position of the furniture. He plans to be accompanied to the hearings by his wife and several of their eight children as well as a contingent of policy aides. (*The New York Times,* 1989)

Prior to all this, Baker had held private meetings with every member of the committee. He had thus prepared them and himself for the session. Furthermore, he made no secret of these detailed preparations. He wanted the Senate and the country to know that he took this assignment seriously.

You want your representative and his staff to know you are every bit as serious about HR 213. That is what will make them take you seriously. In addition to boning up on the substantive issues, you will review your background investigation of the congressman and his staff aide responsible for dealing with mental health issues.

### Preparing the Presentation

In putting together the brief (discussed in Chapter 4), you were guided by the inherent logic of the argument, each issue being a necessary building block for the next. The presentation to the target is different, and its organization is based on what is most salient to the person you will be talking to. For example, if your representative is preoccupied with the threat of violence by ex-patients, you may want to begin by addressing that issue head-on. Or you may decide to focus attention on the majority of ex-patients who are not violent. If your target has spoken eloquently of the need for services, but has taken a stand against any new programs because of the urgent necessity of lowering the federal deficit, you may decide to lead off with arguments regarding the economic feasibility of the plan—and the costs of doing nothing. Figure on having a very limited amount of time in which to present your case and make every minute count.

Finally, prepare a one-page summary of the major points you want to make about HR 213. This you will leave with the congressman or the staff aide with whom you meet. Like everything else, it should include the name of the bill, its subject matter, your name, address, telephone numbers, e-mail address, and fax number. Again, you are building up a linkage in people's minds. The same kind of pains should be taken with the appearance of this as with the rest: neatly typed, not crowded on the page, and limited to a single page, no more.

## *Tracking Down the Hard-to-Reach Target*

What if you can't get an appointment? Don't give up. Figure out a way to meet the target. One good approach is to learn about meetings where the person will appear. U.S. representatives frequently come back to their districts (not just during recess) to address citizen groups. State legislators are even more accessible. Go to the meeting early and find a seat near the front. If you can get the floor during the question period, state your name clearly, and ask about the progress of HR 213, which would provide services for the chronically mentally ill. Be sure to get that all in. You are reinforcing an association in the minds of the representative and, at least as important, a staff aide, who is also likely to be there. This is also a way to alert others in the audience, possibly the news media, to the importance of the bill. After the meeting, try to corner the representative to shake hands, state your name clearly, and reiterate your interest in HR 213. Do not worry about getting into arguments for the bill right then. Those can come in your follow-up letter. If you can't get to the representative, who will be surrounded by other people with their own concerns, talk with the staff aide. This is likely to be a senior staff person and worth establishing a connection with. If it is impossible to get to either, write a follow-up letter anyway, saying you were there, how interesting you found the representative's remarks on such-and-such, and then going into your case for HR 213.

There is not a well-developed set of rules for cornering public officials. A professional lobbyist I know has had to learn by experience. One of her biggest assets, aside from an engaging personality that puts people at ease, is a lively imagination. For example, there was a time when a legislative committee chairman she was trying to see kept avoiding her. Finally tracking him down to a committee caucus from which she was barred, she planted herself outside the men's room, knowing that sooner or later nature would direct her quarry in that direction. Sure enough, eventually he walked right up to her, having no other choice.

Experienced lobbyists have no monopoly on that kind of creativity. One student sat for hours in the outer office of a state representative, whose secretary kept assuring her that the representative would be back "any moment now." Meanwhile, the student knew from a variety of clues that the legislator was right there on the other side of the door taking phone calls. In this case it was the secretary who had to obey the call of nature. As soon as she was gone, the student knocked on the door of the representative's office, was admitted, and got a respectful and friendly reception. She may not have convinced him of her case, but she most certainly managed to impress him with her dedication to her mission.

## The Visit

Like dentists, public officials are chronically behind schedule, especially as the day winds on. It is an unfair exchange, in which you should make it a point to be there when you say you will, even though you will have to sit in the waiting room for a while. Everything you do from the moment you enter the outer office should convey respect and persistence, regardless of the kind of response you get. Everyone is important, starting with the receptionist. It is a time for authenticity, not cuteness. You are there on serious business.

Don't be surprised if, after all this preparation, you get to talk with a staff aide instead of the representative. Treat her or him as if you were dealing with the official. Begin by making sure the person knows your name, that you are interested in HR 213, and that the bill concerns services for the chronically mentally ill. Your target has to keep track of many things at once and may forget which issue this is.

The individual with whom you meet will be trying to size you up: Who are you? How important are you to the representative politically? What is your interest in this bill? The staff may have checked with people in your local area to see if they know you. If you can make a connection to a known person, such as a local party activist, that will help. But be sure you know that this person is on good terms with the representative, not an old enemy.

Start by saying who you are and why you are interested in the issue. Then tell simply and directly why you favor HR 213. When you make a general statement, follow it with concrete illustrations. Assume you are talking to an intelligent person who knows little or nothing about the bill. A good rule of thumb for advocates, teachers, and writers: Never underestimate the audience's intelligence, but never overestimate its knowledge of what you are communicating. If the representative or aide is familiar with the bill, he or she will let you know that soon enough. Just be sure he or she has the right one and not some other that sounds the same.

If you want to make a real impression, alert the person to a few of the points he or she will hear from the opposition and answer these. Don't worry about giving ammunition to the other side this way; chances are the representative is already aware of these arguments. But you will come across as really informed, fair-minded, and not afraid of open debate. More important, you will be prepping your target to handle such issues when discussing them with colleagues. In any event, take only a few minutes to lay out your case, then invite questions. Here are some of the responses you may get:

*Target already supports your position.* You are delighted to hear that. You know that some members of the House are opposed to it; maybe cite by name a specific one you know to be opposed. Could the representative speak to that colleague about the bill? If you know this representative has cosponsored such legislation in the past or has a generally "good" voting record, it would be good to cite that, showing that you are keeping tabs on the legislator's performance. Does the target have any suggestions on strategy? Do you have findings from your research that might be helpful to the target?

*Target generally favors the bill but has specific concerns.* Acknowledge that the concerns are important and then give your arguments regarding them. If they are issues to which you have no answers, stick to your basic position and say you would like to check the matter out further and get back to the target. (It is essential that you do the follow-up, of course.) You must not let the specific concerns overshadow the main thrust of the bill. End the conversation with appreciation that the representative understands the real value of the legislation. In other words, you and the target are still basically on the same side.

*Target is on the fence or noncommittal.* Present your case. Try to get at the specific issues about which the target has concern. Don't press for a definite answer. Offer to get additional information. Plan to come back to the target in the future with more information supporting your case. It may well be that the target needs information to justify taking a stand either way or simply has not thought much about it.

*The target is opposed to the basic thrust of the bill.* State your case. Respond to specific arguments against, but don't allow the meeting to turn into a debate, which the target will either "win," no matter how well you perform, or will resent the implicit put-down in being out-argued. Keep bringing the focus back to your issues. For example, when the target cites the horrendous cost of the program, acknowledge the importance of the fiscal issues and then pull out another case history of a person whose life was devastated because of lack of services. Leave the target with some arresting case histories seared into his or her brain. They may come back to haunt the target after you have left. Of course, it is just possible she or he is playing devil's advocate to see if you (1) are committed and (2) know what you are talking about. You can play a useful role by giving good arguments.

*The target tries to fill up the time by giving you a mini-lecture on the bill and what is happening to it.* Play along with this for a while, but then move in and give your pitch and ask how the target feels about it.

*The target would rather talk about other things.* For instance, your uncle whom he or she knew many years ago, the fortunes of the Boston Red Sox or the Pittsburgh Steelers, or his or her bill to rid the sidewalks of America of jewelry vendors. Play the target the way an angler plays a fish. Go with him or her for a little bit, but then pull things back to your agenda. Chances are the target will get the point after a while, but even if the two of you end up carrying on separate conversations, the target will know that you are serious about HR 213 and cannot be diverted from your mission.

*The target is impatient or frequently interrupts to take phone calls.* You have been given time with the target and you have a right to be heard, so don't be intimidated if this person continually checks his or her watch. If it gets too bad, or the interruptions are preventing you from making a coherent case, you might suggest rescheduling the interview. If you have to be kicked out, he or she will do so; the schedule is the target's problem, not yours. But when you leave, be sure to express thanks to this person for taking the time to talk with you, and don't allow a note of sarcasm to creep into your voice when you do it.

*The target is just plain rude.* Model nice behavior and pretend not to notice. You may be surprised to learn later that you made a good impression after all.

In any of the above cases, remember to leave your one-page summary with the target. Leave the door open for future contacts regarding HR 213. And always make your exit gracious, so that the final impression is positive—on the office staff as well as the target.

### After the Visit

As soon as possible, write a letter to the representative expressing thanks for his or her time, making sure once again to include the magic words: HR 213, for services to the chronically mentally ill, your name, address, and telephones, etc. If you have run across any friendly editorials, news items or the like, enclose a copy. If you have talked with a staff aide instead of the boss, address the letter to the representative, Attn.: the staff aide. You should tell the representative how helpful the aide was.

If you are working with an advocacy group on HR 213, be sure to send them a copy of the follow-up letter, with a cover note telling about the response you got. This will help them get the greatest mileage out of future contacts and multiply your own impact.

Remember, you have had not one contact with your target system, but four—the initial call, the confirming letter, the visit, and the follow-up letter. It's five if you count the one-pager, which is likely to be passed among different system members. Given politicians' natural ability to remember names, yours is by now well-known to the target, linked indelibly to what? Yes, to HR 213.

## GROUP VISITS

Going to see a policymaker as part of a delegation has several distinct advantages and also a few hazards. We should consider both.

### The Advantages

*The impact of numbers.* Politicians, as the old saying goes, may not be able to think too clearly but they all count exceedingly well. You and the target know that five constituents don't amount to much in terms of votes but, psychologically, facing several people at once is vastly different from meeting a lone individual. Depending on the composition of the group—for example, reflecting a diversity of interests or including big contributors or known political heavy-weights—the effect can be substantial.

*It is usually easier to get an appointment.* Not unrelated to the first point, delegations can command a piece of the target's time in a way that one individual, especially an unknown, may not. But don't expect to walk in unannounced and find the target sitting around waiting for visitors. The meeting should be scheduled ahead of time, just as with the individual visit.

*There is comfort in numbers.* Even the shyest among us feels safe in going to see policymakers as part of a delegation. Especially when you are trying to recruit other people to lobby, the knowledge that they will have company makes the job many times easier than it would be if they thought they would have to face the target alone. However, don't overwhelm the target with a mob. Five is a good number, though I've seen delegations of a dozen or more also work.

### The Hazards

*Internal dissension.* Nothing will wipe out the effectiveness of a delegation quite so fast as a disagreement within the ranks in front of the person you are trying to impress.

*"Don't everybody speak at once."* The opposite problem: The group settles down in the awesome presence and no one speaks up. Eventually things will get unplugged, perhaps with the help of the host, but the impression is one of an unprepared delegation.

*Generally sloppy planning.* The increased sense of security, cited above as an advantage, can turn into a minus factor if it lulls everybody into assuming the task will be a piece of cake. Not only is the delivery of the pitch weak, but the impression can be that the folks just wanted to be able to tell their friends back home that they met with the Great

Person. Autographs, anyone? And let me have my secretary give you tickets to the gallery. The paintings in the rotunda are really. . . .

## Putting the Delegation Together

If your goal is to maximize your impact on policy decisions, then who goes can be as important as how many. One sign that the target is taking this seriously: the secretary asks for the name and address of each person who will be attending. He or she may put it in terms of security, but the real reason is to check out the political potential of the meeting. People with political clout or who are generally respected in the home district are an asset as long as they understand the purpose of the meeting and are known to be supportive of the agenda.

It's not just that they are present in the room. In all likelihood the target, being naturally attuned to political influence, will turn to a known quantity and ask him or her to state the case for the group. As soon as that happens, you have no control over where the discussion will go. You can chime in with corrections along the way, but that may simply create the perception of internal disagreement mentioned above. So if you decide to take along such a person, be sure he or she is well prepared.

Inviting members of allied groups to join the delegation can add a lot of clout to a visit, but it also carries some risks with it. Try to insist on a joint planning session with everybody planning to attend.

## Preparing for the Visit

This is one place where you should be very forceful in stating your opinion. Stake out a firm position at the outset as the group defines the situation. The purpose is to influence the decisions of the policy-maker, and everything else should be subordinated to that goal. Team players only, and anyone wishing to attend the session with the target should be expected to attend at least one prior session in preparation.

Briefing materials, both on the subject matter and the target, should be distributed before the warm-up meeting. People should bring their questions to that session. Have it understood that if questions are not raised then, people will keep the doubts to themselves and not bring them up midway through the visit to the target.

You should spend some time at the beginning of the meeting helping first-timers deal with their anxiety. Emphasize the kind of positive
awareness of strengths discussed in Chapter 1, then on to the business
at hand.

Spokespersons should be chosen. It is wise to have one person act
as chief of the delegation and lead off the presentation. Allow time for
role-play and discussion of what happened in the mock exchange.

### Conducting the Visit

If possible, have the group rendezvous near the target's office fifteen minutes to a half-hour before the scheduled appointment. Coffee
shops have the advantage of allowing delegates to put something in
their stomachs to relax them, but they don't allow privacy in case
there must be a final briefing. Bars are a definite no-no, because you
don't want to walk in smelling like a distillery. Alcohol on one person's breath may be noticeable; in a group it can be overpowering, especially if nobody else in the room has been imbibing.

Assume that anything that can go wrong will go wrong and plan
accordingly. Have more than one person ready to take the helm, in
case the designated hitter is down with the flu or held up in traffic.
The same goes for the one-pager. Have two people charged with
bringing it in case one falters. Perhaps most important, be ready to
step into the breach in case others forget their lines or decide to use
the opportunity to lobby for a controversial measure that is not on the
agenda.

After leaving the target's office, the group should go somewhere
together to reflect on what has happened. If it has gone well—for
some the fact of having been able to carry out the mission at all will
feel like a success—you will want to celebrate. If things went wrong,
people need to be put back together. In any event, this is an opportunity to assess what did happen and make clear this one visit was not
the end of the process but only a beginning. Members should look
forward to continuing the work. This time the setting matters very little. Maybe that bar would be a good idea. At the least a coffeeshop, so
the group can reward itself.

## *Follow-Up*

In addition to making sure the thank-you letter gets sent soon afterward, send your own thank-yous to all members of the delegation. Let them know they did a good job. If you have any additional news regarding the target's subsequent action, be sure to include that. Helping delegates feel they have accomplished something and are appreciated will assure that they will have an appetite for more. Remember, it is awareness on the target's part that the advocates are serious and will stay around for the long haul that gives the group real power. Policymakers count on people to lose interest in an issue. You want to be able to demonstrate that this group of people is different.

## WRITING LETTERS

Please note: I did not say e-mail. More on that subject shortly. There are two kinds of letters, and they are is different as night and day. One is the solicited letter, the other the unsolicited.

### *The Solicited Letter*

In the course of your visit to your representative or that person's staff aide, you have been asked to put your thoughts on paper so they can be passed along to the boss or colleagues, depending on who is making the request. Or your organization has asked you to draft a letter to your congressman, to be signed by the designated hitter.

This kind of an invitation calls for what I will call a "serious" letter. It must be written with even more care than would go into the preparations for a face-to-face visit. Why? Because whatever appears on the page is what the target will see. No chance for corrections or answers to follow-up questions, to clarify your position. Moreover, in both cases, other people's credibility is on the line as well as your own, so you have to be doubly sure the letter is accurate and says what you want it to say.

You must be very clear about what you are being asked for. In the case of a request from a sympathetic representative or staff aide, does that person have any suggestions about issues to stress? Same question if an organization is making the request.

## Tailor It to the Task

There are few standard rules for writing to a policymaker. An opening paragraph should establish clearly what you are asking for (if regarding a bill, include the number and title) and your (or your group's) credentials. Following this are the arguments in favor of your position, with evidence to back them up. A few major points are better than a laundry list, which will only serve to confuse the reader.

Pay attention to writing mechanics, and have at least one other person proofread your work. Through your handling of the mechanics, you speak volumes about yourself and the importance you attach to the letter itself.

Remember what was said about the face-to-face exchange with a target. What is that person looking for? How will your opening sentence trigger off a definition of the situation inside the target? What will convince the target to modify that definition?

Try to avoid arguments and evidence the target already has in abundance. Try to think of an original twist, a personal experience or acquaintance who can shed new light on the problem.

Arguments are a way of persuading the target to do something. They can also be used to supply the target with talking points and supportive evidence, as does the following excerpt from a letter to a senator urging support for health care legislation:

> My four-year-old son has had recurrent bouts of bronchial asthma, and needless to say, his high fevers, wheezing, along with numerous (and expensive) trips to the doctor and pharmacy are stressful for my husband and me. However, we are blessed that we have both the cash flow to pay the doctor and pharmacy bills as they occur and a good medical insurance policy (my husband's employer pays the full premium) that reimburses us a full 80 percent of all outpatient and hospital and prescription expenses. . . .
>
> But my friend E, a 35-year-old divorced mother of six children, is not that lucky. She works at least 40 hours a week as a secretary, but her $13,000 salary doesn't stretch that far. Until a year ago, she received Medicaid, but she always had difficulty finding a doctor who would accept her card. Now . . . she is no longer covered under Medicaid. Instead, she has a pretty pitiful health insurance policy offered through

her employer: She pays $520 a year in premiums, but the policy pays for hospitalization only, no doctor's visits or prescriptions. As a result, her kids don't always go to the doctor when they're sick or get the prescriptions they need, because sometimes E simply doesn't have the money. Also, the kids don't have regular eye and dental checkups. . . .

In general, the shorter and more concise, the better. Just about any document can be tightened up without losing essential content. Try to keep the final version to one page or less. That's not always possible, of course. You must say enough to make your point. In the letter above, for example, without all those personal details, the basic impact of the message would have been lost. Or you may be discussing a complex bill or set of regulations that require extra space in order to be understood. Always assume you are writing to people who are not familiar with the subject matter, unless you know for a fact that they are. It would be smart, especially with a complex subject, to get a layperson unfamiliar with professional jargon to go over the letter. If that person has trouble with the language, assume your target will too.

### Unsolicited Letters

The ground rules for these are entirely different from those for solicited letters. The only thing you have going for you is authenticity— this is a message from the heart. Write it by hand and focus directly on what the proposed policy change means in your life and the lives of people you know and love. Forget canned talking points, statistics, etc. If you have had a previous contact with the target or his or her staff aides, mention it; name recognition may help your cause.

If brevity is important in solicited letters, it is many times more so in an unsolicited personal epistle. Figure on fifteen to twenty seconds to make your case.

### Letter-Writing Campaigns

These rely on large numbers for their effectiveness. The easier and more painless you make the task, the more people will pick up a pen and actually write. Getting them in one room, for example at a conference, supplying representatives' addresses, pens, paper, and envelopes (different sizes and colors), and offering to pay postage will increase the amount that actually get mailed.

It is common practice to hand out lists of talking points at such sessions, or send them to members of an organization with a request to write to one's representative or senator or the president. Talking points can be helpful in educating letter-writers, but they should not be quoted in the letters themselves. That looks canned, which is the quickest way to make the whole operation an exercise in futility. People should tell the target in their own words why House Bill such-and-such would hurt them or their children or suffering people they care about.

You will probably get an answer from the representative—written by a machine—thanking you for your letter and explaining where House Bill such-and-such is in the legislative process, and very likely not committing to vote one way or the other on it.

If the representative receives a large number of letters on this subject, it can have an impact. Letters are better than preaddressed postcards with a message already printed on them, leaving a space for you to fill in your name and address. But in both cases, they are most likely to get tallied as "yes" or "no" without ever having been read by the intended recipient.

## *LOBBYING BY TELEPHONE*

This is not my favorite form of lobbying, but it's better than nothing. It can actually be very effective if you have established a relationship with someone on a representative's staff. That is the person you should talk to. Otherwise, phoning your target's office works best if you have a specific staff member to call (not the elected official, unless he or she knows you and will recognize your name). Be prepared for telephone tag and maybe some long waits. By putting up with this routine and hanging in there, you are demonstrating your commitment to the target. Unless you know the elected official personally— sometimes even if you do—it's best to try to talk with the staff person who specializes in the issue you are calling about. He or she will understand what you are talking about and be able to respond. Have your pitch organized and ready to go, so you don't waste the person's time. You may be asked to send a letter. Whether you are asked to or not, you should definitely follow up with a letter thanking the person for his or her time and making sure to include the number and subject of the bill you called about. If you're lucky, the person on the phone will ask questions or comment on your message. Most of the time, you'll get a perfunctory thank you for calling, the senator/representative likes to hear from constituents, etc. One clue as to whether they are paying attention is whether they ask for your name and address.

### Telephone Campaigns

These are a lot like letter-writing campaigns. They are dependent on large numbers for their effect. Since they take less effort than writing a letter, they are less likely to impress the target. However, they are relatively painless. Sit at home, pick up the telephone, and dial your representative. You can call the local district office and convey the message that way. If the issue is hot and they are down to counting the yeas and nays, you will be asked to state your position.

## OTHER TYPES OF LOBBYING

### E-mail and Fax

Unless explicitly requested by a policymaker, e-mail seeking to influence him or her is a generally a waste of time. Even when your legislator or congressmember invites people to send their views via e-mail, this may be intended primarily to show that he or she is being responsive to the opinions of the folks back home.

Organized e-mail campaigns? They may work if the numbers are very large. But more commonly e-mail is used not to send messages to policymakers themselves, but to rally the troops to communicate by more traditional means.

E-mailing your representative is not the worst form of lobbying. That distinction in my judgment belongs to faxing. E-mail from unknown constituents will just be deleted without reading. Faxing requires paper at the receiving end, so imposes an unwanted burden on the recipient.

## Petitions

Petition drives, except for those designed to get someone's name or a referendum question onto the ballot, have very limited impact on policymaking. They have all the disadvantages of the obviously orchestrated letter-writing campaign with none of the virtues. Politicians know that many people who sign petitions are doing a friend a favor, or are flattered to be asked, or just have a hard time saying no when someone shoves a clipboard and a ballpoint pen in front of them.

Petitions have one important function, of course: They provide names and addresses for mailing lists. If you signed a petition on an abortion issue, you are a prime target for an antiabortion or pro-choice organization's direct-mail campaign. Depending on how the computerized lists are shared, you will also start getting mail on everything from banning handguns, to saving the whales, to attending a rock concert for the benefit of children in the Sudan. The causes may all be worthwhile, but we are into a different kind of lobbying, where you and your check book are the real target.

## LOBBYING APPOINTED OFFICIALS

From Chapter 3 we know that appointed officials are much harder to lobby than elected ones. They are not looking for your vote. They are specialists who are very well informed, have heard all the arguments, no doubt, and start off by assuming that you know less about the subject than they do. However, they handle that all-important phase of policymaking, turning enacted laws into regulations, so they are worth trying to influence.

### The Action Agenda

Work on regulations is detail work, not a matter of broad, general principles. You are most effective if you carve out specific points to focus on rather than a total piece of legislation. Needless to say, it should be something with which you are very familiar. You are not going to try to play one-upmanship with the professionals, but you at least have to demonstrate that talking to you is not a total waste of time, because you do have something to contribute.

It is helpful in this kind of lobbying to work closely with advocacy organizations that have already established working relationships with certain administrators. As was suggested in Chapter 2, this may affect your precise position on the subject matter, because now you are not the only one setting the agenda.

## The Target

Here again, experienced insiders are necessary allies, because the general public doesn't know the people who churn out regulations. You may be dealing with a cadre of people rather than a single individual. Ordinarily, there is one key person who, either because of strategic position, old friendships, or professional affiliations, is the link to the system. It is very likely that this person is looking for feedback from trusted sources, which can only help the advocates to make their input. The key word here is "trusted." A stranger offering advice may get a polite, even cordial reception, but is unlikely to register much impact on the decisions being made. In addition to representatives of advocacy organizations, staff aides to legislators considered friendly can also open the door to the regulation writers.

## Preparing the Case

Sound a bit intimidating? What could you possibly have to offer a policy wonk who is steeped in the finer points of the subject matter? For one thing, if you work with people who are or will be on the receiving end of the policy in question, you know something the target is unlikely to know of or even be dimly aware of: how it feels to the average individual caught up in the day-to-day reality of policy-in-action.

This is a good time to use case examples, to turn the abstractions of policy into concrete reality. But that is not enough. You also have to show that you have enough of a grasp of the policy itself to be worth listening to. You will have to wade through those numbing details you love to hate. And this is no time to pretend you know more than you do. Make liberal use of friendly experts to bring you up to speed. That is one reason a collaborative effort, not a solo performance, is essential.

Since legislative intent is an overriding consideration in writing regulations—the touchstone that everybody will use to justify a particular interpretation of policy—you must be prepared to research what led up to the final enactment of the bill. (See Chapter 5 for more on doing policy research.)

At the state level, you may have to rely much more on personal contacts with the people who lobbied the legislature before final enactment. Staff aides to friendly legislators are another potential source. Aside from legislative intent, your case needs the same thorough investigation required for any brief. The fact that you are dealing with an expert on the subject should not daunt you. The worst that can happen is that your message will fall on deaf ears.

### Presenting the Case

All the rules that apply to lobbying elected officials are equally relevant here: making the initial contact; writing a confirming letter; finding out everything you can about the person you will be visiting; making sure to get to your destination on time, but being prepared for a rescheduled appointment or talking to a person you did not expect to; being short and to the point; being gracious, whatever the response; providing a one-page summary before leaving; writing the follow-up letter.

Lobbying by letter may be the only way to get your message across—for example, if the target is in Washington, DC, and you are in Salem, Oregon. But because the appointed official has less need than an elected representative to curry your favor as a potential voter, it is easier for them to ignore a letter. At least if you see the target in person you know you had his or her attention, if only for the moment.

### Letting People Know

Because of the hidden nature of this phase of policymaking, it is doubly important to let others know you made the contact. Your representative and senator should be informed. Having a say in the agency's budget appropriation, they have a kind of clout you lack. Remember that fear of having the agency's budget cut is the first concern of an appointed official.

Friendly advocacy groups also need to be informed of your contact, though the foray into the bureaucracy should be planned in conjunction with such groups if at all possible.

## POINTS TO REMEMBER

1. Lobbying involves an exchange between you and the target. Be clear about what you want from the target and try to figure out what the target wants from you.
2. Your power base determines your potential ability to influence decisions. Coordinating your work with allied advocacy groups multiplies your power base.
3. In lobbying an elected official, get as much information as possible regarding the target and his or her constituency. In particular, what forces affect the target's political fortunes? What are his or her special concerns and biases? How much weight does he or she carry with colleagues? In the case of an appointed official, look for the same kind of information, but remember the "constituents" are his or her bosses and co-workers.
4. Careful preparation, prior to any kind of lobbying, pays off many times over.
5. Your presentation should be organized around the issues that are most important to the target.
6. Take along a one-page summary of your case when you visit the target.
7. Everything you do, from the moment you enter the outer office until you leave, should be intended to maximize the positive impression on the target and all staff members, including secretaries.
8. Follow up the visit with a letter of thanks, with copies to all advocacy groups with which you are involved on the issue.
9. Group visits have several advantages over solo visits, but they also have risks. To minimize the latter, insist on careful selection of the delegates and thorough preparation of everybody involved.

10. Letters written in response to a request by a policymaker, a staff aide, or an organization demand as much preparation as in-person visits. Unsolicited letters have their place. They should be hand-written, very brief and to the point, and should emphasize personal experiences, yours or those of someone you know.

11. Telephone calls to policymakers, petitions, e-mail, and faxes are much less effective ways of influencing policy decisions, unless you personally know the recipient. But they may be better than nothing.

12. It is harder to gain access to appointed officials than elected representatives. Don't feel insulted if someone seems to be talking down to you or trying to avoid you altogether.

13. In lobbying appointed officials, stress ways in which policy impacts people's lives. You will still need a thorough knowledge of legislative intent and the details of policy.

14. It is especially important to alert your congressional or legislative representatives as well as allied interest groups to the fact that you have been in contact with the appointed official, and to the of nature of your input.

# Chapter 7

# Testifying in a Hearing

Public hearings before legislative committees can be very exciting. The witnesses, sometimes well-known public figures, give their testimony, then are exposed to a withering barrage of questions from committee members. Exciting like a television drama and often about as spontaneous and unrehearsed. At the very least, everyone involved is acutely aware that this is political theater.

The official purpose of committee hearings is to provide vital information to committee members, but opinions on the extent to which this is true vary widely. Especially in Congress, the information gathering function tends to be secondary. Committees have staffs of experts who spend months researching the subject, briefing witnesses, and preparing questions and answers for committee members.

As for the interest groups that provide the testimony, if they were interested only in imparting information they would send their technical experts. Instead, they are likely to send high-visibility spokespersons, who are often colorful public figures.

Historically, state legislatures lacked strong technical staff support, compared with Congress, so they relied to a greater extent on committee hearings for an understanding of policy content. "The committee hearing is generally the most important source of information for legislators," wrote two political scientists in 1969, "and lobbyists tend to flock to the committee rooms as the focal point of their contact with legislators" (Zeigler and Baer, 1969:162-163).

In recent years, legislatures, particularly those in large states, have developed technical capacity rivaling that of Congress. Then why has this venerable institution of the legislative hearing persisted all these years, if anything taking up more of lawmakers' time and energy?

*Lobbying for Social Change*
© 2006 by The Haworth Press, Inc. All rights reserved.
doi:10.1300/5782_08

Obviously, they must serve a purpose for committee members or they would have been abandoned long ago. If we broaden our conception of information to include the political as well as the substantive, their significance becomes more clear.

This is one way for legislators to hear directly from the range of viewpoints on a given issue. Staff tend to screen out certain information in response to what they perceive their bosses want to hear. Here, in the space of one or two days, a committee member has paraded before him or her all the major players in the game. Furthermore, the actors are talking policy more than politics. This is a great way for the lawmaker to hear the major arguments that constitute the debate on the question. He or she has an opportunity to challenge or support witnesses.

It's not only those giving testimony who are on stage. Elected officials, whose careers depend so much on public exposure, have a fine opportunity to look wise and statesmanlike. The news media are willing partners in this process.

Beyond the purely political aspects, by holding public hearings a committee chair can generate support for a bill or expose it to public outrage, speed up or delay action. Particularly as legislative staff, administrators in the executive branch, and outside interest groups work in concert, they can do much to orchestrate support for a course of action through the hearing process.

There is also a more subtle use of committee hearings: providing a safety valve for strong emotions. Given its "day in court," a vocal faction may be more inclined to let the movers and shakers have their way. Clearly, that can subvert the democratic process, but it also allows action to proceed on some issues that could end up in gridlock.

As an advocate you don't have to decide how socially redeeming legislative hearings are. They are an integral part of the process, and there is every likelihood they will continue to be in the future. Your task, then, is to see how to make the most effective use of them.

## YOUR AGENDA AND THEIRS

In Chapter 2, we saw the importance of knowing where you want to go lest you discover you are in someone else's territory. The first thing, then, is to see whether you want to testify at all. You don't want to be a punching bag for a hostile legislator. You may, however, decide to represent the minority opinion in a hearing tilted away from your side, willing to allow a biased chairperson to look fair-minded for letting you testify as the price of getting your own views out to other committee members and the public via the news media. The media like controversy, and newspapers in particular look for quotes from the opposition. This prevents the majority from creating the illusion that people are all of the same mind on an issue.

Try to figure out why the hearing is being held on this subject at this time. Assume the scheduling has been carefully thought out by the chair and majority committee staff to get maximum mileage. (Each party has staff, but the committee staff director is always in the employ of those identified with the majority party.) Friendly lobbyists and advocacy groups can help you understand the reasons behind the scheduling.

You will not automatically have a chance to testify. As you are trying to figure out their agenda, they will try to figure out yours. If you think the committee chair and his staff will want to keep you off the roster, you might try the minority staff, who will have some slots available. Your chances of testifying are best if you can go as the representative of an organization identified with one side of the question or the other. The more powerful the organization, the better the chances, but then you have to find a way to interest the group in having you represent it.

Check the list of committee members. Is your representative or senator on the committee? That may be a way in. You won't be invited just because you are a constituent, of course. Somehow you will have to convince someone that what you have to say is vital enough that they should hear you instead of one of the dozen other would-be witnesses anxious to speak.

If you are not allowed to testify, you can still submit written testimony. By circulating copies to the news media you can have nearly as much impact as if you appeared in person. If you have material worth sharing with the committee and its staff, your written information may be used in the deliberations.

Keep focused on what you want out of the hearing. Does it appear to be mainly an opportunity for a legislator to feed a gigantic ego? So what? You are not there to build character or give lessons in modesty. Keeping focused is even more important in the hearing itself. It may be tempting to score points in a debate with a committee member. The news media will, of course, eat it up. However, winning arguments with a committee member in a hearing is a little like a teenager winning a debate with a cop on the street. It rarely happens and winning may be worse than losing. Your opponent will insist on somehow having the last word.

Neither should you be put in the position of conceding that your viewpoint is wrong or of coming out looking beaten. More on that later. Testifying in a hearing is different from one-on-one lobbying in one crucial respect: It goes on in a goldfish bowl. Maintaining one's own dignity and allowing committee members to keep theirs is a must.

It has been said repeatedly that policy advocacy is not a solo activity. Particularly since hearing testimony is public and may become part of a permanent record, it is important to find out in advance who else is testifying and touch base with allies. In this way, your approach can be consistent, if not coordinated. It may be possible for two or more witnesses to divide the territory in order to cover all the important points. How do you find out who is scheduled to appear at the hearing? The staff director (who can be reached through the chairperson's office) will be willing to share that information. Knowing who the friendly and unfriendly witnesses are to be will help you decide where to focus your own remarks.

## AUDIENCES

While figuring out why you should testify and what you want to achieve, you will have been thinking about where you want to aim your message. Are there issues on which you can educate the committee, say, out of your work experience or personal situation? If so, why are you using the hearing route, since you could share this content with staff members directly? Are you interested in providing ammunition for friendly committee members? If so, you will want to alert them in advance, so they can be prepped to ask helpful questions.

One potential audience for any public hearing testimony is the news media and, through them, the public. Sometimes they are the real audience.

You will need to prepare enough copies of your written statement (discussed in the following) so they can be distributed to all committee members, with additional copies for reporters, allied advocacy groups, and your own representative and/or senator.

Not only do you want all these to see your material, but you want them to be aware that you presented testimony. In the eyes of your representatives you cease to be merely one more vote. Elected officials always pay attention to constituents who are informed, articulate, and willing to express their views in public. Your potential role at election time is not lost on them.

Your main pitch will be to the priority audience, but you must keep in mind the secondary targets as well. Regardless of your priorities, there is one group of people who warrant particular attention: the committee members. By being thoroughly familiar with them, their biases and concerns, and especially the makeup of their districts, you are in the best position to anticipate the kinds of questions you will get from them.

In Chapter 6 we looked at ways to case an individual lawmaker. The process is essentially the same for committee members. Be sure to check beforehand and find out if this is to be a meeting of the full committee, a subcommittee hearing, or an inquiry conducted by a single legislator. As you gather information on the committee members, keep in mind that they will be in the public eye, not talking with you in the privacy of an inner office. Everything is on the record, and they are keenly aware that they are performing in front of an audience.

## PREPARING TESTIMONY

You have two tasks at the outset: establishing your credibility (you are knowledgeable and sincere) and focusing the audience's attention where you want it. As in the case of one-on-one lobbying, your aim is to get your audience to define the situation the same way you do. The task is complicated by the fact that you are communicating simultaneously with several audiences, and what you say is likely to become part of the permanent record. From the beginning of your testimony, you must seize the initiative in order to carry out those two basic tasks: establishing your credibility and focusing your listeners' attention.

### The Written Statement

Although, as we shall see, some witnesses submit no written statement, there are several good reasons for doing so. As Sharwell (1978) points out, the document states very clearly that you have approached this task in a professional manner; in short, you mean business. With such a statement, you can provide a more extended discussion of the issues, with added evidence, than is possible within the time constraints of the hearing itself. It is the written material the news media are most likely to use, unless you are sufficiently good theater to warrant live coverage on television. Since the statement will become part of the permanent record, committee members and others can consult it later. Most important, perhaps, in writing the statement you are forced to be very disciplined in formulating and expressing your ideas.

Great care should be taken in preparing the written statement. You will draw heavily on your policy brief (see Chapter 4), but the statement for presentation to the committee will be different in several respects. You will not present the opposition arguments, unless to set them up to be knocked down. Initially, you will want to establish who you are, whom you represent, and basically why the committee should listen to you. In the main body of the statement you should organize the major points specifically for the audience to which they are directed. If the need for action is generally conceded, you may even bypass that portion of the argument entirely. If feasibility questions are paramount, you may decide to lead off with those.

Sharwell (1978) suggests starting and ending with the strongest points, leaving the less crucial ones for the center of the paper, the idea being that a strong start and finish leave the best and most lasting impression on the audience. Kleinkauf (1981) says the written statement should be short, no more than two typewritten pages, and should focus on broad principles rather than be too specific. Her reasoning is that in the constant jockeying that goes on in the legislative process, one should have maximum flexibility.

It may be desirable to think in terms of two written documents: a basic position paper that one's sponsoring organization can support (one couched in generalities), and a statement prepared explicitly for a particular hearing. However you decide to go, the most important thing is that your reasoning be tight and your evidence convincing.

In 1979, the late Senator Daniel P. Moynihan held hearings in Buffalo, New York, on toxic waste cleanup in Niagara Falls (U.S. Senate, 1979). The announced reason for the hearings was to gather information to assist ongoing deliberations on a proposed Superfund for cleaning up hazardous materials.

We shall see how three witnesses representing different interests approached the task of giving testimony. The first was Bruce D. Davis, a Hooker Chemical Company official. The second was Lois Gibbs, president of the Love Canal Homeowners' Association. The third was Glen Haughie, MD, of the New York State Department of Health.

I shall present excerpts from their testimony and look at what they were trying to do and how they went about it. Both Davis and Gibbs provided written statements, prepared with the help of experts. The experts could have done the testifying, but the impact of a senior official of the company and the woman whose name and face had become well-known was important.

First, Davis of the Hooker Chemical Company:

> Hooker is deeply and vitally concerned with the problem of the disposal of wastes—what we as individuals and a society no longer want, no longer need, or no longer use—not just locally, but nationally, for this is indeed a problem national in its scope. I understand that various federal legislative proposals have been brought forward, and I am pleased to see the beginning of discussion for possible national solutions to this problem. . .

Davis describes the work of Hooker in cleaning up toxic wastes and developing new technology for that purpose. The testimony is detailed and at points technical.

> Finally, I will share with you some thoughts and concerns about legislation dealing with the disposal of hazardous wastes. In developing legislative approaches . . . we believe it essential

to keep in mind that in both origin and scope, these problems run far more broadly than Hooker, or the chemical industry, or even industry as a whole. They run far more broadly than the Niagara Frontier and New York State.

The recommended approach in the bills introduced in Congress thus far is a superfund or ultrafund. We believe this is a viable financial solution. However, it does need considerable refinement. . .

Davis ends his testimony with a set of recommendations for limiting the uses of the Superfund, for example reserving it "for emergency and imminent hazard-type situations and not as a monetary source for total reclamation of the land." He also proposes a limit on total payouts "to prevent abuses of the fund."

This witness has two audiences to deal with. One is Senator Moynihan, who as chair of the Subcommittee on Environmental Pollution has a pivotal role in shaping the federal government's toxic waste policies. The other is the citizenry of the Buffalo–Niagara Falls region. The local news media are sure to report extensively on this hearing. Davis must rely on media representatives to carry his message to the public, possibly adding their own editorial "spin" in the process.

He begins by addressing the latter audience. Rather than dwell on who did what at Love Canal—a debate in which Hooker is bound to lose, no matter how valid its arguments—he focuses on his company's image as a concerned and responsible member of the community. He defines the problem as national, not local. In fact, the local waste disposal sites are not even mentioned until well into his testimony, then only as illustrations of certain types of pollution problems.

We are all culprits when it comes to toxic waste, says Mr. Davis. Note the early reference to what "we as individuals" do. Later, "I urge you not to let the focus of recent public attention, or the focus of my remarks today on the chemical industry, lead you to believe that the problem of hazardous wastes is limited to industry alone."

The terminology is carefully chosen. Never does the word "toxic" (poisonous) appear. Wastes are at worst "hazardous," which puts them in the same category as cigarette smoking.

For his other audience, Senator Moynihan, Davis is more specific, at points technical. He knows enough not to oppose the proposed Superfund legislation outright—another losing debate, given the public mood. Instead, he urges a number of "refinements," mainly aimed at limiting the potential cost to companies like his own.

The witness is defining more than the problem. Throughout, he is also defining himself as a trustworthy source of information. He does this partly by going into technical matters in some detail, in effect becoming the patient teacher of the senator. Rather than be affronted by this implicit role reversal, Senator Moynihan, a former university professor, appears to welcome Davis's testimony and even submits to him a list of questions for further elaboration after the hearing.

Bruce Davis has the company's counsel, Thomas Truitt, at his elbow during his testimony. Lois Gibbs, the Love Canal Homeowners' Association spokesperson, brings along Dr. Beverly Paigen, a cancer researcher who has been a consultant to the citizens' group.

> First of all, my name is Lois Gibbs and I am president of the Love Canal Homeowners' Association (LCHA). The LCHA is a citizens group consisting of over 1,000 families, representing more than 90 percent of the residents of the area. LCHA was formed to deal with the problems of living near the Love Canal dumpsite.
>
> I would like to address the issue of the adequacy of present local, state, and federal government response to hazardous waste emergencies. At the start I would like to say that upon learning of the situation at Love Canal, the state moved very quickly to begin health and environmental studies. They also put into effect a remedial construction plan which would attempt to reduce chemical migration from the Love Canal. Although there are many problems which I could discuss, I will limit my testimony mainly to the experiences I have had in dealing with the different state agencies involved at Love Canal. . .

Midway through her testimony, Lois Gibbs is asked a question. Dr. Paigen, who has been sitting with Gibbs, then interjects a comment and from then on questions are directed to her instead of Gibbs. Clearly, Dr. Paigen rather than Gibbs is seen as the real party to deal with.

Senator Moynihan's staff has filled him in on what Lois Gibbs will say. They may have even given her suggestions on what to say. She is not there to instruct him on toxic waste disposal but to give him leverage.

Even within the Buffalo area, the senator is no doubt receiving conflicting messages. Environmentalists and members of the LCHA are telling him to take strong action, maybe to crack down hard on companies like Hooker. But chemical companies are big employers in that part of New York State, so there is bound to be a sizable faction telling him to go slow. Graphic descriptions of the plight of Love Canal residents, picked up and amplified by the news media, make it easier for the Subcommittee on Environmental Pollution to act.

Lois Gibbs may or may not have calculated this, but a U.S. Senate subcommittee hearing in her own backyard is a banner opportunity to get out her message. She doesn't have to fight for media attention, a chronic problem of grassroots organizations. The senator, being an experienced politician, knows how to maximize the media coverage of an event. He thus helps Lois Gibbs in her task of getting exposure. The hearing is sure to get good play in the local press, but in addition the wire services may air her remarks nationally. Her task is simpler than that of Bruce Davis. She has a single, straightforward message: The little people, having been the unwitting victims of industrial carelessness, are now suffering unnecessarily from bureaucratic callousness and incompetence.

This is the same message she has been presenting in state hearings, television interviews, and news releases. Everybody in the news business knows what she is going to say, but it still has a freshness and authenticity that means it will make the headlines again. This is not unlike the stock campaign speech that becomes boring to reporters accompanying the candidate on the campaign trail but still sounds new when it is shown on WMBD in Peoria.

The introduction is probably something she says in her sleep by now: "[M]y name is Lois Gibbs and I am president of the Love Canal Homeowners' Association . . . a citizens group consisting of over 1,000 families, representing more than 90 percent of the residents in the area." Senator Moynihan already knows that, but there could be reporters around who don't.

She then goes directly to the theme of her presentation: Official foot-dragging and incompetence are disrupting and in some cases endangering human lives. The Hooker Chemical Company is ignored. The real villain, she says, is the New York State bureaucracy.

By this time, Gibbs herself is news. Beverly Paigen could just as readily say, "This is especially alarming since on March 9, 1979, thick, black, oily leachate was found running off the north section of the canal onto the street." The word "leachate" would probably seem more natural coming from her; she may in fact have written all or part of the statement. But when Lois Gibbs says it we can visualize her children being exposed to the demonic brew, her house slowly sinking into the morass. It is effective theater, which in large part is what this hearing is about.

Dr. Glen Haughie, a New York State health official, uses a different approach. He brings no written statement and will rely on the questions and answers to bring out his message. As long as the focus is on the appealing housewife from Love Canal, the state officials are on the defensive. When it is Dr. Haughie's turn to speak, he tries to shift the ground of the dialogue by emphasizing what Lois Gibbs lacks, professional credentials.

DR. HAUGHIE: Yes, Senator. My name is Glen Haughie. I am a physician. I am a graduate of Harvard College, Harvard Medical School, and I have a Master's in public health from the Harvard School of Public Health. I believe this is a university dear to you, sir, as it is to me.

SENATOR MOYNIHAN: Particularly that school of public health, if I may say. We will call you an epidemiologist.

DR. HAUGHIE: Well, sir, I do not carry that title easily. I have spent a couple of years with the Center [sic] for Disease Control serving as an Epidemic Intelligence Service officer.

SENATOR MOYNIHAN: In Atlanta?

DR. HAUGHIE: Yes. I was assigned to the state health department in Albany in the late 1960s. I have served as director of the Monroe County Health Department of Rochester, New York, for a period of time. For the past three years, I have been employed. . .

SENATOR MOYNIHAN: We will accept your credentials, Doctor.

DR. HAUGHIE: I have no written statement, Senator. I am prepared to answer questions that you may have for the department. I may offer a couple of comments concerning the discussion of the definitional terms "requisite nexus." They are definitional because from an epidemiologist's point of view, I think what we are saying is, is there a causal association between exposure for a given chemical, or group of chemicals, and an adverse health effect. This, of course, has been the concern on our minds in the investigation of the Love Canal situation. . .

Up to this point, Dr. Haughie has presented himself, not as a combatant but merely a highly qualified resource to lend his expertise to the proceedings. He has brought no written statement. He is not trying to argue anything, just be a helpful presence. Then he steps out of character, as he responds to what he perceives as a criticism of his department by the senator:

DR. HAUGHIE: If I may, sir, I respectfully disagree somewhat with the comment you made earlier regarding the department's apparent lack of effort to obtain information from residents of the area about their health status.

SENATOR MOYNIHAN: Doctor, I do not recall myself saying that.

DR. HAUGHIE: I think the issue has related to our blue-ribbon committee. You may or may not be aware that we have convened a blue-ribbon committee on four occasions. This group of experts to which I just referred were gathered together in order to obtain their best expert advice on our data.

SENATOR MOYNIHAN: I am going to exercise the right of the chair to say again, what was it I said? I do not recall. . .

DR. HAUGHIE: I think, Senator, in response to a comment made by Ms. Gibbs concerning the closed-door policies methods by which the department has. . .

SENATOR MOYNIHAN: Oh, I did say something to the effect I wondered about the question of excluding persons who were not professionals. I meant not in the least an aspersion on anyone who is professional. You go ahead and correct the record.

DR. HAUGHIE: I am intimately familiar with the concern Ms. Gibbs raised. I am also intimately aware of the numerous efforts we have made to conduct public meetings and to try to explain to a lot of very anxious people the nature of our studies, the progress or lack of progress, and the efforts I think the department has made in trying to unravel a most difficult problem.

SENATOR MOYNIHAN: Let me, then, correct that record to show that no aspersion was intended and that none remains. Explain that blue-ribbon committee to me. Did you have a question of data analysis that you wanted a jury to say is this the way to go about it?

DR. HAUGHIE: From time to time, Senator, we asked physicians, toxicologists, statisticians, chemists, geneticists and epidemiologists, and others to give us advice on the design of studies, methods of collecting our data, and also sought their advice in trying to interpret our data.

SENATOR MOYNIHAN: Would you tell me for this record—and we are trying to get a record here—what you have done in the way of data collection in the Love Canal?

Dr. Haughie goes into an explanation of current steps being taken by his department and the difficulties involved in carrying them out. Senator Moynihan continues to interject questions for clarity. He ends by urging cooperation between the state's efforts and those of Dr. Paigen.

One gets the sense that Dr. Haughie knows where he wants to go but is not always sure of how to get there. His attempt to distance himself from the embattled housewife via professional credentials, his strength and her weakness, is a sound strategy, but he appears to have overdone it as Senator Moynihan in effect says, all right, we accept your professional credentials, let us move on. One basic rule of thumb is never to gratuitously irk your inquisitor. It is his show, not yours.

Dr. Haughie then proceeds to remind us of what is the state's most vulnerable point, its failure to sufficiently inform and consult the Love Canal residents. The question is one of indifference to the plight of ordinary citizens, not limitations in scientific expertise, which could perhaps be justified in the arcane world of toxic waste disposal. This is a classic case of focusing your audience's attention on the wrong issue, forcing yourself on the defensive. If Dr. Haughie wants to set the record straight, he can simply describe in detail the exhaustive attempts his department has made to involve the people affected.

Dr. Haughie is in a difficult spot. In defending his department, he can't attack Lois Gibbs, the embattled housewife. Instead he quarrels with something Senator Moynihan is supposed to have said, putting him on the defensive. Some committee chairs would have made it a point to administer their own put-down at this juncture, basically nullifying anything else the witness had to say. But Moynihan is not about to be diverted by this nonissue and the hearing proceeds. His final admonition to the two sides to work together could be interpreted as a subtle downgrading for Dr. Haughie, since Dr. Paigen has no official standing and the state officials have tended to dismiss her work as lacking in scientific credibility.

## *GETTING READY TO TESTIFY*

Given the fact that the purpose of holding such a hearing has a large, if not exclusive, political component, it is wise to bring a written statement and spend a little time laying out one's position. Bring enough copies for committee members plus extra copies for media people. The news media may or may not be interested in the content, but the chances are good that by the time you get to testify they have left the hearing room, with or without a document from the presenter.

Especially if you have never testified before, you will probably die a few deaths on the way to the witness chair. The nice part is going through the experience and discovering that you did not actually die. Generally, the more anxious you are going in, the more of a high you will feel afterward.

The first thing to do to boost your confidence is have a little conference with yourself. Mirrors are good for this sort of heart-to-heart. Look yourself in the eye and say (out loud), "I am scared." At this point you have taken the most important step of all: admitting to yourself that you are afraid. Next, say (also out loud): "I can do it." Not just once, many times—preferably with increasing volume. When your roommate gives you a strange look afterward you can say, "And I'm not afraid of you, either."

Now get your mind off yourself and onto business. Practice a little focusing, as in definition of the situation. If there is any information you lack about the hearing setup time, place, which committee members are likely to be in attendance, who else will be testifying, where you come in the order of appearances, how much time you will be allotted—get it from the staff director's office.

Have you done your research on the members? Have you decided how they are likely to define the situation? How you want them to?

Once you have all this information, you are ready to plan your presentation:

1. Open with who you are. If your work or past personal experience is pertinent, be sure to spell that out clearly. This is where you will establish your credibility as a witness. If you state your position title, be sure to make clear whether you are speaking on behalf of the organization, another group, or merely on your own behalf.
2. If you plan to speak about a particular issue, state that fact.
3. Make your major points concrete by using illustrations, preferably from firsthand experience, but don't neglect to state what it is you are illustrating.
4. At the end, summarize briefly what you have said and offer to answer any questions.
5. Practice delivering your testimony several times. Having a friend listen and make suggestions can be useful, but only if the friend doesn't have so many ideas that you begin to get rattled. A more useful role for your friend is to act as devil's advocate, raising questions both of you think the committee members might ask. Practice answering those, too.
6. Do you plan to make a Powerpoint presentation ? If so, make sure to let committee staff know in advance. They may supply the equipment. In terms of the content of your presentation, make sure it is appropriate for this audience (the committee). A canned presentation that works with the hometown PTA may come off as condescending to lawmakers already steeped in the issues.

## GIVING TESTIMONY

On the day of your actual appearance, try to reduce stressors to a minimum. Give yourself extra time to get to the hearing room so you won't feel rushed. Cecilia Kleinkauf (1981) suggests getting there in time to listen to others testify and see which legislators ask what kinds of questions. The last thing you want to do is arrive in the hearing room out of breath, while everybody else looks mellow and bursting with self-confidence. If you know any friendly witnesses who will also be testifying, you may want to link up beforehand and go together.

Friendly co-testifiers are like friendly roommates. Avoid getting a lot of last-minute suggestions from them. It will tend only to confuse you. However, they can point out who is who among the committee members and opposition witnesses if any are scheduled.

When your turn comes, take your time walking to the witness table. If you are shaking, chances are nobody else will notice, least of all the committee members. If there is water at the witness table, take a sip. It will help clear your throat and give you something to do with your hands. Avoid fidgeting, rattling papers, and other distractions. You can always fold your hands in front of you.

The chair will introduce you. If your name has been mispronounced or incorrect information given about your job title, quietly state the correction. It will be appreciated. Assuming there is a microphone, speak loudly enough so you hear yourself coming back through the sound system. If it is too soft, move closer to the microphone. If it shrieks at you, move back a little.

Initially speak to the chairperson. Thank him or her by name for inviting you to speak. If you are reading written testimony, bring your eyes up periodically to meet the eyes of the chairperson, then other committee members.

Above all, don't allow yourself to be rushed. If the chairperson asks you to wind up your presentation, jump ahead to your closing paragraph. If any vital details have to be omitted, tell the committee they can pick those up in the question period. Remember, the committee members and the news media will have access to the full document.

When you have finished, say you will be happy to answer questions and sit back. That may be it. It's more likely that at least one member, probably more, will have questions. Rather than see this as a threat, look on it as an opportunity to expand on what you have already said.

## FIELDING QUESTIONS IN A PUBLIC HEARING

When a committee member asks a question, take a moment to be sure you understand what is being asked. If it is not clear, ask to have it restated or clarified. Naturally, that can be overdone. Address your answer to the person asking the question, preferably by name. Make your answers brief and to the point and bring in concrete illustrations wherever possible. Don't ramble. If you haven't fully answered everything asked, the questioner will probably follow up, asking for more.

Many questions will be friendly or neutral—at least you should start with that expectation. People really do want to know what you have to say about the subject. But there may be some questions which are not friendly. Here are a few problematic kinds of questions. In all cases, keep cool, treat all questioners with utmost respect, regardless of how abusive or off-the-wall their behavior.

*Legitimate debate.* When you take a position on a controversial issue, you can expect to be challenged at points. That, after all, is an important function of public hearings—to air opposing points of view and expose them to critical evaluation.

*Response:* Chances are, if you have done your homework, you are already aware of the major criticisms of your argument and have prepared responses. Plug in your answer and see if it holds. The questioner may persist. If so, see if the further questioning really advances the argument or is simply a rehash of what was already answered. You may want to restate your position on that issue, possibly adding an illustration, then let it go. If the committee member will not give up, shrug and say, "I guess we should agree to disagree."

Following is an excerpt from a hearing on welfare reform in which two representatives of a public employees' union try to respond to questions about mandatory work requirements. They are opposed to making them mandatory. Some committee members feel otherwise. One in particular, Representative Brown, persists in focusing on that issue. The witnesses must respond to this, like it or not.

MR. BROWN [a committee member]: Thank you, Mr. Chairman. Mr. McEntee [witness], I appreciate your coming this morning and look forward to working with you to develop a bill in this area. I noticed you indicated a concern about making jobs mandatory. Does this same concept transfer over to mandatory education and training? Do you feel it would be inappropriate to make those mandatory?

MS. MEIKLEJOHN [a colleague of Mr. McEntee]: Well, I think again you have a problem.

CHAIRMAN FORD: Pardon me. Would you state your name for the record? I do not know whether you did earlier, but. . .

MS. MEIKLEJOHN: I am Nanine Meiklejohn, and I am in the legislative department of the union. I think while that may be theoretically a desirable thing, again you have the problem of trying to do something with the limited amount of resources. You would be choosing to cover everybody and diminishing the quality of services that you are providing, and that is unavoidable in this current fiscal climate. So, again, we think it is better to start off with motivated people who do well in the program, and as the program gains credibility with the welfare and the general public as a whole, that, in turn, produces more support for program expansion.

MR. BROWN: So, you think it is wrong to require people to attend a work program or a training program or an educational program as a condition of receiving welfare?

MR. MCENTEE: I think it would probably be one of the worst things in the world to give them the training and the education and no place to go. I think it would just be tremendously frustrating and, once again, that is why the scope should be limited. . .

MR. BROWN: Well, that was not really my question, but I appreciate your comment on that area. I wonder if you share my concern for what happens to people when you provide them with welfare benefits and ask for nothing in return.

MS. MEIKLEJOHN: I think that presumes that the recipients are not motivated to improve themselves, and I think that most. . .

MR. BROWN: No, no. I am sorry. I am not presuming anything. I am simply asking you what happens when you provide welfare benefits and do not require something in return.

MS. MEIKLEJOHN: Well, I think you have to look at what is involved in, for example, requiring a young teenage mother with a child to finish her education. We have to be prepared then as a society to make sure that her children are in a decent child care arrangement while she participates in the program. We have to make sure that she has transportation that does not involve her spending two hours going back and forth. We have to make sure we cover her other needs.

MR. BROWN: Yes, but if I understand your statement, your position is that even if we provide adequate child care and transportation, you are still opposed to mandatory participation in work, training, or education programs—is that right?

MR. MCENTEE: Go ahead.

MS. MEIKLEJOHN: I think our concern is that we will write a law which will have the mandatory participation requirements and not in the end be able to follow up with the dollars to provide the services, and, so, when you are left with a range of activities that includes workfare and job search, it will draw the system into these activities because they are not as expensive.

MR. BROWN: I am not trying to put words in your mouth, but am I hearing you say now that if there is money available in a particular program, then you feel that mandatory participation would be appropriate?

MS. MEIKLEJOHN: No. I do not.

MR. BROWN: That is still a concern for others.

Later another committee member picks up the mandatory versus voluntary issue.

MRS. KENNELLY [a committee member]: Let me ask the legislative person something Mr. Brown asked you about. Did you still have reservations, did you have reservations about mandatory education as well as mandatory taking of a job? How many children do you think would go to school if it was not mandatory that they go? How many people do you think; I do not know if you have got children.

I had children. Unless it was mandatory for that person to get educated, to become literate, to be able to get a high school equivalency, who would go unless it was mandatory? Let us talk about who we are talking about.

MS. MEIKLEJOHN: It is hard for me to believe that a person who has a dependent does not want to seek a way to be self-supporting, and it is hard for me to believe that if she was given an opportunity, a real opportunity with a real promise to it, that she would not take it.

Further along in the hearing yet another committee member comes back to the mandatory work issue. It is clearly the focus of their definition of the situation, despite where the witnesses may wish to lead them.

MR. CHANDLER: I think that it is fair then to ask if we are sending a negative message to a person by requiring a work element of those asking for and receiving assistance from society, what kind of a message we are sending when we do just the opposite, provide assistance without any requirement for anything, for any contribution in return?

MR. MCENTEE: I guess we just keep going back to the same situation. If we had a situation where we could provide all of these things with the promise of a job, then that most certainly is one set of circumstances. . . . We are trying to deal with the realities here. That is what we are trying to do, and not with a theory or what could happen or what may happen. We are trying to deal with the reality that the federal government only has so many bucks, only have *[sic]* so many dollars, and to get as many people as we can in a voluntary way off those rolls, and let the American people see it as an unqualified success then maybe down the road a little bit, we can do other and more things. (U.S. House of Representatives, 1987)

The congressman then picks up on something McEntee has said about defense spending, and the focus shifts away from the mandatory/voluntary participation issue. The two union representatives have been queried by three different committee members on the mandatory/voluntary issue. In assessing the witnesses' argumentative strategies, we should begin by looking at their initial posture, which defined the battleground in the first place.

McEntee devotes about two-thirds of his opening statement to the mandatory participation issue, so he is inviting dialogue on that issue. His basic argument is that success is more likely if one starts with those who volunteer to participate. Mandatory participation without sufficient investment of government funds in day care and other support services would end up hurting the children, he says, and there would be a temptation to stress workfare, to the detriment of real job preparation.

Representative Brown asks if the witnesses' opposition is to mandatory education and training as well as mandatory jobs. The witnesses appear to be on the defensive, Meiklejohn saying the congressman implies that recipients are not motivated to improve themselves. Brown persists: What if you were assured of adequate education and support services? Would you still be opposed to the mandatory feature? He forces them into a corner, weakening their position.

Brown will not be put off. He wants them to address the mandatory feature head-on. He doesn't say, but might have, "Can you think of any circumstances under which you would favor mandatory participation?" The witnesses skirt that central issue, and they suffer for it.

What should one do in response to this kind of questioning? The most important step comes before the interrogation. Decide in advance where you are ready to draw the line in the dirt. Either you are categorically opposed to mandatory participation, in which case you simply say so, or you decide under what circumstances it would be acceptable. Above all, avoid seeming to waffle.

McEntee could have said under no circumstances would he support mandatory participation. He could have said, yes, if you will guarantee adequate education and training, or guarantee a job at the other end, then I have no problem with mandatory participation. Instead, his strategy is to keep focused on the circumstances themselves and say we must deal with reality, not some hypothetical wonderland.

Representative Kennelly raises the question of mandatory education: Do you think children would go to school if they did not have to? She has challenged the witnesses' stance at perhaps its most vulnerable point: not wanting to require people to enroll in educational programs which presumably can only help them escape from poverty, and which in any event are akin to apple pie and motherhood in this country.

Meiklejohn detects an underlying message in Kennelly's comments, a view of welfare recipients as unmotivated, and seeks to meet that head-on, as she did with Representative Brown. But the exchange ends on an inconclusive note.

It is possible to challenge Kennelly's underlying assumption that one can isolate a particular part of the total package—education—and ignore the rest. But what about her comparison of school attendance laws and mandated participation in educational programs by welfare recipients? When presented with an analogy—in this case between schoolchildren who might prefer to play outside than go to school and welfare mothers—it is important to consider whether it is an appropriate comparison. Is making your teenager abide by compulsory school laws that apply to everybody the same as requiring female heads of households in poverty to attend programs with a dubious record of achievement?

Representative Chandler voices a common concern: You send the wrong message to the poor when they can get something for nothing. McEntee could have challenged the underlying assumption that the poor pay nothing for their status as recipients. That, of course, would not have satisfied the congressman and could simply lead to a protracted argument about whether welfare recipients are motivated—an argument in which the witnesses would remain on the defensive regardless of how good their evidence. Instead, McEntee stays with his theme that the questioning assumes a world removed from reality; the reality is too little commitment of resources for services and no assurance of a job at the other end.

The respective parties to any debate want to score points and show that the opponent's position is wrong. But this airing of honest differences is an essential part of the winnowing process in policymaking.

We now turn to argumentative tactics that resemble legitimate debate but really are distortions of it. There is nothing unethical about them. They may seem unfair, but in the policy arena fairness is an elastic notion. Like beauty, it tends to be in the eye of the beholder.

*The outright attack.* Understand that in this case the quarry is not your arguments, but you. You can tell the difference by the fact that reasonable responses meet a deaf ear, the questioner shifts the ground, always in a way that makes you personally look bad. You can usually tell by the tone of voice and the facial language, although your judgment of those qualities may be too subjective, especially since you are under attack.

*Response:* First, make sure it is an attack, not simply difficulty in understanding what you had in mind. If you are asked, "Do you really expect us to believe that . . .?" and that is what you intended to say, stick to your guns. People can disagree. However, chances are it is not what you intended but has been pulled out of context, taken to absurd extremes or simply distorted. State what you did intend to say, possibly adding an illustration. Don't get into a debate—it is probably one you can't win, given the hearing format and the fact that you are on their turf. The best you can do is demonstrate that you are a credible source of information and let people draw their own conclusions. Don't assume others will agree with your assailant.

*The extraneous issue.* You get a question about something entirely unrelated to your testimony. Often this is an oblique attempt to raise doubts about your credibility as a witness. Again, the issue is not the subject matter but your image. Or it may be an attempt to put words in your mouth—a statement instead of a question, using you to corroborate the committee member's biases.

*Response:* Answer briefly and get the focus back to the main track. Don't try to spar with the questioner. If it is your image he or she is after, demonstrate your image by treating the questioner with respect and maintaining your own dignity.

On one occasion I testified before the Pennsylvania State Senate Public Health and Welfare Committee on a welfare reform proposal. I had a general knowledge of the makeup of the committee but had not done my homework on the individual members. Unfortunately, the ranking Republican member of the committee knew who I was. When I had finished my testimony and invited questions, he asked me if I had previously been the chairperson of the board for one of the State Department of Public Welfare's county assistance offices. (Yes.) And was it true that the State Auditor General's office had found a particularly high rate of suspected fraud in our caseload? (Yes. Implication: How could I be trusted as a witness since obviously we had not been sufficiently concerned about protecting the taxpayer against welfare cheats.)

It so happened this senator and the auditor general had issued a series of reports on fraud in the state welfare rolls. I knew the senator was shifting the focus away from my testimony and onto me, but I had no choice but to respond to his questions. Rather than get into a major argument with him—for example, by pointing out that many cases of "suspected welfare fraud" are really staff errors and in most such cases outright fraud is not proven—I decided to try to keep the exchange brief and get back to the main thrust of the testimony.

Then I got a break. He asked me what we did when we were informed of the suspected fraud cases. We did two things, I said. The first was to tighten up on procedures in the office to minimize the risk of fraud. The second thing we did was remind the State Department of Public Welfare that our county had the highest ratio of cases to staff of any in the state, because of limited allocation of staff positions by the state. (Implication: If we had more staff, we would be in better position to monitor the caseload.) We were soon back on track with the discussion about the proposed welfare reform legislation.

*Questions you can't answer.* These may be friendly, neutral, or hostile. They are sure to be unsettling. Here you have come before this panel as an expert and suddenly you can feel very awkward and unsure.

*Response:* Rule Number 1: Never fake it. Legislators can detect phony responses, and if you are caught in a misstatement, however innocent, your credibility will plummet. Say you don't have that information and you will try to get it for the person who asked. Then be sure to follow through promptly (and accurately!).

This should not be seen as negative. You now have an opportunity to extend your influence with members of the committee. As you acknowledge that you don't have all the answers, you come across as authentic and trustworthy. Information supplied to the committee staff later lacks the dramatic punch of testimony in the hearing, but it can actually have more impact, since it is not vying for attention with everybody else's testimony.

While testifying on welfare reform before a legislative committee, I mentioned in passing the economic impact of suddenly cutting tens of thousands of persons off general assistance—the certain result of the bill under discussion. I referred to a reverse multiplier effect. In economics, the multiplier effect is the tendency for additional spending to have an impact on income greater than the original increase. Even small increments in spending can thus multiply the effects (see Heilbroner and Thurow, 1975:384-387).

According to the multiplier effect, placing a dollar of public assistance in the hands of a consumer generates more than a dollar's worth of economic activity. I reasoned that cutting back on the assistance would have a greater negative impact on economic activity than the original amount withdrawn. I called that a "reverse multiplier." Actually, it is a multiplier, regardless of whether it is an increase or decrease, but I thought saying "reverse multiplier" added a little impact.

In the question period, the staff director of the committee asked me if I had any evidence regarding the reverse multiplier as it applied to public assistance. I said I did not but would try to get that information for him. I am not an economist, had only a general notion of the concept, and had no idea whether anybody had ever applied the principle to assistance payments.

A few days' research in the library produced an obscure study done a few years before for the U.S. Department of Commerce (Stein, 1975). Its author, an economist, had found that aid to families had a multiplier effect of 2.05. That is, every dollar in welfare payments generated about two dollars worth of economic activity. General assistance, a nonfederal program that varies from state to state, was not included, but it stood to reason that its multiplier effect would stand somewhere between the other welfare programs, since it included some families with children. The most impact was on (1) rents and real estate and (2) wholesale and retail trade; that meant a predominantly local impact.

With the help of the staff of a poverty law center, I put together a report which described the reverse multiplier that would result from a sudden reduction in general assistance. We broke it down for each county in the state, so individual legislators could see the potential impact of welfare reform on their local economy. Articles describing these findings found their way into six different newspapers in the state. None of this would have happened if I had not been asked that question I didn't know the answer to, or if I had failed to follow up.

## *POINTS TO REMEMBER*

1. Decide in advance what you want to achieve by testifying, and to whom your remarks are really directed.
2. Do your homework: Analyze all targets thoroughly and figure out how they are defining the situation. Be sure of hearing time and place and any special rules to follow.
3. Prepare your testimony carefully and practice delivering it until you are comfortable with it.
4. Stay calm. You do know what you are talking about.
5. In fielding questions, be sure you understand what is being asked. Be honest. Keep your attention and that of your audience where you want it.
6. If you don't know the answer to something, admit it and offer to get more information on it. Then be sure to follow up promptly.

# Chapter 8

# Using the Mass Media

Question: What is it that has the power to make or break aspiring presidential contenders, that large corporations pay millions for, but that you can get at no cost?

Answer: Media exposure. That is the subject of this chapter. Media exposure may mean using the traditional forms of communication: newspapers, radio, and television. Nowadays, it also means transmitting your message via the Internet, thereby both speeding up and greatly expanding your reach.

Why are Americans such news addicts? Why do they keep buying newspapers that are primarily rehashes of old news and watch the television news show while getting ready for work and listen to radio news on the way to and from work and catch at least one and maybe two television news programs after they get home?

According to Paletz and Entman (1981:16-18), the answer lies in the fact that we are driven by two complementary forces: threat and the need for reassurance. News keeps telling us about threats to our safety and our well-ordered world, and then holds out reassurance that things will be all right or will get better. It is clear that we are never satiated. No amount of reassurance is enough; there will always be new threats tomorrow.

That we are so obsessed is not surprising, considering the wrenching crises this country has been through over the past three-quarters of a century: economic collapse in the 1930s; World War II and the advent of the nuclear age in the 1940s; Cold War in the 1950s; civil strife in the 1960s; the resignation of a president in disgrace, not to mention our first acknowledged military defeat, in the 1970s; war in the 1980s; near-impeachment of another president in the 1990s; then 9/11 and a new war after the turn of the century.

No wonder we are so hooked on potions to calm our nerves—and on news. That helps to explain the power of news and news organizations, and also the intense competition from all the people wanting to get their messages out to the public.

## *TRADITIONAL MEDIA*

Let's start with the kind of media just about every person who reads this book grew up with: newspapers, radio, and television. If you are to use these potent tools to full advantage, a major part of your task is getting the attention of the people who gather and transmit information. It is also important to be aware of certain risks in dealing with the media. One is that, once you share information, you have no control over how, when, or whether it will be transmitted. An innocent offhand comment can touch off a furor with some injured constituency. A reporter can garble a statement and give it an entirely different spin from the one intended. There are ways of cutting down on such errors, but the risks can't be eliminated.

Then, too, one is always at the mercy of totally unrelated events. When General John Murray, the highest ranking U.S. military officer in Vietnam, publicly denounced congressional cuts in military aid to Saigon on August 8, 1974, he probably expected to make a splash in the news media that would generate pressure back home on wavering members of Congress. He could not know that his remarks would be virtually eclipsed by the resignation of President Nixon.

Similarly, when the British Labor government lost a vote of confidence in the House of Commons on March 28, 1979, setting the stage for Margaret Thatcher becoming the prime minister, it would normally have been page-one news. But the fact that the crisis at Three Mile Island happened that same day relegated the fall of the British government to the inside pages of American newspapers.

You can see this phenomenon for yourself by checking the newspaper archives in the library. Go back to the edition of any major daily for September 12, 2001, or April 20, 1995 (the day after the bombing of the federal building in Oklahoma City), or July 8, 2005 (the day after London train-bus bombings). What else were people trying to publicize (or divert attention from)? Whatever it was, for the moment it was eclipsed.

The Blather Corporation holds a news conference to announce that it is underwriting low-income housing to the tune of $1.5 million. The event rates fifteen seconds at the end of that evening's newscasts and an item on page twelve of the next morning's paper. Five activists with so little capital among them that they could qualify for some of that housing hold a prayer vigil at City Hall and get a full sixty seconds at the beginning of the evening news and a three-column photo on page one of the morning paper. Why? Because the Pope died on the day of the Blather Corporation's announcement, while the City Hall prayer vigil happened on a very quiet weekend.

Audience size means just about everything to the news media. Every day something has to make headlines or that audience will shrink. But it can be a matter of feast or famine; some weeks everything breaks loose at once. Except on rare occasions, the coverage will be limited to the same newscast format and the same headline type size. Some weeks very little happens and reporters have to scratch for a newsy angle.

Some material—for example, features on a human services organization—can be put on hold; the interest is essentially timeless. The item may be shown days or even weeks later, or not at all, depending on what else is vying for attention at that particular moment. That can be frustrating to the agency staff members who took valuable time to be interviewed and photographed. They need public support now, not some other time of year. They should understand it is equally frustrating to the news staff who wrote the story.

News is a callous and fickle master. The task of the advocate is not to wish it were otherwise but to learn to work with it and use its maximum potential. That is the purpose of this chapter. We shall start with the print media (strictly speaking, something of a misnomer, since most newspapers and magazines offer their readers an electronic version as well these days). We'll then move from there to the broadcast media, before looking at the Internet. While a majority of Americans still get most of their news via the tube, the people who bring it to them get their news from printed sources and the Web. If we can understand the newspaper business, we have one important key to the news business.

### Cultivating News Contacts

It's important to get to know who is assigned to cover your local area and/or your organization's priority issues. In a metropolitan area, the major news wire services will have their own stringers. Get to know these reporters. You want publicity. They want news. A perfect mix, but be aware that their job is to get the story, not boost your cause. On controversial issues, they will also be interviewing the opposition and will avoid siding with anyone. They are also hypersensitive about being used. Only by maintaining a respectful distance and being totally honest can you become a trusted source.

### Deciding What to Say to Whom via Traditional Media

As with lobbying and testifying in hearings, the advocate's first task is to determine what he or she wants to say and to whom. While the shotgun approach may yield some fleeting benefit, you can make more efficient use of your time if you target your message to specific populations. There are special editions of large daily newspapers aimed at readership in specific geographic areas. There are small weeklies limited to a certain suburb or ethnic group. Just about any organization has a monthly newsletter. There are radio stations that specialize in music for a particular age group or musical taste. There are radio stations that are all news (though much of the time is devoted to content that could be characterized only loosely as news). There are ethnic radio stations, likewise a variety of television channels.

Your local chamber of commerce may have a directory of media outlets. The Yellow Pages are another source. You can ask someone in an advocacy group that shares your interest. Think who is likely to be sending out news releases; chances are they can give you a media list.

From time to time in this book I have emphasized the importance of working with friendly advocacy organizations. That is especially true when it comes to the mass media. Unless you are rich, famous, or a recognized expert on the policy question, the media are not likely to be interested in what you as an individual have to say. That doesn't mean you can't get into print or on the air by yourself. Radio call-in shows love to hear from you; the more off-the-wall the better. Letters to the editor are from individuals, by and large. But your input begins to have real impact when it is part of an orchestrated campaign involving allies.

## SEEING THE WORLD THROUGH THE PRINTED PAGE

Increasingly over the past few decades, control of the media, for all intents and purposes, has become concentrated in a few large corporations. Cities that once boasted several competing newspapers have become one- or two-paper towns. The ownership is more likely to be vested in a company based in another part of the country altogether. And, yes, selection of editors and reporters, as well as syndicated columnists, is affected. If you are a reporter on such a newspaper, you can't help but be influenced by the fact that your job may be dependent on these relationships.

That doesn't mean that all reporters slavishly follow the party line, nor that dissenting views will be uniformly excluded from coverage. Some major newspapers make it a point to insulate the newsroom from the boardroom and run op-ed pieces by one or more columnists with a bias different from that of top management. Thus there is constant subtle pressure on staff at all levels of the news organization to play along, or at least play it safe.

What about the more blatant kind of pressure from local businesses on a news organization, the kind Hollywood loves to depict: "Fire that guy or we'll never buy another inch of advertising in this paper!" That certainly can happen, but often it would be suicidal on the part of local businesses to boycott the means of getting their message out.

There is one way, however, that advertisers rule the roost: the makeup of the newspaper format. Except for page one, the first pages of major sections, and the editorial and op-ed pages, the news department fits its material into what is left over after the ad department gets through with layout. Look at your own daily newspaper. Turn past the first page and notice how much space is taken up by actual news. *The New York Times* is looked upon by many as a textbook example of a good newspaper. In a typical weekday edition, the majority of space in the first news section can be taken up by ads. Sunday editions are worse, with some pages filled with ads, including only a single column of news. In the period between Thanksgiving and Christmas the domination by ads is even more extreme.

So your first task is to fight for a piece of that shrunken space. What will make the news editor decide to use your material, as opposed to all the other urgent messages he or she is bombarded with? Is the issue sufficiently controversial to pique readers' interest? Is there a man-bites-dog angle to your story? Where is the human interest? A person recently released from a mental hospital, telling about conditions there, has a better chance of getting the editor's attention than an expert reciting alarming statistics. How will the issue affect the average reader? Is this going to show up in my tax bill? If so, can a comparison be made between the tax bite and the payoff for the kinds of people I care about?

You should get over your fear of reporters. They can be a tremendous asset to you. You should seek opportunities to be interviewed. Are you bringing in any high-visibility people for a meeting? Depending on how widely they are known and whether they have published books or are recognized experts, they may make excellent copy. More on this later.

### Press Releases

Newspapers are deluged with press releases, so don't count on much coverage from them, especially in the large dailies, unless there is a very newsworthy angle. The dailies will rewrite (and condense, usually) them. The weeklies, which run on a very small staff and are hungry for news that has special relevance to their readership, are more likely to print the release, probably verbatim. Because they go to a specialized constituency, it is best to prepare a release specifically aimed at that audience. Lawmakers' staffs read these papers assiduously, because they know their constituents do. So it's a great way to reach both audiences.

One caveat: Don't overdo the press releases. Make sure there is potential news value in anything you send out. I once ran the newsroom of a small radio station. A cancer research organization used to send us "bulletins" almost daily, sometimes two in the same day. After a while, any envelope with the magic logo was dumped without being opened. As it was, the wire services already carried the more news-worthy items. I won't say that the experience has made me any less ready to make donations to cancer research, but it certainly has not helped the cause.

The spelling, grammar, and punctuation should be impeccable. Editors won't take time to give a course in Composition 101. A poorly written piece will go directly into the circular file. Some people whose English mechanics are flawless don't know how to write news English. If you can find a reporter who is willing to help, that is prob-ably the best way to be sure of getting copy that grabs the reader's attention and therefore the editor's.

Above all, avoid professional jargon and initials for agency names. To you they may be basic English; to a large part of your audience they are a foreign tongue. Assume that the editorial staff as well as the readers have no understanding whatever of your subject matter. Take the time to explain what is meant by "base service unit" or find other language with which to refer to it.

An editor is a reader with a very short attention span and an intuitive sense of what the public wants. Some editors will stop reading your press release by the end of the headline, more after the first sentence, still more with every succeeding paragraph. That means your "lead" (beginning) must be arresting and punchy. Punchy but not cute. A lead such as, "I wonder if you've ever thought what it would be like to be seven years old and mentally ill and have no opportunity to meet friends," will make a quick trip to the wastebasket. "Susan Martin says seven-year-old Billy has been a new person since he started going to the Grant Street Mental Health Center" has at least a fighting chance.

Writing with excessive words is bad writing. Excessive words in a press release are worse than bad. Here are some suggestions for putt-ing together a press release:

1. Start with a headline. Your release should have one anyway, and putting the headline down first will help you focus you on what you really want to say. Keeping focused is a must.
2. Write the release as if you were writing a news item for the pa-per you are sending it to. It would be good to look at a few cop-ies of the paper and see what style its editors prefer, then follow it.

3. Set the release aside overnight, then reread it. You may be shocked at what you wrote. Squeeze out every word you can without losing the meaning. Then go back and squeeze again. Try to keep it to one page maximum, including the heading.

4. Ask someone to look at it and make suggestions, but don't commit yourself to follow any of the advice unless you are mandated to by your organization. You can specify that you merely want to check for accuracy. Above all, don't let a group write the release. News items written by a committee come out looking that way.

5. The final copy should be clearly labeled as "NEWS." Either use your organization's letterhead or put contact information where it's clearly visible.

6. If the release is earmarked for a particular newspaper—for example, an ethnic weekly—you should make that clear at the top.

7. The chances of getting the release published are greatly enhanced if you can send it to a specific individual. Unfortunately, there is a lot of turnover in the news business, and editors' names on media lists soon become obsolete. It might be wisest to call the news organization and ask to whom to send the item, as well as check the address and the news deadline. Send the release to only one person in a particular news organization.

8. More and more, press releases are e-mailed. It might be worth calling and asking if that is the preferred route.

9. If possible, monitor—or have someone else monitor—the publication to see if your release appears. If it doesn't, you can call and ask why. Either that will remind them to run it or let you know why they turned it down. If it does appear, drop a note to the editor, thanking him or her for publishing it.

10. If your organization is sending out a press release to several publications, send an extra copy to each representative and senator in whose district the organization is located. It is an inexpensive way to let them know you are alive and are communicating with their constituents.

### Print Media Interviews

You should welcome these as opportunities to get the message out, but you must also be on your guard. If possible, get the chief spokesperson for the organization you're working with to do the talking. If you are interviewed, limit what you say to what you feel it is safe to say. Prefacing your remarks with the fact that you are only handling arrangements and can't speak for the organization is meaningless. You may still find yourself being quoted as the president or a spokesperson and your statements treated as official.

It is probably best to huddle with the official spokesperson in advance and prepare him or her in two ways: help to figure out the key point to get across—the phrase that will catch the reporter's attention—and get him or her ready for possible questions.

Ideally, a reporter should prepare for an interview by researching both the subject and the interviewee in advance, but time pressure rarely allows this kind of preparation. You will endear yourself to the reporter if you provide the background material. In that way, you also have a chance to influence what kind of material the reporter reviews beforehand.

Don't ask to review the story before it is published. Reporters are very sensitive about being censored or even having their work reviewed by interested parties. You can ask the reporter to call you if he or she is unclear about anything or needs further information.

Then go home and pray that (1) the material is used and (2) it is reasonably accurate. Anything beyond that, in terms of prominent location, large headlines, etc., is pure gravy.

If the mountain will not come to Muhammad, then by all means Muhammad should make the rounds. I have walked into some city rooms, handed over my press release, shaken hands, and walked out. I have also been asked to stick around and answer questions. In both cases, our story has appeared in the paper. It is not a bad idea to visit a newspaper city room anyway. You get a real feel for what it is like on the other end. A press release and an offer to be interviewed will get you inside, whereas just a social call may get you turned away at the door.

## News Conferences

Calling a news conference is one way for an organization to get out its message, but the message has to be newsworthy. It is important to have a short written statement available for distribution at the conference. Don't hand it out in advance or you will end up with no conference. Reporters are under pressure, as are the rest of us, so if they can get a story without leaving the office they will do so.

If your organization is sponsoring a public meeting with a guest speaker, why not set up a news conference with the main attraction? The speaker must of course be willing to do it and be given a graceful opportunity to decline. So clear it with him or her well in advance of the event. The biggest risk is that nobody will show up to interview your speaker, an embarrassment to both of you. It might be well to call around and find out if news organizations have any interest in coming before scheduling this event-within-an-event.

### Photo Opportunities

If you want to know how powerful news pictures are, watch how eager politicians are to be photographed. One picture may not be equal to a thousand words, but it can reward the effort a thousandfold. Even small organizations' newsletters include pictures. When planning any kind of event, be sure to alert news organizations to picture possibilities. Obviously, street demonstrations and famous people have the greatest interest. But newspapers also like to feature hometown folk. The more localized the readership, for example a neighborhood or an ethnic or professional group, the more interest in pictures of members. You may find the ever-present straight-on group photo boring, but readers love to see themselves in the newspapers and have something to send to relatives. One caveat: Don't overdo the offers of photo opportunities; they can sound like part of a highly orchestrated effort, and that may become the focus of interest rather than the subject matter itself.

Weeklies and specialty papers will often accept your photos, but be sure to ask ahead about requirements such as print finish, whether color or black-and-white, and what size.

### Letters to the Editor

One of the most avidly read sections of the newspaper is the letters-to-the-editor column. Writing a letter is also the easiest way to get into print. The ones most likely to be published are related to something that has already appeared in the same publication, short, to the point, and well written. You can get a good sense of what the letters department looks for by reading a sampling of what gets printed.

Don't worry about writing too many. Some newspapers have regulars. Occasionally, you will see a letter from outside the local area, one which is obviously part of an organized campaign. It probably means the newspaper was hard up for letters that day.

To find out how to submit your letter, check the box on the editorial page. If you lack information of this sort, call the city desk and ask. Some newspapers ask you to include a phone number so they can verify that you really submitted the letter and agree to have it published. Most papers now accept letters by e-mail. They are just as welcome as the snail-mail kind.

Because access is relatively easy and the readership so high, letters are a superb way for a group to advance its cause. And lest you think this open forum for everybody is somehow *too* open, merely an opportunity for the riff-raff to vent their spleen, be aware that high public officials and corporate executives use this medium as well.

Letters are most effective when they (1) are part of an organized effort involving several persons but (2) don't look that way. Once having settled on an issue, each group member commits to writing a letter within a given time frame. Every letter begins with a reference to something that has appeared in the paper, citing the date it appeared. When one of the letters appears, it can be the hook for succeeding letters.

I once heard of a group in New Jersey who organized a letter writing campaign to put a moratorium on prison construction. They had this down to such a fine art that different letter writers would argue with one another. For example, one writer might say prison construction was bad because it was too expensive. This would then be responded to by another writer who expressed disagreement with writer number one because the expense was not the issue, the real problem was that prisons were self-defeating because they turned first offenders into hardened criminals.

In the same way, pro-choice letter writers might argue with one another about whether the real issue was a women's right to choose or equal rights of rich and poor or the fact that tight abortion laws would lead to a rise in the number of back-alley abortions.

Most letters sections strive for balance, so you may find your letter followed by one on the opposite side of the argument. Good. That increases public interest. There is nothing to prevent you from writing another letter in response to that letter. Or a few weeks later, when one appears criticizing your stance, don't hesitate to respond with still another letter. Each time be sure to cite the letter that triggered your reply.

All the rules of good argument apply here. Know your agenda, and decide what audiences you want to reach and how you can help them change their definition of the situation. Concrete illustrations of general points are a must. Absolute accuracy is also the rule, although you will see many letters that violate this canon.

A cardinal principle of argument is to seize and hold the initiative. You want others to respond to your issues, not the other way around. So one thing to avoid is reminding people of the opposition's strong points. Your letter will appear several days, probably weeks, after the news item or letter that caused you to write in the first place. The readers have long since forgotten the original argument. The trick is to connect with that earlier statement without restating the other side's case.

Here is an example of this technique. A previous letter by the writer called for the defeat of a harsh welfare reform proposal (House Bill 2044). That provoked a response from another reader who asked, if the poor were out of work why didn't they go to the Sunbelt, where there were plenty of jobs? The letter below is a reply to this reply. Note how it merely picks up the hook but doesn't dwell on the previous writer's argument.

> To the editor:
>
> Regarding the letter on welfare reform that appeared in the June 21 issue, one can certainly sympathize with the writer for wishing that the welfare problem would "go elsewhere"—e.g., the Sunbelt. But with the whole country looking down the barrel of the worst recession in more than a decade, there is really no place to hide. In the face of the economic realities, the Governor's plan to deprive 81,000 poor people of General Assistance is as foolish as it is cruel.
>
> General Assistance employables are no strangers to work. According to testimony of the Secretary of Welfare before a House Committee last August, 92 percent have been employed previously. Three out of five stay on the welfare rolls for less than a year; four out of five for

less than two years. And, reports the Secretary, when they are able to find work, "employables leave the General Assistance rolls."

As the recession deepens in the coming months, many more employables are going to find themselves out of work. This has dire consequences for them and for the rest of the people of this county. Shutting off income from thousands of destitute persons means removing a cushion for the region's entire economy—at the worst possible time to do so.

There is still time to prevent this monstrous and ill-timed action. Readers should urge their state senators to defeat House Bill 2044.

In effect, the opponent's letter has been used to further the original argument against the legislation. If this newest letter provokes additional reactions, they will simply be used as hooks for one more exposure of the writer's position.

It is not only readers who look at the letters column. Editorial writers, local columnists, and reporters do as well. Occasionally, an editorial will refer to a letter to the editor. Like anything else, letters are a tool of policy advocacy. Their use must be seen in the context of an orchestrated campaign, in which other media, direct lobbying, and testimony all play a part. That is the way they become more than simply an opportunity to let off steam and see your name in the paper.

### *Getting Extra Mileage Out of Printed Matter*

News items and letters to the editor should routinely be copied and sent to allies and elected officials. It is an easy way to spread the word on an issue and let people know you are actively interested, as well as one more way to remind your legislator that you are alive, well, and still in there pitching.

## RADIO: THE EVER-PRESENT VOICE

When television became popular in the 1950s, there were dire predictions that radio would go the way of vaudeville and the buggy whip. It didn't happen. Instead, radio adapted to no longer being the chief home entertainment medium and is now more intrusive and influential than ever before. It has become our constant companion, the background music to our lives—music, literally, but also information about the world around us. Everybody from the lawyer commuting to work on the train to the teenager hanging out in a shopping center to the weekend jogger wears headphones. An automobile without a radio is an oddity.

How does the advocate tap into this powerful tool of communication? By understanding radio, especially radio news, from the inside. Today radio stations are very specialized in their target audiences. You can often get a pretty good idea about the audience by listening to a station at different times of day.

Some stations don't do regular newscasts. At some stations, "news" is whatever comes in over the wire service ticker. But every station must allocate time to public affairs and allow the presentation of opposing views, although they may interview you Wednesday afternoon and play the tape at 2 on Sunday morning. Call-in radio, which is a special breed unto itself, is discussed below. We will start with the basic staple of the advocate: the news release.

### Radio News Releases

Everything that has been said about releases for newspapers applies here. Keep in mind that radio works by the quarter hour, not the day. You may want to aim for a particular time of day when your target audience is most likely to be listening. Radio stations often have community calendars, an excellent means of promoting a coming event.

Many organizations simply send the same release to everybody and count on station staff to do the editing. Such releases-for-all-occasions may just as simply be tossed in the wastebasket. They are sometimes read verbatim on the air. In most cases this is too bad, since radio writing has its own requirements. I shall assume that you want to write a news release specifically for broadcast.

### Writing for Radio

The first difference to note between print and radio is what it takes to get audience attention. Since radio is background to other things going on at the time, most people half-listen most of the time. What catches their attention is a word or phrase that links to something they are interested in. If I hear "social workers" in the middle of a newscast or ad, I suddenly start listening, because that's my profession they're talking about. But already the speaker has moved on to the next sentence. I can't ask that it be repeated. Radio writing thus must not only use words that will hit listeners hard, but it must give the message after it has caught their attention. Keep in mind also that senior citizens make up a large part of the radio audience. They are also the people who write letters to their representatives and vote. And many are hard of hearing.

So a second, even more fundamental, difference between print news and radio news is that the audience has to catch the latter the first time around. You can be a slow reader but not a slow listener. No going back to reread what you half understood. No finding a reference to "Dr. Spencer" in the tenth paragraph and checking paragraph one again to see who Dr. Spencer is.

To a great extent, newspaper items follow a formula in which the who, what, where, and when come in the lead sentence. Try to cram all that into the lead sentence of a radio news item and you will confuse your listener; a confused listener is going to tune out.

The third point to remember about radio news writing is the need for brevity. Audience attention fades fast. Commercials, with all their use of gags, sound effects, and appeals to self-interest are typically thirty seconds long. Except for audiences with a special interest in the subject matter, fifteen to twenty seconds is a long time to hold the listener. How many words is that? Forty-five to sixty, or three words per second (Yorke, 1978:38).

Does that sacrifice depth? Indeed it does. If you have more material than can be contained in such a brief format, you might consider enclosing a background piece along with the release, making clear it is not part of the release itself. A better way to have in-depth coverage is to arrange to be interviewed.

## Radio Interviews

While everybody is under time pressure, newspaper reporters have the luxury of, in effect, having a conversation with the interviewee. The discussion need not be grammatical or logical. There can be backing and filling as a later comment reminds the reporter of something he or she forgot to ask. It is less likely to work that way in radio. Imagine your interview with a newspaper reporter being broadcast live.

Regardless of the medium, your message should be focused, with you choosing the points to emphasize rather than leaving it to the interviewer to try to pluck a lead sentence out of the morass. Ned Potter of ABC-TV News puts it this way:

> In most media, you get to make one point—just one. So decide what it is, and make it abundantly clear. A reporter is looking for the quintessence of your argument. I've interviewed plenty of confused people in my time, and gone on endlessly, desperately, trying to coax one fifteen-word summation out of them. I am sincerely trying to give them a good hearing, but I cannot put words in their mouths. Worse yet for them, I may instead use one of their digressions to illustrate an issue in my story that has little to do with their cause. So know your argument well enough to give ten one-line versions of it. The reporter will pick the most concise one. On a talk show or in some letters, you may get to make secondary points, but if you are part of a reporter's story you generally won't get more words into print than you will on the air. (Potter, 1987)

Radio tries to put the listener at the scene of the action through a live or taped interview, so the reporter becomes a performer. There may be general discussion of the interview beforehand, but reporters and commentators don't want a canned performance, nor any implication that the interviewee can veto a question in advance (see Yorke, 1978:110-113).

If you are interviewed by phone, ask whether the call is being taped and how it is to be used. You don't want to blurt out some state secret for background, only to hear yourself on the late-evening roundup.

## On-Air Interviews

These range from on-the-spot interviews that will be woven into regular newscasts to guest appearances on talk shows. In either case, the interview may be conducted by telephone or in person.

Many points in previous chapters about responding to questions are relevant here. As to talk shows, we shall assume that you have had a chance to prep the host and have a general idea of what is to be asked. The host wants your help in putting together a story. An experienced interviewer will avoid queries so wide-open they invite the respondent to ramble, or so narrow as to call for a simple yes or no answer.

The host has something you want: public exposure of your views. You have something she or he wants: content that will attract listeners. Depending on the program and the intended audience, it may be a serious effort to enlighten, or an on-air equivalent of the garish tabloids one sees at the supermarket check-out counter.

If there is something you prefer not to have aired, better not say it in the first place. Once you are on tape you are on tape. The interviewer is then not bound to delete any of the material. What to you may seem like common courtesy may look like censorship to the interviewer.

Talk shows typically have a call-in segment. There you can expect questioners who are not bound by any standards and tend to have an ax to grind. Your biggest problem may be trying to understand what the caller is asking, or how it relates to what you have been discussing. If so, don't hesitate to ask for clarification. Talk show hosts will generally try to be helpful.

In the case of on-the-spot news interviews, normally a great deal of the interview will be edited out before it is broadcast. You know your subject. The news department knows its audience, which as we have said is the paramount consideration for them. You may have definite ideas about what ought to be used, but what you think is important may not be seen that way by the news people. If you think a particular point should be stressed—for instance, the demoralizing effects of funding cuts on staff—explain why that is important in terms the reporter can understand.

### Language

I talked earlier about jargon in relation to writing press releases. Avoidance of special language is triply important in radio, because of the half-listening phenomenon and the fact that it's a case of once-by-

and-never-again. Good interviewers will ask for a translation of obscure terminology, but you are way ahead of the game if they don't have to.

We all fall into the habit of using inside language; in some settings it is impossible to operate without doing so. It is well worth the effort to break that habit, whether one is being interviewed on talk radio or visiting a senator's office. There are usually simple and understandable ways of saying the same thing.

### More About On-the-Spot Interviews

These are great opportunities to get licks in at a point of high interest in the subject matter. They are also hazardous because nobody, interviewer or interviewee, has time for preparation. In general, try to stay factual. Opinions uttered while standing on one foot at the back of a convention hall are unlikely to be as thoughtful as those coming out in a planned interview. Regardless of how you define yourself, you will be defined as speaking for your organization. Because the reporter is under pressure to find someone to interview and under time pressure to get in and get out, the questions may seem more curt and provocative than they are intended to be. But on-the-spot interviews are still a wonderful way to be heard.

### The Radio Provocateur

There is a brand of talk radio whose ratings depend solely on its ability to shock. Anybody is fair game for slurs, be they ethnic, gender, or political in nature. Listeners who call in are regularly insulted. If you haven't had the pleasure of listening in on this slice of Americana, you've missed an important piece of your basic education.

I should make clear what I am not talking about here. There are serious discussion programs with call-in segments that are in an entirely different league from the "shock jock" variety of on-air journalism. The former can be particularly good venues for your message. Typically I find them on public radio, but not exclusively. But let's go back to the latter kind of interviewing.

Before you write off this form of diversion as no more than a haven for neo-Nazis, sick people, and elderly shut-ins, you might want to listen a while. Between all the off-the-wall clatter you will discover lucid people making lucid comments, some of which you may find yourself agreeing with. That means someone is out there listening, a lot of people as a matter of fact, and it is one more way of getting the word out.

The individuals who conduct these adventures in arms-length combat actually run the gamut, from obnoxious and abusive know-nothings to sharp minds with a social conscience. By and large they tap directly into the modal outlook of the station's listening public, which is why they continue to be employed. The listeners, if they are treated with a modicum of respect, do actually listen, which means they can learn. They are the people who talk to other people whom you may never be able to reach directly.

How do you play? You call the number they keep announcing, give your name (maybe only your first), get put on hold for what seems like forever, finally are told "Okay, you're on," then you are on your own. Fred or Jane or whoever will ask you what you think about the subject (or if it is an open microphone, you pick the topic).

Talk show hosts specialize in knowing a little bit about a lot of things, but chances are they will know very little about your subject. So you educate them along with their listeners. Many also specialize in being provocative or argumentative, which is what makes them so popular. Regardless of the host's behavior, you should model good behavior. Always remember that you are selling yourself—even in the anonymity of two-way radio—as well as your views.

In this kind of setting it would be particularly important to talk in concrete examples rather than abstractions. The case of Mary X will continue to bounce around the discussion after you have gone off the line.

Stick to your position; agree to disagree if necessary. Don't give in to the temptation to tell the host off. They are past masters at turning put-downs around and making you look dumb.

Even if you decide not to play, it would be worth listening in once in a while. It is an opportunity to see another part of the forest. Many of those people vote and a few work for candidates on election day.

### Mike Fright

It can happen to anybody. There are veteran performers who go into a panic just before airtime. They have learned to manage it. Most important, they know that it passes virtually as soon as they begin talking. Practice will help, but it can't eliminate mike fright. If you happen to have this reaction, be sure to alert your interviewer or host, who is as anxious as you are for a smooth performance. They know techniques for putting a guest at ease. Just the act of admitting the truth to the host will be a step toward conquering the problem.

## TAMING THE ONE-EYED MONSTER

What words are to radio, pictures are to television. In 1960, John F. Kennedy and Richard M. Nixon were in a tight battle for the White House. Then came the first presidential debate. Some say this one event turned the tide in Kennedy's favor. The most striking thing about it is that the people who were polled after watching the confrontation on TV thought Kennedy won. Those who heard it on radio said Nixon won. Clearly, it was the visuals that licked him.

Is it, as the late Marshall McLuhan (1964) said, that Nixon's persona was just the wrong one for the tube? Or was it the fact that Nixon looked pasty because he had just gotten over a bout with the flu while Kennedy was tanning off the Florida Keys? Or that Nixon's gray suit blended in with the background while Kennedy's navy blue stood out? Who knows? The real lesson in this episode is that what people saw stayed with them and very likely influenced their vote.

We hear a lot about sound bites, short quips that get picked up on the evening news. Sound bites are essentially captions for the visuals they accompany. Television news is basically picture news, not word news. If television has to explain a change in the economy it does it with colorful graphs.

What is the lesson for the social policy advocate? Never forget the visuals. More positively, make them work for you. You will find television people delighted to cooperate, because they need what you need: good images that capture the attention of viewers. There are endless opportunities to get images of children using services, homeless people struggling to keep warm, ex-mental patients working or lobbying their legislators, pregnant women running the gauntlet to enter an abortion clinic.

The kind of image is important. Who is it we want to reach and what will make them identify with our position? Street demonstrations that seem to be getting out of hand, speakers reading from a script, slouching posture instead of visible confidence: These are the visuals that hurt the cause.

Words are not unimportant. They coach the viewer on how to respond to the visual image. Television writing is like radio writing except that it works around the picture, supplements it, instead of being the central carrier of information. Much is made of the effectiveness of former President Reagan's one-liners. But more powerful than what he said was the style with which he delivered it, that and the rugged good looks that belied a man in his seventies.

## Interviews on Television

*Guesting on a talk show.* If you are asked to participate in such an interview, try to schedule it when you are not under excessive time pressure, so you can come across as relaxed and confident. You should plan to watch one or two broadcasts to learn the interviewer's style. Find out the color of the backdrop so you can dress appropriately. More than with other kinds of interviews, it is desirable to do dry runs with friends, having them lob the kinds of questions you think might be asked.

In all likelihood the person who will arrange the interview won't be the interviewer but the producer. Find out as much as you can from the producer about what they are looking for. Unless the interviewer is coming to your home or office, arrive early enough to reconnoiter the physical layout. If you can bring a friend along, that is desirable, because you can take up the position you will occupy in the interview and have the friend see how it looks. If the lighting works against you or there is a busy background that will distract attention from you, don't feel bashful about asking for a change. The worst they can do is say no. At the very least, you will have established yourself as someone who knows what he or she wants, a healthy climate to set at the outset.

If possible, you should meet the interviewer before the actual broadcast and go over what will be discussed in general terms. If that's not possible, then corner the producer and get a final briefing. They won't be offended. They want a good interview as much as you do.

During the interview, look at the interviewer when answering, not at the camera or the light fixtures. Refer to the interviewer by name a few times, but don't overdo it; that sounds amateurish. Be sure you know what is being asked before answering. Don't be afraid to elaborate. If you are going on too long, the interviewer will cut in.

Audiences like humor, so interviewers like humor. Try to work some in if you can do so without making it seem forced. Self-deprecation is effective as long as it's not overdone. You want to come out looking as if you know what you are talking about.

Remember that you are in a visual medium. Help the viewer picture what you are talking about. If you are discussing economic hardship, give an example of Fred or Mary or Sam, with enough detail for the visual image to be formed in the viewer's mind. If you are talking about environmental pollution, bring along a prop, such as a bottle of sludge. If that is not feasible, at least ask the interviewer to suppose, "What would it be like if you found the ugly black stuff in your basement?" Viewers will be picturing their own basements, of course.

You should be polite but not subservient. And of course when it is all over, thank your host for the invitation, even if the person has been rude to you in the interview. You may well have the audience on your side.

A follow-up note, with an offer to come back some time, will help to set you and your cause apart from the steady stream of visitors to the program. It can never hurt to enlist the good will of a television personality.

Such programs are always on the lookout for good interviewees. You and your group might send out the word to producers that you have something worth listening to and are available. You should not, however, be indiscriminate about which interview shows to appear on.

Similar to what was said in the section on radio provocateurs, there are a few TV talkfests whose main purpose is to use guests as punching bags. On-camera mayhem and goon squads in the guise of studio audiences can do nothing to advance your cause. It is a no-win situation. The appeal is the same as that of television wrestling; ditto the potential educational value.

## The News Interview

The news department of a television station is working on a documentary that concerns your area of interest. You are contacted for an interview. If there are good potential visuals, be sure to suggest them. These might range from shots of children in a day care center to a location for the interview itself. As for the latter, it should be relevant to the story; otherwise it is a distraction. The time constraints may not allow the same kind of preparation as in the case of the interview show, but you should try to approximate.

Breaking news events don't allow for much preparation, but you should not hesitate to seize these opportunities to be interviewed if the content is germane to your issue. The reporter is bent on finding someone to question, and you and your slant on things might as well be it. As you establish yourself as a good information source, you will be more likely to be sought out when they need an on-the-spot reaction. All of the caveats regarding radio interviews apply here.

## The Panel Discussion

This is like the solo appearance on an interview show in many respects, but the presence of other participants adds new opportunities and new risks. Some such shows deliberately seek opposing views and provoke a confrontation among panelists. Others also use diverse opinions, but are more interested in light than heat. Still others will put together a like-minded panel to delve into a particular viewpoint in greater depth. You should research the program carefully to find out its agenda and the style of the host. You also need to know who else is going to be on the panel and what to expect from them.

I once walked into a show without sufficient advance preparation. The topic was welfare reform. The other panelist was an attorney in the administration pushing the bill I was opposing. I had in mind a genteel discussion of the issues in which each side listens to the other's arguments and responds in a thoughtful manner. The other panelist had something else in mind. The first question was to me, and I started to give a stock response. The co-panelist suddenly broke in with a sharp attack on my position, and for several seconds I just sat there and listened. Then I noticed the interviewer motioning me to jump in, and I realized that I had been operating under the wrong ground rules. I was able to pick up the beat and we ended in one of those impasses in which each side can take something away.

Advocates need to know themselves and the environments in which they operate best. Some people relish shouting matches. I do better where people listen to one another.

### Television Coverage of Events

In the late 1960s, many activists operated on a simple rule of thumb: the more media exposure the better. They quickly discovered how to increase the amount of time on the video screen: Provoke confrontation; dress and speak in outlandish ways. Television news departments loved them for it, even though their commentaries would castigate the performers. Since then, activists have become more sophisticated. (See Chapter 9 for more on the use of special events to dramatize issues.)

It is clear that the quality of exposure is at least as important as the quantity. In some cases, legislators make it a point to vote for or against a measure not because of strong feelings about the content of the legislation, but to teach obstreperous advocates a lesson. There are times when a quiet corridor conversation or a phone call can yield far more than a widely publicized event. With that in mind, let's consider how to milk a public event for maximum television coverage.

Put yourself in the place of the assignment editor (the one who decides who will cover a story), the reporter, and the camera operator: the three standard actors. Advance notice explaining why the news department should want to cover the event is of course essential. A news release followed by a telephone call will help get the staff there in the first place.

Having the name of a person for the television crew to connect with when they arrive is helpful. The offer of a cup of coffee can only help. Be ready to give background information, on the spot.

If the event is a scheduled program with a guest speaker, a brief written biographical statement is useful. Media people pay more attention to organizational affiliations than credentials, which the viewing audience is less likely to be familiar with. Be sure to include a brief description of the sponsoring organization—emphasis on brief.

If an advance copy of the speech is available, give that to the reporter. Don't try to edit or underscore; it makes it look as if you are dictating what is to be covered. It may be wise to point up a highlight or two orally.

Facilitate the work of the television crew to the extent feasible. If more than one station is represented, try to keep everybody happy. You also have to keep your members and speakers happy. Having the roving camera operator come up behind the speaker in the middle of a presentation and shine a light into the eyes of the audience may lose you more than it gains in rapport with the news people. It would be best to establish some ground rules with them before they start.

Someone will need to monitor the station afterward to see what is shown. Don't expect a lot. A public meeting with a guest speaker at best rates a brief shot of the speaker, audience, then back to speaker, while the newscaster gives the bare essence of the message, ending with a few seconds of the speaker's own voice mouthing a particularly punchy line.

## Invitational Events and Visits to Agencies

If the event is an open house or the opening of a facility such as a golden age center, the television crew will be most interested in seeing the clientele using the facility, secondly any prominent public figures who are on the board of directors. Try to set up interviews with the clients themselves or their families. You should also keep in mind local politicians who might like to be shown shaking hands with the customers.

Public demonstrations, picketing of a facility, people boarding buses to visit the state capital to lobby, and the like are all naturals for television. Used wisely, they can yield big dividends. Facilitating the work of the reporter and camera operator and making people available to be interviewed are especially important. Just keep in mind that you don't control the kind of coverage you will get, and be sure you want this type of exposure. (See Chapter 9.)

## Camera Shyness

Like mike fright, discussed earlier, camera shyness can happen to the bravest among us. Its origin may be different, for example, self-consciousness about one's height or complexion. Again, experience in front of the camera can help to erase it, but that may all leave you when you are about to be interviewed. In addition to warning the interviewer or host, try to focus on the people you are trying to reach and why you want to reach them. Visualize a person and talk to that person. You will be so busy trying to convince this person that you will have less time to be frightened.

## *ELECTRONIC MEDIA*

Just imagine being able to broadcast your message to unnumbered thousands of people, as often as you want to, at little or no cost. The lobbyist's dream come true. Why, with a little ingenuity and the click of a button, you might "speak" to every member of Congress and the president, too. At the very least, you could instantly summon dozens or even hundreds of like-minded souls across your home state, or the country as a whole, to the barricades. Who needs to corner reporters at meetings, write press releases and letters to the editor, set up interviews on the local TV station, and do all those other burdensome things?

Sound too good to be true? As my grandmother used to say, if it sounds too good to be true it usually is. The electronic media have indeed opened up a vast new world of communication that was unknown when this book was first published. And as Howard Dean demonstrated in 2003-2004, it's possible, via the Web, for someone to be catapulted out of relative obscurity to instant name recognition across the country. The same way it is possible to hit the jackpot in the state lottery and become an instant millionaire. The problem in both cases is same: That easy avenue to success is open to everybody else, so you are competing with many other people for the prize. The advantage in the case of lobbying on the Web is that it costs next to nothing and you can increase your chances by the skill with which you put together your message. And—aside from the remote possibility that you will inadvertently share too much personal information with the wrong party or be hit by a hacker—Web sites, e-mail, chat rooms, and blogs are relatively risk-free.

The bigger problem with using the Internet in this way is that the intended audience may dismiss the whole enterprise as what it is: lobbying on the cheap. Or at the very least get fed up with being inundated by your marvelous rhetoric. I'm not saying don't use these ways of communicating with a mass audience. But they should not be looked upon as anything more than a new tool with which to try to affect policy. A very potent tool, to be sure.

## A New Ball Game

Fitzgerald and McNutt (1999) make a useful distinction between traditional uses of electronic technology in political action and a new generation of techniques. Traditional methods include direct mail using integrated data bases, computer-enhanced telephone campaigns, and certain innovations in TV broadcasting. Among the newer tools of the trade are e-mail and Web sites tailored to specific audiences.

The older methods tend to be more costly, not an insignificant consideration for grassroots groups. But the real advantage of some of the newer approaches is their speed, reach, and flexibility.

*Speed.* Imagine that you are attending a legislative committee hearing on House Bill 209. Things are not going the way you were hoping. Representative Pander, who was considered a safe vote on HB 209, has been coming off as an opponent, or at least a waverer. You step outside with your cell phone and call a colleague back at home base, letting her know the situation. Within minutes she has alerted hundreds of supporters via e-mail to call Representative Pander's office at once, urging him to stay the course on 209. Back in the hearing room, you settle back to listen to the testimony drone on.

When Representative Pander returns to his office during a recess, his staff tells him the phone has been ringing off the hook. Calls have been coming in regarding HB 209. His constituents want to be sure he will support the measure. Later, when the hearing resumes, Representative Pander makes it clear that he still supports the basic thrust of the bill and is merely asking questions for the purpose of clarifying certain sections. His comment, in turn, helps shore up support from another committee member who tends to follow Pander's lead.

This scenario may sound a bit fanciful, but it's not at all improbable— if one has a cadre of loyal activists with the time to check their e-mail several times a day and the motivation to make the all-important phone call when asked. That it could happen at all is one indicator of the revolutionary changes in communication technology that are transforming political action these days.

*Reach.* In politics, numbers are what count. They are what lawmakers live by. Your representatives may not know what time it is, but they can tell you with remarkable accuracy the number of registered Ds and Rs in their districts.

The ability of organizations operating on a shoestring to reach vast numbers of people in a hurry is truly amazing. But guess what: If everybody is doing the same thing and inundating allies as well as target officials with e-messages, it tends to dilute the impact and can actually be counterproductive. More later on the thoughtful use of this newfound capacity to reach people.

*Flexibility.* One of the biggest advantages of the new technology is the ability to target your message to specific people, not the whole world. Newspapers, radio, and TV are for communicating to mass audiences. Although these audiences are increasingly selective—Do you concentrate on an NPR affiliate, a gospel music station, or a Fox news outlet?—the audiences are still wholesale, not retail.

Along with targeting comes the ability to move messages directly from point A to point B without interference or distortion by intermediaries. That becomes even more important because of the speed with which information travels, permitting greater chance of misinterpretation as a message is handed on from one person to another. As communication technology becomes more sophisticated, the ability to target will be even greater.

The flexibility also allows a group to create an illusion of spontaneity, so that the public official in its sights assumes that an orchestrated campaign is a spontaneous outpouring.

## Gang Mail

This is my term for the use of e-mail to contact a slew of people all at once via what was traditionally a one-on-one affair. You are sending your message to exactly the people you want to reach—members of your organization, for example. They may pass it on to kindred spirits, but that just adds to its impact.

We are talking about reaching supporters and potential supporters, not public officials themselves. At the beginning of this section, I mentioned instantly contacting all members of Congress plus the president with the click of a button. Yes, you could gather all those addresses, set them up in an e-mail group, and fire off your missives. But unless you are personally known to them it would be a colossal waste of time.

Even lowly state representatives have been known to chuck anything like that in the delete file without reading it. In fact, your loyal supporters may ignore your e-messages after the first one or two. I regularly get urgent appeals for action from associates who are forwarding them from someone else. And I must confess that just as regularly I delete them without opening. If you want me to do something, send me a personal message. Better yet, pick up the phone and call me.

On the other hand, if an action alert comes from an organization I'm actively involved with already, I pay attention and am likely to respond. E-mail is a great way to conduct other organizational business: notices of upcoming meetings, minutes of past meetings, and specific events the group is organizing.

### Chat Rooms

Not a physical place, of course, but a place on the Web where like-minded souls can get together and exchange their ideas on everything from good sex to cancer cures to the state of the world and the existence of God. And they do. The advantage is that you get to pick your topic or political point of view and then plug in to a vast network of kindred souls.

One disadvantage, if you're thinking of using this medium to rally the troops, is that the troops may be scattered over the United States and probably other parts of the globe. Even assuming people on the other end were moved to do more than chat back, this would not be an army likely to impress Representative Votegetter, who can run in only one district at a time.

### Blogs

Blogs are no longer just online personal journals by which individuals can share their inner thoughts with whoever is curious enough to read them. Everybody from private industry to a political action group now uses them to spread the word. For a long time, blogs, like chat rooms, were assumed to be appropriate for national but not local campaigns. They were not seen as a tool for bringing pressure to bear on specific policymakers. Unlike a chat room, a blog doesn't allow you to pick your audience. Now blogs are going regional, opening up new possibilities of targeted campaigning. Local candidates in Philadelphia and Pittsburgh have used bloggers as a way of offsetting the power of established politicians to recruit dollars and volunteers (Fitzgerald, 2005). You no longer have to be a Howard Dean or a National Rifle Association to capitalize on this growing technology. As with other electronic media, what you do need is someone who knows the technology as well as the territory.

### Web Sites

Web sites are great for getting out information to your own members and others you've already targeted by other means. The biggest advantage of a Web site over a printed newsletter is its flexibility. You can post frequent updates on breaking issues and give background information to people who are new to the game. Social studies teachers might be encouraged to steer their students to you for an understanding of an issue or the way government works. By promoting your Web site in all your literature and public appearances, you can pick up additional devotees who will click on your site for updates and advice on what bills to back. If you're lucky, one or more major search engines may list you among resources.

Putting together your own Web page is such a good idea that millions are already doing it, trying to have that little creative edge that will thrust them forward as different from all the rest. So keep in mind that it's a crowded field, and, like all other marvels of the information age, this one can be tuned out by the overloaded recipient.

Are electronic media worth the effort? Yes, particularly for keeping allies posted, rallying supporters to an activity in a hurry, and recruiting new blood. And in coming years it may be necessary to master these new media in order not to be left in the dust by the competition.

But, as with all lobbying tools, it's important to keep things in perspective and your eye firmly on the ball.

Cardinal principle: Don't pretend to be more sophisticated than you really are. There's no shame in asking the experts for help. In fact, it's the height of intelligence to do so. And if you don't understand the advice, insist on a user-friendly translation.

## *POINTS TO REMEMBER*

1. You must first decide what audience you want to reach with what message. Once you "go public" you have only limited control over how your words are used.
2. You must catch the attention of the people who prepare the news and convince them their audience will be interested in what you have to say.
3. Writing for newspapers must be concise and understandable to the average reader. The lead sentence must pull the reader in.
4. Keep in mind opportunities for photos.
5. Letters to the editor are most effective when done as an organized effort rather than as an opportunity to see your name and opinion in print.
6. Even though you use a previous letter as a hook, keep the focus where you want it, rather than reminding people of your opponent's arguments.
7. Writing for radio demands strong attention-getters at the beginning, ideas reduced to short takes, and overall brevity.
8. When interviewed live or on tape, formulate your own "sound bites" in advance. Be sure you understand the question before trying to answer it.
9. Avoidance of jargon is especially important on the radio.
10. Visual images are the key to television. They should always be paramount in your thinking.
11. Prepare thoroughly for participation in an interview or panel program. Research not only the subject matter but all the key actors as well.
12. If you are planning a special event, consider the possibilities for television coverage, especially of activities other than formal speeches. Always keep in mind the messages, intentional and unintentional, you may be sending.

13. The electronic media are a powerful tool but not a cure-all. Use them for contacting allies, not for lobbying targeted officials directly.
14. In using any kind of media, be ready to ask experts you can trust for help.

# Chapter 9

# Taking On the System Through Direct Action

The kind of lobbying we have been talking about up to this point is unlikely to bring about fundamental change in the social, political, and economic order, certainly not by itself, though small steps may indeed contribute to fundamental change. Avalanches, after all, can start with a few rolling stones. However, skeptics may argue, not without justification, that this kind of lobbying can help to keep the basic status quo in place by making it marginally more tolerable. I won't get into that debate here.

By direct action I mean any form of social protest in which people physically confront the established order. It may range from public demonstrations to dramatize an issue to civil disobedience in which people knowingly and publicly violate the law. I am talking about nonviolent direct action. If you want to learn how to use violence to bring about change, you have the wrong book.

Typically, direct action focuses on fundamental causes of injustice. When young black students sat in at whites-only lunch counters during the civil rights struggle of the 1960s, their purpose was not to be served lunch but to force the community to face the underlying racism in its segregation laws.

A group of homeless people who occupy abandoned housing may be doing it to obtain temporary shelter for themselves, but they are also acting on behalf of the much larger number of families and individuals deprived of decent housing.

Antiwar protesters who block factory gates don't assume their action will actually stop the factories from producing munitions. Rather, they are forcing the larger society to face the consequences of what is being produced.

Environmental activists who chain themselves to trees in the path of the clearcutting bulldozer know they will be unchained and moved elsewhere, while the cutting goes on. But they hope to bring to public attention the decimation of the forests in a way that mere words cannot.

Direct action moves the political debate from the theoretical to the actual. It dramatizes the conflict between the forces of social justice and injustice. It can help clarify who or what is the source of the injustice. In many cases, its intent is to disrupt normal operations. Civil disobedience may involve the violation of laws that in themselves are considered unjust (e.g., breaking segregation laws), or violating lesser laws to draw attention to an injustice (e.g., tying up traffic with a street demonstration during rush hour).

My first street demonstration was in Chicago in 1953. It was Hiroshima Day (August 6, the anniversary of the first use of an atomic bomb in war), and we were calling for an end to nuclear testing. Having prepped ourselves for the possibility of arrest ("If the cops tell you to stop handing out the leaflets, keep on handing them out while you talk to them") and made our hand-lettered signs, we marched through downtown. All twenty-five of us. It was quite a sight.

We weren't arrested. Not even harassed. In fact, the police held up traffic so we could troop through. The other thing we had been prepared for was that people would throw away the leaflets as soon as they saw the message. We even had a plan for running around and cleaning up after ourselves so as not to hurt our image as good citizens. To our amazement, people held onto the fliers, read them, stuffed them into their pockets or handbags. A few even gave us a thumbs up.

Having scored this victory for world peace, we assembled for a hastily called news conference. One reporter showed up. His first question, "What are you planning next?" was greeted with stunned silence. One of the organizers mumbled something about events yet to be scheduled, there were a few more questions, and the news conference ended. We had been so preoccupied with failure that we had no idea what to do with success.

Twenty-five peace activists walking through Chicago's Loop with picket signs at lunch hour actually got a small item in a major newspaper. That says something about how times have changed. Street demonstrations with hundreds and even thousands of participants have become so commonplace these days that they hardly make a blip on the radar screen. Even sit-ins and arrests for civil disobedience are quickly forgotten. That has pushed organizers to try to up the ante in two ways: Go for very big numbers and become ever more outlandish.

### Potent Medicine

As in the case of radical surgery and chemotherapy, the payoff from direct action may be enormous, but the risks are also great. It is essential that the advocate enter this territory with eyes wide open, ready to accept the consequences. If you are encouraging others to join in, be mindful that you are not the only one with something to lose. A university student joining a group of welfare clients in an act of civil disobedience may miss out on some class time or even have to make up course credits. The clients, on the other hand, may be risking their means of support for themselves and their children.

### Pluses and Minuses

Direct action definitely has its place. Handled wisely, it can get media attention and mobilize kindred spirits who have been sitting on the sidelines. When I see children at a demonstration, I'm encouraged, because I know they are getting a kind of political education they will never get in the classroom. But it's not just the impact on the youthful marchers. For many adults of all ages, the act of getting over their concern about what family and friends will say, putting their bodies on the line, allowing the public to see a different side of them can all add up to a transformative experience. And once having crossed that line of respectability, they are unlikely to go back.

One of the biggest pluses in direct action, then, is its impact on the participants themselves. It is indeed exhilarating to take part in confrontations of this kind. This fact carries with it certain risks that will be discussed below.

Confrontative tactics also have a more tangible impact on participation: They are an excellent way to recruit people for future action. An orderly march through downtown can be the "toe in the water" by which a person tests his or her resolve. If you have taken part in such an event, you may remember that at some point you were handed a clip-board and asked to write down ("print, please!") your name and ad-dress and phone number and maybe your e-mail address. Or perhaps the sign-up sheet was taped to the top of a table. The purpose, of course, was not to help find you if you got lost in the ranks of the marchers. You were being recruited for future work for the organization.

As to the impact on the policymakers, that will vary a lot. The di-rect impact of a single event may be nil. Unless this is a mammoth outpouring right at the doorstep of the policymakers who are the tar-get of all this attention, they may not even be aware it has happened. On the other hand, a sustained series of demonstrations, especially by constituents of a particular lawmaker, can show the official the power of the group to affect his or her political future.

The indirect effects are something the confronters have no control over. A march through downtown with picket signs and leaflets may hit the evening news and rate a picture in the next day's paper or may be largely ignored by the media. The people who witness the demon-stration may pay attention and mention it at the dinner table that night or may quickly forget it. The possibility that this will translate into lobbying by anyone out there is next to zero.

Reactions may be friendly or hostile. Or people may not take seri-ously the specific message the group is trying to convey.

Sit-ins and civil disobedience are different, in that they are hard to ignore. Occupy my office and I am damned well aware—furious, too, of course. But these more militant tactics aren't meant to win the hearts and minds of the public officials against whom they are di-rected. Rather, their intent is often to provoke a reaction by the target or else heighten the awareness of the issue among those who sympa-thize but have yet to become actively involved.


## THE IMPORTANCE OF ADVANCE PREPARATION

Throughout the book I've stressed the importance of preparing in advance of the actual engagement with targets. In the case of direct action, advance work is crucial because of the many things that can go wrong without it. Here are some guidelines if you are part of the rank-and-file, or if you are leading the charge. The requirements are different.

## If You Are a Participant

1. Think through very carefully whether this particular event is something you want to be part of. Once you are in it, you can't just suddenly decide to be uninvolved. Also, it is so easy to become caught up in the fever of the moment and leave judgment behind. Besides, individual discretion is not what direct action is about. Once the event has begun, unless you are prepared to be a good soldier and follow orders, you can be worse than useless to the organizers.

2. Pay close attention to all those picky details on the instruction sheet and in the prep sessions. They may cover only mundane things like water bottles and rain gear and whom to address questions to and what number to call if you get lost. Depending on the type of event, they may also include what to do in case of medical emergencies or if you are arrested, how to deal with tear gas, and how to avoid injury if you are attacked by police or a bystander. The time to digest this information is before the event, not in the midst of a crisis.

3. If you are asked to be a marshal or take some other special responsibility, don't hesitate to decline the invitation, regardless of the pressure to say yes, unless you are truly prepared to take it on.

### During the Action

1. Once in the march or sit-in or other event, focus totally on what you are about. The distractions can be enormous. You will get a lot of advice from self-styled experts. Unless they are designated leaders, ignore the advice.

2. Above all, keep your cool. Under no circumstances is this a time to give vent to feelings. Just as the action is usually intended to provoke someone else into reacting, they in turn will try to provoke you into being reckless.

3. In general, your role is to strictly follow instructions from whoever is in charge. But if you discover you are into something different from what you were expecting (e.g., a peaceful demonstration that gets out of hand and becomes violent), you have every right to walk away.

## *If You Are an Organizer*

1. Make sure the goals are clear and agreed upon by everybody involved in the planning. The goals have to be shared goals, which means you may have to give some ground. But as to the need for absolute clarity, you should be adamant.
2. There has to be a definite group structure so that it is clear throughout the event as to who is in charge. You may be that person or part of a leadership collective. If the latter, make sure everybody is on the same page. Does all this sound a little military? So be it. Command structures are a necessary part of any joint operation of this sort. In the middle of the action, who will call the shots? If that person is sidelined, who takes over? Who will talk to the police, the news media, and anyone else needing to be talked to?
3. There is a clear plan of action from beginning to end. That having been said, prepare for something, maybe many things, to go wrong at points along the way. Being prepared for the contingencies is, of course, an essential part of direct action. Writing the script may be a collective enterprise, but, once it's agreed upon, everyone must buy into it.
4. If there is any chance of running afoul of legal or administrative rules, make sure there is legal assistance available, and prepare participants for the legal "what ifs."
5. Nonviolence training is essential. Anyone—the police, the opposition, or curious onlookers—can be very provocative. The first place to look for help with training is organizations and individuals who are experienced at this sort of thing. Make sure they are experienced *and* nonviolent. There are good Internet sources on the subject. Check your favorite search engine for them. Your library may also have materials but is less likely to.

### How **Not** *to Do Direct Action*

*Poor planning or no planning.* The issue was education. The meeting included parents enraged by an unresponsive school bureaucracy. For some reason the nominal leaders were not present, but the meeting went on anyway, with the one who could outshout the others taking charge. "We have to shut the thing down!" said one. Another called for blocking traffic at a busy street intersection. People were ready to go to jail if necessary.

What were their demands? To whom would they present them? How could the system respond to the pressure if it wanted to? Those questions were never answered.

It was a classic case of unplanned confrontation politics. Fortunately the meeting ended without a specific battle plan. This would give cooler heads a chance to have their say and counsel a more thoughtful plan of action.

*Action as an end in itself.* Direct action is serious business. It requires people who have succeeded in subordinating their need for adventure or revenge to some higher cause. The least helpful participants are the ones who see this sort of thing as a lark or a chance to get back at the evil ones. The rhetoric is often angry and focused on past sins of the system. But the purpose is to change things from here on out.

It's a good time for individuals and the group as a whole to do a lot of soul-searching. Are people calling you chicken for not signing up for duty? Let them. The most courageous act is to do what you know in your heart is right when your friends are trying to goad you into doing something that's not right. They may simply be trying to shore up their own backbone by challenging you about yours. That's *their* problem.

About what is right or wrong, there is no easy answer. Every year on Martin Luther King Day, a friend of mine leads a group of people in a protest at a plant making military hardware. Each year they cut the fence surrounding the facility, trespass on company property, and get arrested. On occasions they have smeared blood or red paint on the corporation's files to make their point about the evils of war.

They are acting out of a deep-seated conviction, not a desire for the limelight, nor a wish for revenge against anybody, nor a need for self-punishment. I respect them for what they do. I share their abomination

for war. I hope they score some points in their campaign. But I have
no interest in participating. I'll do my confronting in other ways.

## GOOD COP, BAD COP

A group engaging in direct action in the streets may also hold
negotiations with the target system. These meetings may simply be
window-dressing, so the officials can show how reasonable they are.
Or they may result in serious concessions. The labor movement has a
long history of sitting across the table from management in bargaining sessions, even while the pickets block the gates outside.

A variant on this insider/outsider strategy involves different constituencies operating independently. The confronters may provide
the nonconfrontative advocates a kind of leverage they would not
otherwise have. In this case, we are talking about different sets of actors. Let us say your group goes the direct action route and thereby
eliminates itself from any role in the negotiations inside the tent.
However wise or committed to the cause, it may discredit itself in the
eyes of potential allies. Conversely, if your group is seen as willing to
bargain with the "enemy," it may lose the support of the more militant
faction. That is when it is useful to have allies operating on the other
side of the gate.

These complementary roles of insiders and outsiders may not even
be a result of a conscious strategy on the part of either. While Group A
is outside disrupting traffic, Group B is inside negotiating with the
enemy. The fact that Group B is not "those other people" may work to
its advantage. Both groups may be oblivious to how they are helping
each other perform their respective "assignments."

I once sat in on a meeting attended by a welfare rights veteran who
had participated in a noisy demonstration during the debate over a bill
in the state legislature. At the same meeting was a union representative who had been part of a lobbying team visiting legislators on the
same bill at the same time. The union member said the demonstrators
had helped the inside lobbyists get more of a response from the
legislators.

As a deliberate strategy, insider/outsider alliances are highly risky.
Especially in the eyes of members of a direct action protest group, the

people who disdain this kind of activity may be looked on as traitors to the cause. And they may be viewed as worse than the out-and-out opponent.

The core leaders of the respective groups may see the value in such an alliance, but they may lose their constituencies in the bargain. And, for the outsiders who are urging people to take risks in direct action, trust is everything. Add to this the reaction of legislators if they feel they are being manipulated by a behind-the-scenes alliance.

On balance, then, I would vote for letting the good cop/bad cop alliance happen but not deliberately trying to make it happen. Appreciate the value in what other groups with different tactics are doing and how, together, you are making a difference. But leave it at that.

## DIRECT ACTION IN THE INFORMATION AGE

Electronic media have transformed direct action politics into something entirely new. As was discussed in the previous chapter, it's possible to summon vast armies of sympathizers to an event with lightning speed and at little cost. This capacity, unheard of only a few decades ago, creates its own dynamic. Demonstrations, quickly organized, keep getting bigger. If organizers are going to get maximum attention, they have to go for big numbers. The Internet provides this kind of reach and speed.

Therein lies a major hazard. Your own ability to check out who will be involved in an event is minimal. Once out on the Internet, word about an upcoming event will get handed on to others who weren't on the original mailing list. So groups with their own agendas, and their own ideas about acceptable tactics, are free to join in.

This does not suggest that the Internet should never be used to recruit people for an event. But among the questions you may want to ask yourself is whether the sponsors have the know-how to handle what they may be unleashing.

Even assuming the event goes well and the unscheduled troublemaking is restricted to a few people bent on causing havoc, the sponsors have no control over how the media will cover the proceedings. Aside from their need for a compelling story that plays well on TV, they bring their own biases to the party. The running debate in subsequent days over whether Group X's behavior was accurately portrayed or whether it represented the main thrust of the action will do little to change that first impression about the event in the public's mind.

## THE ULTIMATE LOSS OF CONTROL

I recall a cartoon from the 1960s in which a person is applying for a job with a civil rights organization. He is asked, "Have you ever been arrested? If not, why not?" Those were indeed the days when putting in jail time was a badge of honor among many activists. Martin Luther King Jr. was the most famous ex-con around, a wonderful role model for the rest of us. Later Nelson Mandela filled that role.

This book approaches the subject of arrest and incarceration in the cause of social justice the way it approaches everything else: Think things through, with as much information as possible, before you take the plunge. Afterward will be too late. Relevant advice for writing a letter to the editor or visiting your congressperson's office—many times more relevant in the case of getting involved with the criminal justice system. So here are some things to think about if you are so inclined.

1. This is indeed the ultimate loss of control. Once arrested, you relinquish any authority over your body. This is not to say you are powerless. When Nelson Mandela was nearing the end of his twenty-five-year imprisonment in South Africa, government representatives came to his quarters to negotiate with him. He invited them in, offered them tea, and in every way was the perfect host. His most powerful weapon was, ironically, his refusal to gain his freedom on the government's terms. So here was a man wielding tremendous power over the people who, in an official sense, had total control over him.

My late wife used to lead Alternatives to Violence (AVP) workshops with prison inmates. The sessions were about avoiding violence, but they were much more about empowerment. In the face of the most extreme provocation, these men whose whole lives had put them on the short end of the power equation

discovered how much leverage they could actually wield in
dealing with authority.

All that having been said, once under arrest you are no longer
a free agent. For the moment, even your constitutional rights,
over which you may try to sue someone later on, are not a sure
thing. And later, in court, when it's your word against their
word, we know how that is likely to go.

2. You may be roughed up. You may be strip-searched in a way
   calculated to be maximally humiliating. You may be separated
   from friends and associates. Even if you are held in detention for
   only a few hours, you may find yourself in the company of folks
   who don't necessarily share your politics or your lifestyle. (That
   may in fact be a rewarding and enlightening experience.) You
   may have to wait your turn for everything from a toilet to food
   and water. Depending on the season of the year, your surroundings may be hot and humid or freezing. I say these things not to
   scare you off, but just so you go into it armed with the facts.

3. An arrest record is an arrest record. Same with jail time. It will
   be there long after the cause that brought you to this point has
   been forgotten. Admissions directors, personnel managers, and
   loan officers down the road may find this item in your application inspiring. Then again, they may not. Or will you omit that
   information and risk having it discovered? John Kerry wasn't
   even breaking the law when he threw those medals over the
   White House fence, but thirty years later, the incident came back
   to haunt him in the 2004 election. It's amazing how the opposition can make a candidate's past heroism look downright sub-
   versive.

4. What is the issue we're fighting over? Punitive welfare policies
   and lack of heath coverage for children, or your right to fair
   treatment by the criminal justice system? Will your arrest and
   detention divert your time and money away from the original
   concern? You may become a cause célèbre, but that doesn't usually last for very long. Court cases can take months or even years
   to resolve, long after the nasty policy has been enacted and your
   fellow advocates' attention has shifted to some other good
   cause.

None of which is to say that arrest and imprisonment can never be worth the risk. In 2005, Judith Miller, a *New York Times* reporter, went to jail rather than violate a trust by revealing a source to whom she had promised anonymity. In the early 1950s, during the red-baiting days of McCarthyism, some people faced the choice of ratting on their friends or going to prison. During every war, committed peace activists serve time behind bars rather than destroy life. They do so knowing this will permanently close many doors of opportunity to them. After weighing all the options, you may decide that the cause to which you are dedicating your life is worth the price.

So, in summary, direct action can be a valuable tool in bringing about change; maybe necessary sometimes. Not a strategy for all occasions, nor a strategy for everybody. Like any potent medicine, it should only be prescribed with full awareness of the possible side effects.

### POINTS TO REMEMBER

1. Direct action can be a powerful tool for bringing about policy change, but it also entails risks.
2. It is essential that the advocate think through the consequences, good and bad, before embarking on an action.
3. The fallout from some confrontation tactics may be there for the rest of one's life.
4. The original cause for which one engages in confrontation politics must remain the focus of attention and not be sidelined by the activity itself.

# PART III:
# CASE HISTORY OF A GRASSROOTS LOBBYING CAMPAIGN

In this final section of the book, I recount the life and death of one grassroots lobbying campaign in a Pennsylvania county. There were successes along the way, but this was by no means the kind of David versus Goliath triumph that the media love to celebrate. Rather, it is an honest portrayal of one lobbying campaign by a small but determined group of people operating on a shoestring budget. It is presented in the belief that we learn as much from our mistakes as from our achievements. Chapter 10 gives the history of the organization nicknamed "Duck Sauce." In Chapter 11 we extract lessons to be learned.

# Chapter 10

# "Duck Sauce":
# Reforming Welfare Reform

The scenario was a familiar one: The state president of the professional association is invited to speak to a local division of the organization and uses the occasion to call on members to put their money where their mouth is. You say you want social change? Then get working for it. He reminds the locals that their county is home to some of the most powerful members of the state legislature. End of meeting. End of subject.

Only this time it turned out differently. The state was Pennsylvania, and the meeting was sponsored by the Brandywine Division of the state chapter of the National Association of Social Workers. The year was 1996. Congress was on the verge of passing a welfare reform bill that was particularly galling to social workers. It would permanently end welfare for families with children who remained on the rolls beyond five years. It imposed other hardships and indignities on the poor. Similar legislation was in the works on the state level.

Located in suburban Delaware and Chester counties outside of Philadelphia, the Brandywine Division was in many ways an unlikely venue for political activism. Its main activity was providing continuing education workshops to help workers hone their clinical practice skills. But in response to the challenge from their state president, a few members of the division's leadership, all of whom resided in Delaware County, agreed to begin meeting to plot a strategy for trying to reverse what was considered an antiwelfare trend in the state as well as nationally.

I was among the five social workers who, along with a feminist activist, began meeting in someone's living room. The majority had

*Lobbying for Social Change*
© 2006 by The Haworth Press, Inc. All rights reserved.
doi:10.1300/5782_11

never considered themselves as policy advocates, and most of us were rank amateurs at the game of politics. But, once involved, the group stayed the course.

## BUILDING AN ORGANIZATION

It was clear that a handful of social workers by themselves would accomplish little. This is how we moved out of the box, so to speak: I called Connie Smith, state chair of an organization of present and former welfare moms and a staff member of the recently deceased State Senator Roxanne H. Jones, herself a former welfare rights leader. Smith had earned her bachelor's degree in social work under my tutelage. She was well-known among welfare organizations and state officials as an articulate and dynamic advocate and had important ties to the African-American community. Her response to my call was immediate and enthusiastic.

You may not know a Connie Smith, but chances are you can think of people who know and trust you and share your zeal for your cause. At this point, put dedication and loyalty ahead of political prowess. You need people you can count on. Elected officials, the successful ones, do exactly the same thing.

Smith recruited Anne Vaughan, a welfare rights lawyer who had won Smith concessions from the welfare system, and Vaughan's husband, Niles Schore, chief counsel to the ranking Democrat on the Senate Health and Welfare Committee. They in turn brought in Martin Berger, a seasoned labor union official with lots of experience in state politics. Marty could reach people who had little use for what they considered "left-wing do-gooders." Priseilla Hopkirk, a political science professor, soon joined the group.

Meanwhile, the people from the Brandywine Division of NASW were reaching out to the professional community, including the state chapter leadership in Harrisburg. That could allow them to tap into an established lobbying operation that up to this point had spent most of its time on issues of social work licensure.

Using the division mailing list and word of mouth, we invited colleagues and friends to a series of public meetings to air the issue of welfare reform. This brought together a range of people who shared an aversion to the new welfare proposal but little else. Everybody had a theory as to where we were trying to go and how we should get there—or if not a theory, at least a vague sense that things were moving in a bad direction and something needed to be done.

Between a dozen and twenty-five people came to the initial meetings at a house of worship in the Delaware County seat. During that initial shakeout period, some people dropped out, never to return, or waited in the wings for "real" action. That included at least one person in the original group.

One key constituency remained elusive throughout the life of the organization: current and former welfare recipients, whose personal stories were critical ammunition in the fight over welfare reform. While the Delaware County effort was going forward, several other initiatives were occurring in the Greater Philadelphia area. They ranged from the shock tactics of the nationally known Kensington Welfare Rights Union (KWRU), which sought to provoke official reaction including arrest, to an older welfare rights organization that accepted government grants for helping to make the welfare system work more humanely and effectively on behalf of the poor. More on this issue later in this chapter and in the next one.

At one of our early meetings, we decided we needed a name that reflected our purpose. In nearby Philadelphia, the main opposition to welfare reform was being led by a loosely organized Coalition to Save Our Safety Net, or S.O.S. Connie Smith suggested that our group become the Delaware County Coalition to Save Our Safety Net. Wanting to get on to other matters, the rest of us quickly agreed, little realizing, perhaps, that we had made a permanent and, for all intents and purposes, binding decision.

It was a cumbersome name, and it soon became shortened to DCCSOS. Still difficult to remember. One member solved that problem by saying the letters spelled "duck sauce." It was a throwaway line that broke up the group at the moment, but the acronym stuck. Though the initials DCCSOS continued to be used in print, everyone from public agency administrators and legislative aides to members of community organizations and the news media were soon referring to "Duck Sauce."

We capitalized on the nickname. During one holiday season, we hand-delivered gift bottles of duck sauce (the Chinese cuisine kind) to the offices of Delaware County's sixteen state legislators. This little gesture was no competition for the baskets of cheer and fancy costume jewelry from high-priced lobbying organizations that adorned elected officials' offices at that time of year. In most cases it was probably a secretary and not her boss who took the duck sauce home. But it's secretaries, after all, who get you on the schedule or neglect to. All in all, not a bad investment, considering that the total outlay for the duck sauce was $20. What had started out as an inside joke became an asset to DCCSOS. Remember, in politics, name recognition is critical.

An image of bipartisanship is also critical. We stoutly asserted that we were a nonpartisan organization, though there was no getting around the fact that we were mostly Democrats in a county firmly in control of the other party. One or two prominent Democrats on the steering committee (discussed below) kept a low profile as we maintained the fiction that fooled no one, least of all the public officials we were courting. When a core member admitted to having registered Republican years before in order to get a county job and offered to switch parties, I urged her not to. I told her she allowed us to say truthfully, "Our top leadership is from both parties."

Early on, we assembled a ten-member steering committee. In many ways this became the heart of the organization, though less intensively involved members also played a crucial role, as is described later. We had four officers, including chair, vice chair, secretary, and treasurer, but most of the time we were an informal group that operated by consensus. As the chair, I ran into a problem that is typical in such bodies: an over-reliance on the presiding officer and a tendency for a few strong personalities to dominate the process. In time I was able to ease myself out of the chair while remaining actively involved, but the problem of participation was never resolved to my satisfaction.

The effectiveness of such a group is highly dependent on unity around goals and good working relationships. We all have egos. From time to time, they are bound to be bruised, no matter how tough-skinned we think we are. A member comes up with a creative idea that gets knocked down by others in the group, sometimes with too little reflection; on more than one occasion, we lost people under just such circumstances. Do what you may, it is bound to happen. What do you do at that point? Try to be tender toward hurt feelings, but then pick up and move on, knowing that the cause for which you fight is more important than people's feelings, including, of course, your own.

Politics makes strange bedfellows. Two individuals who were drawn together by their concern about the new welfare policy had been on opposite sides of a child welfare issue not long before. They came with that baggage, as well as more general views about the human services establishment. I was greatly impressed by their ability to get past this and eventually develop a close friendship that outlived their involvement in DCCSOS.

Participation rapidly evolved into four identifiable tiers:

1. three or four core members who were in frequent communication with one another between meetings and took the lead in charting the course of the organization;
2. a similar number who took on specific tasks, ranging from getting out mailings to making the arrangements for our annual dinner meetings, but who operated largely behind the scenes;
3. a cadre of regulars, maybe fifteen to twenty, who showed up for major meetings and hopefully followed through with calls to their legislators; and
4. all the others on the mailing list, whose involvement and commitment were relatively unknown.

Those four tiers or something akin to them can be found in most voluntary organizations of which I'm aware.

### Lobbying on a Shoestring

It's obvious that money makes a mammoth difference in the world of politics and policymaking. Otherwise presidential candidates wouldn't forgo millions in federal matching funds in order to be able to have limitless opportunities to raise more millions. The folks with big bucks get to write their special privileges and protections into legislation, swing key votes on critical issues, and literally buy members of Congress. Even on the basic step of getting on a senator's busy agenda, money talks.

That doesn't mean that lobbying is a purely pay-to-play pursuit. DCCSOS was created by ordinary people, none of whom had a lot of spare money. Working people and retirees on fixed incomes, even people out of work at the time, they were no match for well-funded lobbyists. At least, not where money is concerned. So they competed with the resources they had, namely good information and the ability to use it where it mattered.

At its highest point, the DCCSOS treasury amounted to no more than a couple thousand dollars. Small contributions, typically less than $100, came from steering committee members and dozens of supporters. Like so many advocacy groups, we were abominable fundraisers. Two benefit performances at a local community theater netted a few hundred dollars. An anonymous benefactor put up annual challenge grants (to be matched by other donations) that started at a thousand dollars and declined each year.

Our biggest expense was postage. Printing costs for our monthly newsletter were next. The cost of paper and envelopes was third. We sent everything first-class, not because we were a first-class operation but because people are less likely to dump first-class mail in the wastebasket than bulk mailings. How did we get our mailings out? Many a Saturday morning I sat at my kitchen table sticking on address labels, stuffing envelopes, stamping and sealing them. No, I didn't lick the envelopes, I used a wet sponge, thank you. Great activity while you're listening to Weekend Edition and Car Talk. Then I had a brilliant idea. Share the joys of this tedious activity with the rest of the steering committee. So after that our meetings had two agenda items: first, discussing weighty issues of welfare policy and our strategies for dealing with them; second, dividing up the envelopes and mailing labels and newsletters and stamps and doing what had to be done. Many hands make light work—and it's a great way of building unity in a group.

We invested $40 a year in a post office box. Along with a printed letterhead (that can be done on your computer), it made us look like a real organization. We also wanted a phone number for the same reason. This problem was solved when a steering committee member with a disability that kept her homebound agreed to serve as our "office." As calls came in she would take down the information and forward messages to the chairperson. That way we were able to respond to inquiries faster than many large, well-heeled lobbying organizations, without anybody being put on hold. Two resources we didn't exploit, but probably would today, were e-mail and a fax machine.

The other major expense item was our annual dinner meeting. We charged enough for the catered meal to about break even. These we saw not as fundraisers but as a way of widening the circle of supporters.

We never sought tax-exempt status, both because we didn't want to restrict our freedom to lobby in any way and because we didn't feel the need for it. Might we have gone after serious money instead of remain a shoestring operation? Yes. Could we have used the extra money? Absolutely.

What might a grassroots lobbying group spend money on, besides the mundane kind of printing and postage items mentioned above? Staffing, for one. A part-time staffer could have taken on the burden of handling phone traffic, mailings, and other routine maintenance activities. Or, depending on her or his talents, a part-time employee could represent DCCSOS at meetings with allied organizations, do research on issues, and arrange speaking engagements. Actually having or borrowing office space equipped with a computer would have increased our productive capacity, as well as providing a place to receive (and impress) other people.

We could have used a bit more style in our brochure, other handout material, and newsletter. As it was, they were done on a computer and duplicated at a nearby copy center. They had a more-or-less "homey" look. Whatever charm or grassroots authenticity that may have conveyed would probably not outweigh the value of more professional materials to match the steady stream of slick propaganda coming out of the State Department of Public Welfare and other organizations.

Additional money would have allowed us to send more people more often to roam the corridors of the state capitol or cultivate relationships across the state. It might have made it possible to do more in promoting organization of welfare clients and ex-clients.

A tax exemption would have allowed us to seek grant money with which to carry out projects such as educating the welfare poor or the general public on the issues. As long as we kept it "educational," such activity would have been legitimate.

And of course, with real money we could have hired a professional lobbyist or two. Inevitably, even the most dedicated corps of volunteers begins to look to the paid professionals to do the real work of contacting policymakers, sitting through hearings, and applying political pressure. At that point it is no longer a grassroots effort of people who care. The people who will see the difference immediately are the ones you are trying to influence: the policymakers. But unless you are ready to pay-to-play big-time, forget it.

One advantage of not making money a major concern of DCCSOS was that it allowed us to focus our time and energy on the issues that had brought us into this fight in the first place.


## *SETTING THE AGENDA*

Initially, DCCSOS had a single issue: defeating the federal welfare reform bill and its Pennsylvania counterpart. It was an effort doomed to failure. Welfare proponents could do little even to soften the measures as they easily sailed through to passage. The organization could have decided to fold up its tents and go home at that point. But we understood that passage of a law is only the beginning of a very involved and multifaceted process of policymaking.

The agenda now shifted to impacting on the nuts and bolts of policy as it was translated into rules governing the administration of public welfare. And, for a number of reasons, it made sense to focus on state rather than federal policy. First, the states would play the primary role in fleshing out the new welfare system. Second, Delaware County was home to powerful leaders in the state General Assembly (legislature). Third, and in some ways most important, Pennsylvania state government was familiar territory to a number of DCCSOS's leaders.

Advocacy groups often coalesce around a loosely defined vision of what they don't like. It is tempting to leave things that way for fear of losing the support of some constituency or other. But it is a dangerous practice, for sooner or later issues will arise that threaten to drive a wedge between factions. Unless a group spells out clearly what it wants to see happen, it is courting disaster. Of no little importance is the fact that the ability to articulate a positive agenda makes a group more credible to policymakers and to the general public.

To the committed advocate, impatient to get results, brainstorming sessions on statements of purpose can seem like a waste of time. Particularly is this so as groups get bogged down on fights over minutiae in the wording of this or that clause. However, these efforts are not a waste of time but an essential step along the way of putting an advocacy organization together.

DCCSOS devoted one of its early meetings entirely to brainstorming its vision for the future. Out of this came a laundry list, the items of which were grouped under five general headings. In subsequent months members hammered out the basic content of each of the five sections. One member with a flair for writing volunteered to develop a draft document. This approach may seem undemocratic, but it need not be. If the drafter sticks to the spirit as well as the letter of what comes out of the group, and then brings the draft material back for further fine-tuning, the completion of the task can be greatly accelerated without sacrificing the group's control of the process. Needless to say, the writer must be willing to follow the group's lead faithfully, however painful that may be personally. Not a job for all people with a flair for writing.

The final document included the five sets of principles in DCCSOS's mission statement and, after each section, a background statement. Here, in a nutshell, was People's Agenda for Pennsylvania:

1. Generation of Real Opportunities to Work (G.R.O.W.)
2. Promotion of Self-Help
3. Protection of Children
4. The Right to Medical Care
5. Citizens' Task Force on Welfare Reform

Each of the five headings was followed by a series of specific demands and related background material.

It was far from a wildly radical agenda, considering that it emphasized the value of making welfare recipients self-supporting, and the State Department of Public Welfare was already in the process of putting together a citizens' task force including representatives of welfare rights and other advocacy groups.

On reading the draft, one member of the group raised the issue of fiscal responsibility: We would come off sounding like pie-in-the-sky do-gooders, oblivious to the woes of the average taxpayer, unless we addressed the cost of what we were asking. Some people bridled at the idea. We shouldn't be playing the antiwelfare crowd's game, they said. Where was our fighting spirit? It was the classic case of two parties to an argument being right. Both sides spoke truth, their own truth. We resolved the matter by taking the issue of fiscal responsibility head-on:

Fiscal Responsibility:

> Draconian measures which hold out the promise of budgetary quick fixes will, in the long run, be detrimental to the state's economy. Children deprived of essential support and services will be less productive and require more costly interventions as adults. Adults deprived of preventive health services and the means to become productive workers will become a greater drain on the state's resources than would otherwise be true. Conversely, what is proposed in People's Agenda would, we believe, lead to a healthier and more productive population, and therefore to a more vital state economy. Any other course would be fiscally irresponsible.

Thus was born "People's Agenda for Pennsylvania," or PAPA for short, DCCSOS's vision of a good state welfare system. We were now armed to go out and present ourselves to a waiting world. No matter that the world was not hanging breathlessly on our words or even paying us much attention at that point. We would create our own attention-getting event.

### Unveiling PAPA

It helps to know your way around the state capitol, or at least to know people who know their way around. That is how you find out that any civic group in the state, however small and insignificant, can reserve the rotunda of the magnificent State Capitol in Harrisburg for a public event, be it a news conference or a children's concert. More specifically, the wide central marble staircase that can accommodate as many as 200 people. You also find out the name of the person to call for a reservation (and the direct-dial number), not forgetting to make sure the podium and public address system will be in place and ready to go. At the appointed hour you arrive with your entourage and wait your turn while the high school chorus or farmer's organization or church group preceding you does its stuff and then, as if by magic, is whisked offstage for you to make your entry.

On January 28, 1997, thirty representatives of DCCSOS and allied organizations stood on the marble staircase while their leaders presented People's Agenda for Pennsylvania to the two or three newspeople sitting there. Then, one by one, seven legislators came to the microphone to give their support. All were Democrats (the minority party in both houses) and all but one were from Philadelphia. The exception was Representative Thaddeus Kirkland, an African-American Democrat from the economically distressed Delaware County city of Chester.

At the last minute, a lone Republican came to pay his respects. It was the venerable Senator Clarence D. Bell, whose district also included Chester. Bell had seniority over most of his colleagues and a reputation as a maverick on issues such as welfare. Rather than speaking into the microphone, he faced the assemblage on the stairs and said quietly, "You know where I stand." It was the politician's classic unstatement. No matter. The next issue of the DCCSOS's monthly newsletter announced that eight legislators, including Senator Bell, had attended the unveiling.

The event was reported in a Harrisburg paper and on a local TV station, but not mentioned in the media in our area. Twenty-one agencies and organizations eventually endorsed PAPA. Not exactly an earthshaking beginning. It appeared that we would have to earn our place in the political spectrum through deeds, not words.

Three years after the original unveiling, PAPA was revised to include other issues we had gotten involved in over time. It was mainly an exercise in fine-tuning. The essential message was still there, telling us—and rest of the world if it cared to know—who we were and what we stood for.

## BROADENING THE BASE

Organizations don't grow by themselves. They are nurtured by constant and assiduous efforts to recruit new adherents. Every person who attended a DCCSOS meeting was added to the mailing list, which included phone numbers and affiliations. Some members took it upon themselves to reach out to new recruits, but this is clearly a job that is more comfortable for some than for others.

Attendance at regular DCCSOS meetings never got much bigger than the initial turnouts. Annual meetings, which featured guest speakers, got as many as fifty or sixty attendees. More important, a particular speaker, such as the head of a state agency, could bring out public officials who otherwise would not want to be present. Clearly, DCCSOS needed to have some way of reaching a wider audience. Critical tools in this effort were the mailing list and the newsletter that went out once a month.

In the early months the mailing list grew incrementally until it reached approximately seventy-five. Still a relative handful of people, most of whom had practically zero political power. The founders knew that some of those on the list would come once, decide this wasn't for them, and drop out of sight. But they also knew that absence from meetings did not necessarily mean lack of interest. Occasionally a person would reappear after having not been heard from for weeks or even months. Although there were periodic attempts to clean up the inactives on the list, the guiding principle was clear: When in doubt, leave the person or organization in. Knowing that a substantial part of any mailing would probably make a quick trip to the wastebasket at the other end, some members of the core group were troubled by the presumed waste of resources. But others considered the cost a worthwhile investment. It is a dilemma that hounds many small grassroots efforts.

It wasn't just numbers we were after, as important as they were. We also wanted to be able to show that our ranks included a wide diversity of constituencies. As a particular issue surfaced, we reached out to new groups that might share our concern about it. For example, in the summer of 1998, a year and a half after DCCSOS made its debut in the state capitol rotunda, the issue was the lack of health insurance coverage for Pennsylvania's low-income children. Some of us met with the board of the County Medical Society in hopes of getting them involved. The reception was polite, but the message was clear: The doctors were not interested in political action, at least on this issue.

Organized labor was approached, in relation to a shared interest in the entry-level job market. In this case, the leadership was responsive, largely due to Marty Berger's intervention, but the rank-and-file were not.

We had more success with the child care industry, which is both well organized and taps into the concerns of women ranging from welfare moms to soccer moms. We knew that, unless they had adequate and affordable child care, welfare mothers would not become students and working mothers in any great numbers without endangering their children's well-being. As long as the issue was child care, some child care advocates stayed aboard. But their agenda was very specific. For the most part, it continued to be the same array of moderately progressive religious and civic organizations that formed the backbone of DCCSOS's constituency.

There were three other initiatives to broaden our base: a so-called Legislative Action Network, which attempted to create a rapid response system reaching into several legislative districts but never really got off the ground; and two conferences cosponsored with nationally known Swarthmore College and a university school of social work, respectively. These latter events gave DCCSOS a kind of visibility and respect it hadn't known before. They were also instrumental in pumping the mailing list to more than 350, where it stayed for the rest of DCCSOS's days.

Public officials, elected and otherwise, are pretty good at sizing up how much real clout an advocacy group has. They know that mailing lists are only that. They are much more interested in the fact that Joe Lobbyist knows and respects a particular member of the group's inner circle, or that State Welfare Official Johnson came all the way from the state capital to address the group's annual dinner meeting. In the sizing-up process, Delaware County's legislative delegation was no exception. It did not get its own political power by accident.

That having been said, it is possible for even a small and relatively powerless group to have an impact, depending on how vocal, persistent, and well-informed it is. How ready the group is to look beyond the battles over legislation per se to rule-making and administration of policy at the local as well as the state level also determines its impact. Policy, after all, is ultimately what happens to people at the receiving end.

DCCSOS sought to be taken seriously by elected officials, government agency administrators, their underlings, the news media, and an amorphous entity known as "public opinion." As it sought to fulfill the difficult role of honest critic, it was bound to offend certain constituencies. Worse yet, it might be written off as naive by some of them. Given its slender resources, in terms of numbers and money, it had little to offer in the way of support or opposition in the world of politics. Instead, its potential lay in its command of information and ability to articulate its message in ways that effectively challenged the opposition and gave talking points to allies.

Initially DCCSOS focused on like-minded groups, which shared its taste for an insider strategy, by and large. Its attempts to reach out beyond that to the more established groups, like the unions, the County Medical Society, and organizations aligned with the business community, met with little success, mainly because its political agenda didn't match theirs. DCCSOS did succeed in earning increased stature through the aforementioned conferences cosponsored by academic institutions.

We also formed working alliances with statewide, regional, and local organizations concerned about welfare and child care policy. This multiplied our impact and allowed the sharing of strategic information across organizations. As an example of this, a statewide anti-hunger organization with strong connections to major church groups used DCCSOS's statistics on an uptick in traffic at local food cupboards. The information, which first appeared in our monthly newsletter, gave lie to the State Department of Welfare's rosy picture of families rising out of poverty thanks to TANF. Similarly, allied groups used our data showing that the Delaware County welfare office was dragging its heels in getting welfare clients into job training and education programs. In general, DCCSOS was carving out an image as an organization that understood the issues and could supply critical information about them.

# THE ACTION PHASE

## Lobbying Lawmakers

Humanizing and moderating welfare reform would be a hard sell to Delaware County's legislative delegation. DCCSOS functioned in a political environment under total Republican control. The governorship, both houses of the General Assembly (legislature), and, even more so, Delaware County government were all firmly in the hands of the GOP. Low-income, predominantly African-American and Hispanic cities in the United States tend to elect Democrats. Not so Chester, where Republican control had been virtually unbroken for the past century.

There were two exceptions. State Representatives Thaddeus Kirkland of Chester, a member of the Legislative Black Caucus, and Greg Vitali of Havertown were card-carrying Democrats. Party affiliation, however, was no guarantee of where a legislator stood on welfare issues. Kirkland followed the party script in seeking to soften the impact of welfare reform. Vitali, whose district was historically Republican, had little interest in or sympathy for what DCCSOS was pushing. Conversely, Republican State Senator Clarence Bell made no bones about his distaste for policies deemed punitive and demeaning to welfare clients. And other GOP legislators, while toeing the party line, were open to considering ways of tempering the harshest features of welfare reform.

One of the things that had helped get that original handful of advocates to form DCCSOS in the first place was the fact that Delaware County was home to perhaps the two most powerful members of the General Assembly: House Speaker Matt Ryan and Senate Majority Leader Joe Loeper. It was natural, then, that they would be major targets for DCCSOS lobbying. It soon became apparent that we were close to the seat of power in a geographical sense but not in terms of political influence.

Speaker Ryan never made himself available for in-person meetings with DCCSOS. Senator Loeper did once. After that it was aides who met with us. As is stressed elsewhere in the book, contact with aides can in some ways be more useful than that with the elected official. For example, the aides are likely to be better informed on what you are talking about and may actually play a more critical role than the elected official in crafting out his or her position on a specific issue. Still, our inability to get time with the main guys told us that we were not high up on their list of priorities.

In retrospect, we may have made a strategic mistake in scheduling these meetings in the legislators' capitol offices rather than in the district. Back home, an appointment with the lawmaker is most likely to result in a face-to-face session with that individual. If the meeting is at the capitol office, it is too easy for the senator or representative to be "tied up" and let an aide deal with the delegation.

The one in-person meeting with Senator Loeper concerned practices in the local welfare office that were undermining clients' chances of getting training and stable employment, which DCCSOS saw as lynchpins of effective welfare reform. The advocates presented their case and waited for the senator's questions. No questions. Instead, the senator made some vague comments indicating he appreciated the seriousness of the problem, agreed to check into the matter, thanked the delegation for coming, and signaled an end to the meeting.

The next day a letter went off to the senator reiterating our main points in more detail and again urging his intervention. In response we got a letter speaking in general terms but indicating that Senator Loeper would leave the running of the welfare system to the welfare system. All of which serves as a reminder of a simple truth best summed up by, "You win some and you lose some." But that, after all, is politics, as everybody from the highly paid lobbyist to the experienced public official is well aware.

Our many meetings with other members of the House and Senate delegations from Delaware County or their aides also yielded predictable results—or non-results. With Representative Kirkland and Senator Bell, we were on the same page. Otherwise, the responses were cordial but noncommittal.

## Testifying at Public Hearings

By the summer of 1997, the effects of the new law on low-income Delaware County families was becoming evident. Three members of DCCSOS testified at a hearing before members of the Pennsylvania

House Health and Welfare Committee, who were wanting to know how welfare reform was working and whether there were bugs that needed fixing.

The DCCSOS testimony cited the fact that food banks and shelters for the homeless in our county were getting more requests for help since the law went into effect. We noted that the highest concentration of clients was in an area with a severe lack of jobs. But the major focus in the testimony was on individual hardship cases. It struck a theme that would be sounded again and again: The state agency charged with dispensing welfare in Delaware County was interpreting policy in a punitive manner. Fixing Act 35, the basic welfare reform law, would take more than tinkering with the language in the law itself. It would require a different way of administering the law at the local level. Since Pennsylvania's welfare system is state-administered, that placed responsibility squarely on the shoulders of the State Department of Public Welfare.

The testimony took maybe ten minutes to present. Committee members asked a few clarifying questions and moved on to the next witness. But if we focus just on the brief appearance before the committee, we miss much of its significance.

Preparation for the hearing had begun weeks before, when DCCSOS members came together to draft a detailed critique of the policy and practice of welfare reform. It was well documented and thorough— and tedious in its specification of detail. A shorter, more "user-friendly" version was created. This was the written testimony that would be distributed to committee members at the hearing, as well as to the entire legislative delegation from Delaware County and reporters from media serving the county. The oral presentation itself was shorter still. One of the presenters wandered off the "script" and gave a moving personal story, which included her own experience with the welfare system.

This project had several purposes. In most cases, if anybody actually bothered to study the testimony, it would be the staff aides, not the legislators themselves. We knew that some legislative staff members, including our own Niles Schore, would welcome such ammunition. There might be friendly journalists out there who could use the testimony as background material.

More important, we were presenting ourselves as an informed constituency that cared enough about this issue to do our homework and then come on a busy weekday to testify. We were new faces, not the same old cadre of regulars who always show up for such occasions. We were beginning to get on the radar screen of lawmakers and senior welfare officials—beginning. It would take many more such occasions for us to have any real impact.

The testimony before a legislative committee also told our own constituency that we meant business. That would help keep them aboard, responding to requests to call their legislators, and contributing their time, effort, and money in other ways.

Many times thereafter, DCCSOS testified at legislative or administrative hearings. I did many of the presentations by myself, mainly because other people's work schedules precluded their making the trek to Harrisburg in the middle of the week. Also, for some members it would have been awkward to give public testimony. In the next chapter we talk about one of the functions of organized lobbying efforts: giving individual members political "cover."

But regardless of who did the presenting, the preparation of testimony—including the handout that often accompanied the oral statement—was a joint undertaking, with a draft being reviewed by the people who knew the subject best. No matter that the legislators or senior administrators on the panel might look a little bored and might have no questions on what we had said. They knew we were there and their staff would probably go over our testimony. We also made it a point to drop off copies of the testimony in the press room, where representatives of media in our area had their own in-boxes. I don't recall one occasion when this resulted in getting our name in print, but it was still worth the small investment to let reporters from our local media know we were there.

Having Niles Schore, a key legislative aide, on the DCCSOS steering committee was a special asset under such circumstances. He would know when hearings were coming up and how important they were.

In time, we became a familiar enough sight at such events that we would sometimes be asked by another organization to get ourselves on the list of those giving testimony at an upcoming hearing. We always made it a point to comply with such requests if we could.

## Lobbying Appointed Officials

Welfare reform's real mission was to slash the welfare rolls, not end poverty. In theory, the idea was to move people into jobs that would support them long-term. That was the rhetoric, at least. DCCSOS and other advocates were determined to make the system deliver on that promise.

There were three major obstacles to achieving the goal of long-term self-sufficiency: a population with little employment experience or training; the need to provide day care for a very large number of young children while their parents were at work; and the fact that the people needing the jobs often lacked transportation to the worksite.

For reasons to be discussed later, DCCSOS focused on the first two challenges. While some members were interested in the transportation issue, that was clearly a lesser priority for the group.

Pennsylvania was neither the best nor the worst in terms of pushing families off welfare. Some states chopped recipients off the rolls well short of the federally mandated sixty months. This was not limited to the Southeast, long known for its animosity to welfare. Even so progressive a state as Connecticut limited family assistance to twenty-one months, with no extension of benefits for the children beyond that time.

The regulations issued by the Pennsylvania Department of Public Welfare supported families for the full sixty months allowed by the federal law. And as the first wave of TANF clients reached the "wall" in 2001, the State sought ways to extend the deadline for those who demonstrated they were trying to play by the rules. Yet the focus in Pennsylvania was on cutting the rolls as far and as fast as possible. The rallying cry was "work first," meaning, first and foremost, get the client into a job, any job. No matter if the job was dead-end or paid less than a living wage or lasted a year or less. The upshot was that some clients were forced to give up nurse's training and other career preparation midcourse to go into an entry-level job with little prospect for advancement. Welfare reform was clearly not about ending poverty.

The State's TANF plan outlined an elaborate system of education, training, and support services to aid the transition to the world of work. But the extent to which any of this would benefit the clients depended heavily on how it was implemented at the local level. Pennsylvania's income maintenance system is state-administered, so in theory the senior officials in Harrisburg could mandate full implementation of its policies. In practice, however, it was easy for local welfare offices to sabotage the whole effort with relative impunity. Delaware County was a prime case in point, so it is not surprising that the County Assistance Office (CAO) became a focal point for DCCSOS pressure.

There were other reasons for the concentration on the local level. Some key DCCSOS leaders had a long history of dealing with the CAO. Anne Vaughan had represented then-recipient Connie Smith in her successful suit to get the educational benefits to which she was entitled. Smith, now a graduate from an accredited bachelor of social work program, was living proof that fighting the system could pay off for welfare clients. Vaughan had near-encyclopedic knowledge of the relevant parts of the public welfare code. Besides, within the local welfare office, she "knew where the bodies were buried." Her reputation as a feisty advocate for the disenfranchised and the trust bestowed on her by the welfare client community provided DCCSOS with a steady stream of horror stories. Well disguised, these personal accounts were effective tools in the lobbying process.

The federal government was not making it easy for advocates like Vaughan. Her legal services firm was no longer able to bring class action suits against the welfare system, a standard weapon against punitive agency practices in an earlier time. Similarly, providing hearing testimony was outside of her official role, so had to be done on her own time. These limitations were part of a larger trend of the powers that be putting more and more obstacles in the path of those working for social justice.

Past history has many ways of impacting on the present. The welfare agency knew Anne Vaughan and others almost too well. The local welfare director would go quickly on the defensive whenever certain DCCSOS members were in the room. More often than not, such meetings would end in an impasse, confirming in the minds of the antagonists the rightness of their respective positions. That does not mean the encounters were pointless. They put the system on notice that it was being watched closely and lapses in proper conduct could not remain hidden. Perhaps as important, the issues raised by DCCSOS were redefining the parameters of the problem itself. Whereas traditionally welfare staff have tended to attribute all the ills of the system to client behavior and attitude, the Delaware County bureaucracy now had to look at its own failure to carry out the intent of policy as well.

There were several points of contention between DCCSOS and the welfare office. One was the fact that the Delaware County operation had one of the lowest rates of referral to education and training programs of any county in the state. It was far out of line with much of the Philadelphia metropolitan area. These programs were a vital means of moving recipients into sustainable employment at a living wage.

Another issue was the Agreement of Mutual Responsibility (AMR), a contract between the agency and the client intended to spell out the responsibility of each for helping the transition to self-dependence. If used appropriately, the AMR could be a useful tool. But contrary to regulations, many workers left blank what the agency would do to help the process along and made only vague references to responsibilities of the two parties. Under these circumstances, the AMR became a meaningless document—a one-sided one, it should be noted, with the onus clearly on the recipient.

Typically, clients were not advised of their right to appeal negative decisions handed down by welfare staff. The lucky ones who found their way to Anne Vaughan's agency were believed by DCCSOS to be the exception: the tip of a very large iceberg threatening to sink welfare clients' aspirations in a sea of bureaucratic red tape.

Given the impasse between the welfare advocates and the local office, DCCSOS increasingly turned its attention to senior welfare officials in Harrisburg. The responses were predictably protective of the bureaucracy and noncommittal. Undeterred, DCCSOS leaders made it a point to travel to the state capital to underscore the seriousness with which they were pressing their case. They also made sure to shore up their arguments with evidence and demonstrated familiarity with the arcane welfare rules. And any information sent to the Department of Public Welfare was also shared with the sixteen state legislators in the county's delegation.

Through the grapevine, DCCSOS became aware that the Delaware County office was becoming an embarrassment to the department. The advocates sought to capitalize on this by continued exposure of what they saw as the local agency's abuse of clients' rights, both directly to state officials and to DCCSOS's wider constituency via its monthly newsletter. That the state was paying attention was confirmed by a series of investigations of the handling of cases by the Delaware County staff and the appointment of a new regional administrator, with a reputation for fairness, to supervise the local office.

In the midst of these developments, an extraneous event intervened to alter the situation. The director of the Delaware County welfare office was forced to take a leave of absence and eventually retire because of serious health problems. The people who now took command at the local office were well aware that the agency was under close scrutiny by senior officials in the Department of Public Welfare and criticism from outside. They were both free to change course and under pressure to do so. To the extent that workers down the line detected a change in formal requirements and the informal climate, they might also be expected to adapt to the new environment.

Let's step back a moment and look at all this in a wider context. By nature, public agencies resist change imposed from the outside. In order to disrupt the status quo, they need public acceptance if not enthusiastic support. Working in the Pennsylvania Department of Public Welfare's favor was a belief that welfare reform was a good thing. In a very strong labor market, in which everybody from stores and restaurants to mail order firms was begging for entry-level staff, TANF seemed to be working to everyone's advantage. Even the negative image of welfare moms began to shift, as newspapers carried feature articles about heroic mothers making it out of the depths thanks to TANF. Beyond all this, the department had a vast array of political and economic resources with which to present its case to the public. Local branches of the operation stood to benefit from this protective cover.

But public good will is a fragile thing at best. If an agency's shortcomings are exposed persistently enough, with good evidence to back up the charges, questions begin to form in the minds of public officials and the public at large. As the agency's image begins to become tarnished around the edges, things can turn around very quickly. Aware of this, the bureaucracy will move, if reluctantly, to repair the damage. It will do so at minimum expense and as modest a change in its modus operandi as possible.

There is little question that DCCSOS and other advocacy groups were having an effect on the administration of TANF at both the state and local levels. One shouldn't overstate the case. Abuses of clients' rights continued to occur in the Delaware County welfare office, but they were less frequent now and the official response to complaints seemed less defensive. The solutions tended to be case-by-case rather than systemwide, allowing the basic patterns to remain intact. Yet such adaptations can send an important message to workers and their supervisors about what is and is not acceptable behavior.

The other side of "work first" was the work itself. Responsibility for job training and placement in Delaware County was divided between the welfare office, a state entity, and the Office of Employment and Training (OET), a county agency. New federal mandates under the Workforce Investment Act (WIA) were supposed to mobilize state and local employment agencies to help welfare clients get into the workforce. A local Workforce Investment Board was presumably the instrument to implement the mandates.

In reality, it was the director of OET who called the shots. It was with reluctance that he approached the task of training marginal workers and helping them find jobs. The primary constituency of OET was not the welfare poor but companies seeking qualified employees, along with displaced workers. Unlike welfare recipients, they tended to have substantial work histories and demonstrated job skills in addition to more political clout.

The WIA plan unveiled with fanfare by the Delaware County OET was vague in many places. It was clear that it had been written so as to meet federal requirements with minimal departure from the status quo. One not-so-vague passage had to do with the geographical location of services. There would be two sites: one in Chester, the county's economic basket case. The other would be at the sprawling, wooded suburban campus of Delaware County Community College (DCCC). Meanwhile, struggling communities at the eastern edge of the county, with large concentrations of non-working poor, would have nothing. Nor was there any easy way to get from those needy communities to the DCCC campus.

DCCSOS urged that the plan be revised to accommodate people at the eastern end of the county. There should be a service center in Darby, where the eastern office of the County Assistance Office was soon to be located. The OET director thanked DCCSOS for pointing out the anomaly and promised to act on its suggestion.

Then, nothing. Finally, after much prodding, an OET staffer was assigned to spend two half-days a week in a small cubicle in the Darby office of the Community Action Agency (CAA). No signs. No indication that anything was afloat except a chair and a desk that were vacant most of the time. When asked about the new operation, CAA staff working in the same office said they didn't know anything about it. Not surprisingly, business was anything but brisk at the OET site. The scenario was clear: After a few months it could be announced that there was no demand for service and so the OET operation would be dismantled.

DCCSOS found an unexpected ally in the same welfare agency (CAO) it had been badgering for months with complaints of client abuse. With a new office soon to open in Darby, CAO needed job placement resources close at hand to fulfill its work-first mandates. After much bickering over security and clearance concerns, it was agreed that the new welfare office would have cubicles set aside for OET computers, so clients could search for employment. There would also be space for OET staff to aid in the process.

When it looked as if progress might finally be made, health problems sidelined the OET staff person who had been assigned to spend two half-days a week in Darby. Pleading a shortage of staff, OET let the project die. That was in 2003. As of the spring of 2005, there was one OET job search computer in the Darby welfare office, still waiting to be hooked up, and no OET staff.

### Our Own "Trilateral Commission"

From early on, DCCSOS began convening meetings with the director of the Delaware County welfare office and some of her senior staff. These monthly encounters, attended by people from other community agencies and organizations, later widened to include the County Office of Employment and Training, hence the "trilateral." Often acrimonious, as welfare clients and their advocates attacked and welfare staff defended, they nevertheless served the purpose of clarifying the issues and laying the groundwork for remedies, mostly on a case-by-case basis.

That the public agency administrators showed up regularly at these meetings suggests that they saw value in subjecting themselves to the monthly round of criticism. The sessions served another purpose: improving relations between the welfare and employment staff, which had their own communication problems. This was an unanticipated byproduct of the proceedings.

Gradually the character of the three-way meetings changed. Junior administrators sat in for their bosses. Anne Vaughan left her legal aid agency and withdrew from the meetings. The attorney who replaced her had to get up to speed and had a less confrontational approach generally. The subject of discussion was less and less about client concerns and more and more about working out wrinkles in interagency collaboration. When DCCSOS felt it was doing little beyond providing a forum that the welfare and employment agencies were fully capable of setting up on their own, it discontinued the meetings altogether.

## Children First

Of all the issues on the agenda of DCCSOS, none was more promising than child care. Here was a problem of vital interest to welfare clients, working-class parents, and suburban middle-class families. The middle-class working mother was just as worried about how her children were being cared for as was the woman keeping to a TANF-imposed training and work schedule. We would harness the political clout of the suburbanites in a grand crusade for that most vulnerable of populations: little children. A number of highly publicized cases of child beating and sexual abuse by child care providers kept the issue on the front burner. Finally, child care was an issue where the social workers in DCCSOS were on familiar turf. They were the presumed experts.

As if to help the crusade along, the state proposed changes in the existing child care regulations that, in the eyes of the welfare advocates, could leave thousands of additional toddlers exposed to everything from physical neglect to sexual abuse, while creating new barriers to the transition from welfare to work. The brunt of the problem would be borne not by current welfare clients, but by those who had made it into the world of work and were afraid of slipping back.

In the eyes of the welfare reformers, lack of child care was no excuse for failing to show up for work. So if it planned to put thousands of welfare mothers to work, the Department of Public Welfare would have to find some way to provide care for more children. One way to expand the pool of child care resources was to relax the restrictions on the people doing the caring. The draft regulations would exempt anybody caring for three or fewer children from physical safety rules and background security checks for the adults. The state cast the care of three or fewer children as simply a matter of family members and neighbors looking after the kids. After all, are we going to investigate Grandma as a possible child predator? The reality was that many a parent, pushed to the wall, was getting a boyfriend or ex-boyfriend to watch the children while she went off to work or training. Or it might be a stranger a few blocks away she heard about from a friend.

Another way to deal with the supply-demand crunch in child care was to reduce demand by upping the cost of care. Child care was already subsidized in Pennsylvania for families meeting certain income requirements. The state proposed to double the co-pay for subsidized care and drastically lower the income ceiling. This was hitting marginal income families across the board. It was a classic catch-22: Pressure families to work to support themselves while making it harder for people of limited means to obtain child care.

DCCSOS found new allies in this contest. Agencies and organizations for which welfare reform was a minor concern were suddenly galvanized into action. Statewide, a politically savvy legal services organization that did not labor under the restrictions imposed on most such operations assumed a lead role in opposing the proposed rule changes. Members of the DCCSOS leadership had old ties with the main strategists of the campaign, helping the collaboration along.

The new regulations were by no means a done deal. They still had to be approved by both houses of the General Assembly (legislature) and by a little-known state commission that reviews all state rule changes. To the extent the opposition held together and stayed on message, the lengthy procedures worked to its advantage. But the protracted process could also wear down its unity and resolve.

State welfare officials responded predictably: Give just enough ground to mollify or divide the opposition without giving up the essential core of what you are trying to accomplish. And count on some of the opposition to lose interest and go on to other causes. But the maneuvering by the secretary of welfare and her staff did result in a less onerous code.

Broad coalitions always run the risk of differences in priorities if not philosophy. Among those challenging the rule changes were for-profit child care agencies catering to middle-class parents. What happened to children on welfare may have concerned them, but as a personal moral issue, not an institutional interest. What did concern them was anything in the regulations that would threaten their right to operate as they saw fit.

In the midst of the fight over the proposed rule changes at the state level, the City of Chester came out with its own reform initiative involving child care agencies. Rigorous enforcement of new zoning, health, and safety codes would require expensive remodeling by the child care providers. Worse yet, the agencies first learned about all this in a newspaper article that listed several agencies, including some of the most venerated, as violators of the rules. All at once, the issue of state rule changes was shoved into the background, as far as the local child care industry was concerned.

A key player in the fight over the state proposals was the secretary of welfare. Not expert on either welfare or child care, she counted on a strong personal trust relationship with the governor to help her take on her critics. Backing down appeared to be a major personal issue for her.

As we in DCCSOS presented our case to legislators and their staff, it became evident that, for the Senate and House leadership, at least, protecting the welfare of children was secondary to fiscal considerations. And trumping everything else was their need to support the governor and the party, wherever that might lead. Despite the odds, DCCSOS and its allies pushed on.

In the end, it was neither the Department of Public Welfare nor the General Assembly that determined the fate of the proposed rule changes in child care but an obscure body called the Independent Regulatory Review Commission, or IRRC. This is one of those agencies whose tremendous power is simply unknown to the general pub lic. Here is where having members and allies well experienced in the intricacies of government pays dividends to a group like DCCSOS. We had to learn the basics: what IRRC's function is, when it meets, what its procedures are, and who actually makes decisions.

The work of the commission is governed by two questions about any set of regulations: (1) Can the Commonwealth of Pennsylvania afford the change?, and (2) Is the proposed set of rules consistent with other regulations, including those emanating from federal mandates? So that's what you raise with IRRC. Forget about all those appealing stories of waifs being deprived of good mothering or issues of the quality of education in a day care center.

Given the fact that this five-person panel must pass on everything from fishing licenses to health care standards, it's no surprise that it depends heavily on staff. Apolitical, honest to the core, and very able, the IRRC staff subjects any rule change to searching scrutiny. The question actually boils down to the one or two employees assigned to review the specific document. We and our allies made it a point to find out who was doing the scrutinizing. In the case of the proposed child care standards, the scrutiny paid off. The IRRC staff member found enough wrong with the rule changes that IRRC ended up sending the whole thing back to the Department of Welfare, calling for a reworking.

The final policy reflected one major victory for DCCSOS and its allies: Background security checks on the people working directly with children would remain in place for all child care providers, regardless of size, contrary to the department's wish to exempt operations caring for fewer than four children. The only exceptions were family members. Otherwise, the state welfare proposals went through pretty much intact.

## THE BEGINNING OF THE END FOR DCCSOS

By 2000, the small group of activists that had shaped the course of DCCSOS from its beginnings was starting to tatter. Connie Smith had already dropped out when she took a job with the U.S. Bureau of the Census, then went to work for the Social Security Administration. The death of my wife and my subsequent sojourn at a study center effectively removed me from the scene for several months. With her departure from her job with the legal aid agency, Anne Vaughan shifted her focus away from welfare and to her other love: painting. She remained on the steering committee but no longer took the lead in challenging the welfare system. Her husband, Niles Schore, developed health problems that forced him to curtail his involvement in DCCSOS. Subsequent to that, he moved from the job of legislative aide to that of policy analyst in the Department of Public Welfare, a position that gave him more clout in some ways, but less freedom to work in the world of politics. The other members of the core group stayed on, providing critical support to the lobbying mission. These behind-the-scene activities were essential to the life of the organization, but not enough to sustain it without a clear political mission.

So for reasons unrelated to DCCSOS, the people who had given the organization much of its earlier momentum no longer fulfilled that function. But something of this sort is almost bound to happen in a grassroots lobbying operation. The issues that bring advocates together in the first place change over time. Then there is the problem of burnout. Working on a shoestring budget over a prolonged period of time, even the most dedicated volunteers may find their enthusiasm flagging after a while. We look at this and related issues in some depth in the next chapter, as we try to extract lessons from the life and death of DCCSOS.

Ironically, as DCCSOS was beginning to wind down, welfare reform was back on the national agenda. In 2002, with TANF due for reauthorization by Congress, the Bush administration submitted a bill that would increase the required work hours of welfare recipients to forty, sharply reducing the likelihood of additional training and education for many if not most clients. Child care provisions would be weakened. And, according to critics, measures designed to promote marriage would have the effect of forcing many women to stay in abusive relationships.

Instead of acting on the controversial proposals, Congress voted to extend the old TANF policy for another year. The decision was prompted in part by a slowing economy that wasn't ready to absorb new recruits to the labor force at the pace it had before. The reluctance to act may also have been a sign that welfare advocates were in fact getting their message across, that TANF had to do more than simply lop people off the welfare rolls. In 2003 and 2004, Congress continued to procrastinate, so that in early 2005, the issue of TANF reauthorization was still unresolved.

DCCSOS had long since ceased to be a major player in the debate. Its members might again go to the barricades, but they would do so under other banners. In May of 2003, DCCSOS quietly went out of business and transferred its remaining assets to an allied group.

In March 2005, Anne Vaughan passed along an e-mail message she had received urging people to write their congresspersons in opposition to the Bush administration's latest revision of the welfare reform law. The memo had all the familiar urgency of past struggles, but it would not be enough to resuscitate the defunct DCCSOS.

# Chapter 11

# Lessons Learned

The first and most important lesson from this case history is that in lobbying you should never listen to the odds-makers. They will scare you off every time. In fact, one of the reasons why bad things happen as often as they do in politics is that good people decide there's no point in trying to do anything about the situation.

Want overwhelming odds? Try five social workers without any resources to speak of deciding to take on the powers that be on an issue where they are clearly in the minority. Put those five social workers in a county firmly under the control of a Republican monolith that is on the other side of the issue, in a state with a Republican governor and Republican-controlled legislature just as opposed to their views. Just to make it a little tougher, the policy in question—the one the five social workers don't like—has been put forth by a Democratic president to a Republican-controlled Congress that enthusiastically supports it.

Now that is what I call a lopsided contest. With odds like that, it would have been very easy to throw in the towel. After all, none of the five was going to be affected directly by welfare reform. We know now that the five social workers didn't give up. Instead they started what became DCCSOS. Did that stop the onslaught on the welfare poor? No, the antiwelfare juggernaut rolls on today. But, because of that first courageous act against seemingly impossible odds, families needing assistance in Delaware County and across the state are more likely to receive fair treatment from agency staff. Many Pennsylvania children in child care have better protection than they otherwise might have. More generally, DCCSOS helped to create a different climate of opinion. Think of that the next time you feel like giving up before you start.

*Lobbying for Social Change*
© 2006 by The Haworth Press, Inc. All rights reserved.
doi:10.1300/5782_12

### The Power of Organization

What if there had never been a DCCSOS? Anne Vaughan would have been just as effective in representing welfare clients in their grievances against the agency. Niles Schore would have used his position as Executive Director for the Democratic minority on the Public Health and Welfare Committee of the Pennsylvania House of Representatives to move policy in a more positive direction. Connie Smith might have been just as vocal and just as articulate in opposing the worst effects of welfare reform. It could even be argued that they would have been more effective, since they would not have spent their valuable time on the nuts and bolts of organizational maintenance. We have all experienced the frustration of sitting through lengthy meetings trying to convince John or Mary that the group should take a particular stand on this or that issue, or soothing the injured ego of Jane, or trying to bring Harry up to speed on the issues.

There are several reasons why the advantages of bringing people like these and others together in a joint enterprise more than outweigh whatever distractions and diversion of energy are caused by the messy business of keeping an organization afloat.

Let's start with what I'll call a "political multiplier effect." You may recall that in Chapter 7 I described what economists call a multiplier effect. This is what happens when a dollar spent in one place goes through several hands as it works its way through the economy, picking up extra value at each transaction along the way. For example, welfare payments eventually double in value as they are spent and then respent.

In politics, the multiplier effect is what happens when a number of individuals, each with a certain amount of political capital, spend it jointly instead of individually. Public officials treat organized lobbying differently from individual appeals. They know that their response will be telegraphed quickly to a host of voters, all of whom are presumed to share a common set of attitudes on the matter in question. A host of voters, it should be added, who are energized enough to get their names on a membership list. Mary may or may not tell her neighbor or her mother-in-law what Senator Small said about the bill she was advocating. If Mary is acting on behalf of an advocacy organization, it is a sure bet that she will tell all the people on that membership list—with an added, "Therefore, we should support (or oppose) Senator Small on this matter (and, implicitly, in the next election)."

In addition, if Mary is there on behalf of her organization, she is more likely to have informed herself on this issue before she made her pitch. She's less vulnerable to being put off or distracted by Senator Small's diversionary tactics. Chances are it isn't going to be just Mary doing the lobbying but Mary and three or more of her fellow members.

DCCSOS made a special point of coming armed with good information when it approached officials and their staff. Not only was good information its biggest asset, it was also the way DCCSOS established itself as an entity to be trusted.

Members of lobbying groups spend a lot of time educating one another. It is often at meetings that you find out the most urgent issues and the talking points with which to promote your agenda. I have sometimes become impatient with the amount of time people spend at meetings telling one another about the sins of the opposition and the horrors of the status quo. But I have come to realize that this is time well spent.

It is the cumulative wisdom of many people with diverse gifts that yields the most relevant information. Some of those five social workers knew little about the intricacies of welfare policy, the legislative and rule-making machinery, and the political considerations that shaped legislators' stances on issues. But they did know a lot about the impact of welfare policies on young psyches and the morale of mothers trying to balance the demands of entry-level jobs against health problems and lack of child care. Combine that with the wisdom of people who knew all this from having lived it as welfare clients. But where would they be without the seasoned political operative who knows neither the subtleties of family dynamics nor the complexities of welfare regulations but *can* tell you how to get a particular legislator's attention? It is that combination of expertise that can really pay off.

## Providing Political Cover

Working through an organization has a special function for people whose involvement might otherwise threaten their jobs or political connections. One county employee was on the DCCSOS steering committee. She never gave testimony in a hearing or wrote a letter to the editor, and her name never appeared publicly in connection with DCCSOS. But this member was actively involved in all phases of the organization. There were others who, for personal reasons, preferred to remain anonymous.

In Niles Schore's case, anonymity protected DCCSOS's nonpartisan image. Niles was staff director for the ranking Democrat on the Public Health and Welfare Committee.

I provided cover within DCCSOS itself for a person who gave money anonymously several times. The person did not want to be known even to the inner circle of the organization. Since we did not have tax-exempt status, there were no reporting requirements for money donated.

## Transferable Resources

Set aside the tangible accomplishments of DCCSOS. Our political assets—a mailing list of 350 like-minded folk, a more intimate connection between members of the steering committee—were resources that could be tapped in a variety of ways. The same was true of coalitions of which DCCSOS was a part.

Take the allies who worked on the issue of child care regulations for so many months. Much time and energy went into this struggle but the yield was modest at best, from the advocates' standpoint. Yet in weighing the value of investing in a lobbying effort of this kind, we have to consider the consequences of not having waged the fight at all. Aside from the benefits of easier access to child care for low-income families and better protection against abuse, the child care issue had brought together a loose coalition of forces that could be mobilized on other related issues.

One such issue emerged in 2004, when the State Department of Public Welfare proposed exempting religiously based child care agencies from state control altogether. Since a majority of child care providers in Pennsylvania are sectarian, such a change would have made a mockery of state regulation in that field. The old alliance came out in force against the measure. That may not be what killed the bill aborning, but it illustrates how alliances forged in one context can be carried over to others.

## Defining the Organization

Those original five social workers knew they had to expand their forces if they were to have any success. One way to do so would have been to base the advocacy campaign entirely within the Brandywine Division of the Pennsylvania Chapter of the National Association of Social Workers. Or they might have at least used that as the foundation and reached out to other groups from there. There was a lot to be said for this approach. NASW was united in its opposition to welfare reform at the national, state, and local levels. The state chapter had a staff person who spent a major part of her time on lobbying, mainly on professional licensure issues. Since licensing cut across party lines, she had many useful contacts on both sides of the aisle in the legislature. An affiliated arm of the chapter, Political Action for Candidate Election (PACE), had endorsed both Republican and Democratic lawmakers in past elections. National NASW could make grants available to its chapters for special projects. Pennsylvania would have been a natural place to invest those funds, since it was a large state and something of a bellwether on welfare issues.

It made sense to capitalize on that built-in connection with NASW, but DCCSOS was moving in a somewhat different direction. More than a decade earlier, the Pennsylvania NASW chapter had joined welfare rights organizations in a campaign against then-Governor Dick Thornburgh's plan to restrict general assistance. The chapter found itself working at cross purposes between its welfare advocacy and its quest for state licensing, which required wooing anti-welfare Republicans.

Would NASW stay the course in the welfare reform fight, if that interfered with its concern about professional recognition? We were happy to work within NASW but felt it prudent to broaden the base to include people more clearly identified with the welfare poor. That was when I turned to my former student Connie Smith. It was she who brought the welfare client advocate, Anne Vaughan, and her husband, Niles Schore, the legislative aide, into the picture, and in so doing determined the direction of DCCSOS.

Anne and Niles brought a kind of expertise that no one else possessed. Without necessarily meaning to, they soon assumed the dominant roles in DCCSOS. I don't mean to imply that no one else had a major impact. For example, I was thrust into a leadership position from the beginning. I saw my special role as shepherding the fledgling organization along, keeping everybody aboard, broadening the base, and increasing our numbers. Also, since writing came easily to me, I edited the monthly newsletter that kept our far-flung support network in the loop. As different priorities and different personalities contended for a place at the table, I sometimes found myself in the role of mediator. On the policy agenda itself, I sought to find common ground where people could unite.

The social workers who had started the whole thing did not disappear. They were fully involved in the activities of DCCSOS throughout its life and often spoke up on issues we were discussing. They also acted as facilitators of our general meetings.

In lobbying, there are groups that operate mainly within the system and others that take an outsider role. The former focus on networking with those in power, avoiding confrontation, and generally seeking to make things work for everyone. They are likely to go after tax-exempt status, which can open up access to financial resources but limits their freedom to speak out forcefully on policy questions. They have ready access to people in power, whom they seek to educate on the issues without ruffling feathers.

Outsiders challenge the official system and are more confrontative in style. They either operate on their own, or form coalitions with other like-minded groups. The range of views is generally narrower than is true of insider organizations and coalitions.

Both insiders and outsiders have a legitimate place in the political process, though each tends to question the legitimacy of the other. For the outsider, an attempt to maximize influence through networking with the high and mighty is seen as caving in. Conversely, the readiness to challenge the system and fight over the "real" issues is written off as so much grandstanding by insiders. That is unfortunate, because together insiders and outsiders can multiply their influence, not by merging but by playing their respective roles. In fact, together they can complement the power of each other.

In retrospect, I think DCCSOS never resolved the question of whether it wanted to be an insider or an outsider. It confronted welfare and employment agency administrators on their practices, assuring that it would never be totally trusted by the establishment. But it refused to join organizations like the nationally known Kensington Welfare Rights Union in taking to the streets and risking arrest, lessening the trust of some elements on the other side. Instead, it sought to focus honestly on the issues and let the chips fall where they might.

Did this in-between role, neither fully inside nor outside, help or hinder DCCSOS in trying to influence policy? I'll leave it to the reader to answer that. But, once its basic direction was set, it was important for DCCSOS to stay on message and stay in character. Any other course would have led to the rapid demise of the organization, as elements within the fold broke away feeling betrayed by being a part of something other than what they had committed themselves to support.

## What DCCSOS Was Not

There were some among us who dreamed of being in the vanguard of a resurgent movement of the disenfranchised—the old welfare rights of yesteryear reborn. But the people who founded DCCSOS were mostly middle-class professionals fighting someone else's battles. An exception was Connie Smith, who knew firsthand the deprivation and indignities of being a welfare client and raising a child in poverty single-handed. While there were clients and ex-clients who were occasionally recruited to give testimony about their plight, this was not a client-centered movement. Bottom-up movement politics was one of those agenda items that tended to get pushed into the background because of seemingly more urgent concerns.

Several months after the start of DCCSOS, Connie Smith brought her friend Othea Maisonet aboard. Like Connie, Othea was an ex-welfare recipient who had been represented by Anne Vaughan in grievance proceedings. At the time she joined DCCSOS she directed a social service operation for the Chester Housing Authority. She served as treasurer of DCCSOS for a period.

Somewhat belatedly, we tried to initiate an organization of welfare clients and ex-clients. With Othea Maisonet taking the lead, the Welfare Coalition of Delaware County was born. It consisted of a half-dozen women from Chester, one of the most economically distressed cities in the country. None were currently on welfare. Their concerns centered on the lack of access to decent health care. They also sought resources to help pregnant teens. For a brief period, there were hopes that the group might initiate a class action suit against the Department of Public Welfare with the assistance of a statewide legal advocacy organization.

In an effort to capitalize on the new initiative, we invited a number of Welfare Coalition people onto the DCCSOS steering committee. Aside from Othea Maisonet, one other member of the Welfare Coalition became part of the steering committee. They were both still active members when DCCSOS called it quits a year later.

But as an organization, the Welfare Coalition of Delaware County never really got off the ground. In part this was due to the multiple pressures that diverted the time and energy of its small core of members in other directions. In addition, DCCSOS, already beginning to go into decline, was never able to invest enough of its own time and energy in what would have been a major organizing campaign.

In retrospect, the idea that an organization like DCCSOS could have been the start of such a revolution from below was probably unrealistic. Such movements typically don't come from outside. The welfare poor tend to mistrust efforts by professional do-gooders to organize them and with good reason. They've been used too many times in the past by well-intentioned or not so well-intentioned outsiders.

Real poor people's movements come from inside, not outside. It is only when the frustration with abuse reaches the boiling point and an authentic member of the army of the poor seizes the moment that you are likely to see such a movement. Is there a role for the outsider in such instances? Absolutely. You will have to be tested to make sure you are the genuine article, and you may never be completely trusted. If you are a professional, you may have much to offer such groups in the way of technical knowledge. It must be on their terms, not yours. Be prepared to let someone else call the shots. Otherwise, stay away and wish them well while you follow your own strategy, be it inside or outside. That doesn't preclude working in close cooperation with the bottom-up movement.

### The Internal Dynamics

It had always been my hope that DCCSOS would become sufficiently institutionalized that it could survive the departure of its early leaders. We continually tried to recruit new blood and reach out to new constituencies. Occasionally we would convince someone to join the steering committee. In many cases they stayed for a few months, then disappeared. The ones who continued never assumed central leadership positions. I insisted on stepping down as chairperson after a couple of years in that post. I became instead the unpaid executive, which didn't help much in diversifying the leadership.

It isn't just that organizations like DCCSOS become increasingly dependent on the tiny core group that founds them. Almost without realizing it, the inner circle creates its own culture. The members may begin to spend time together socially. That is an important cement in the binding process, but it also creates a subtle line between the insiders and everybody else. Newcomers with other ideas have a hard time breaking into that circle. The founders of DCCSOS who were driving the agenda had cut their political teeth on the War on Poverty. A person who "came of age" after that time might have other ideas about confronting the welfare establishment, or other issues on which to focus.

One such person joined the steering committee after the inner group had more or less jelled. He had ideas for reenergizing DCCSOS. It didn't help that he began presenting them at the first steering committee meeting he attended. Beyond this, he was of a different generation from most of the DCCSOS leadership. He didn't lack zeal in taking on the system, but he was also interested in developing job training and employment projects that we might sponsor. He envisioned DCCSOS's acquiring tax-exempt status in order to go after government or foundation grants—"real money," as he put it. He eventually left the organization. The point here isn't that one or another approach was better. It's that, once committed to a particular course of action and style of operation, DCCSOS couldn't shift to a different one.

What eventually led to DCCSOS's demise was clearly its dependence on a few individuals who, for personal reasons, had to drop out. That committed core is necessary, or the ship will never get far from the dock. But it doesn't have to stop there. There are organizations that begin as DCCSOS did and are still in there advocating years, even decades, afterward. Somehow they are able to keep the mission alive—maybe in modified form—and bring along a new generation of leaders.

Grassroots organizations are fragile at best, especially in their early years. There are likely to be strong personalities who put their stamp on the group's mission. One of the strengths of the DCCSOS leadership was that there were no "stars" seeking to hog the limelight. But limelight is not what this kind of lobbying is about; there's usually not a lot of it to begin with.

### *"If We Had It to Do Over Again . . ."*

> For all sad words of tongue or pen, the saddest are these, "It might have been."

John Greenleaf Whittier

It is tempting to try to replay—if not rewrite—history. If only we had. . . . You fill in the blanks. Everything from lost loves to lost elections is fair game in this often pointless endeavor. The fact is, we didn't or I didn't. Time to move on with life. Learn from the past, but don't wallow in it. Pledge to do better next time.

The nice thing about lobbying is that there is a next time. Maybe not if you're knocking down six figures working the corridors for a large corporation. The goofs and missed opportunities might then be the occasion for thinking about a career change. But the kind of lobbying this book is about—the kind that you do out of commitment to human decency and dignity—doesn't carry that kind of awesome burden. Pick yourself up, dust yourself off, leave that pathetic threesome—Should Have, Would Have, and Could Have—behind, and move on.

That all having been said, it is useful to revisit history and consider alternative strategies along the way. In the case of DCCSOS, we might start from the very beginning. What if we had folded the whole effort into the political action agenda of the Pennsylvania chapter of the National Association of Social Workers? As it was, we worked closely with NASW throughout DCCSOS's history. For its part, the chapter used DCCSOS as a model it encouraged its other divisions to emulate. But that is still different from making the local campaign an integral part of the chapter (including its budget), making its activities subject to approval by the board of directors.

For one thing, DCCSOS would have competed with other chapter priorities, the chief one being professional credentialing. As it turned out, the chapter was able to pursue both credentialing and welfare reform vigorously without any problem, though we couldn't know that at the time we started DCCSOS. Did the greater autonomy lead to different tactics on our part? Looking back, that seems doubtful. As it was, the things we were doing were well within the purview of NASW and were similar to what the policy point-person at NASW was also doing.

There is one way in which separate status did help. It brought in people whose professional identities lay outside of social work— lawyers like Anne Vaughan and Niles Schore, and a labor leader like Martin Berger. Within NASW, we might have called on any one of them for advice, but chances are their intimate knowledge of the political landscape and arcane welfare rules would not have had the same influence on our basic strategy.

One would have to weigh that advantage against the possibility of mobilizing eleven NASW divisions throughout Pennsylvania on this issue. Time we spent focusing on the local welfare office might have gone into meeting with colleagues in Pittsburgh, Erie, and Scranton. Our delegations meeting with legislators in Harrisburg might, instead of being limited to people from one corner of the state, have included representatives from across Pennsylvania. Add to that the possibility of a generous infusion of capital from NASW's Washington office for a project that they might in turn use as a model for other states across the country.

The fact is, we didn't and they didn't.

Looking in the other direction, suppose we had seriously pursued an alliance with the Kensington Welfare Rights Union, the militant grassroots group practicing in-your-face politics in nearby Philadelphia. Even assuming KWRU had been interested, some DCCSOS leaders threatened to leave us if we went in that direction. They had had some bad experiences with the organization and were totally mistrustful of its leader. Couple that with the fact that most of the rank-and-file in DCCSOS were less militant than the leadership. A few of us might have joined the campaign in the streets I did attend a few such demonstrations—but DCCSOS would probably not have survived. Our own attempt at grassroots militancy—the Welfare Coalition of Delaware County—never had the legs to become a major movement of the disenfranchised. My guess is that, if we had officially joined KWRU, we would have been absorbed into it entirely, losing any separate identity in the process.

There was another way to go that might have given us the advantage of alliance with KWRU without the costs. I had contact with people who were intimately involved in the KWRU leadership. I had to weigh the advantages of more actively cultivating that relationship against the possible alienation of members of DCCSOS's core group.

The fact is, I didn't, we didn't, and they didn't.

Finally, we didn't avail ourselves of available technology that would have extended our reach and saved this shoestring operation some money. Several times one of our leaders suggested getting e-mail addresses of the 300-plus people on our mailing list. It somehow kept getting back-burnered. Even communication within the inner circle of steering committee members relied to a great extent on phone and snail mail. Though we did finally set up a Web page for a brief period, it is doubtful that many members, including steering committee members, checked it with any regularity. To be honest, we were slow in catching on to the potential of electronic media. It may say something about the individuals who happened to be in on the creation of DCCSOS and remained the moving force behind it to the end. DCCSOS came along during a period of catch-up in the communications sphere.

Anyway, I didn't and we didn't.

If I have any real regret about what we did or didn't do, it is that we closed up shop when we did. Not that any organization should go on forever. But, notwithstanding the likely loss of key players with all their expertise, if DCCSOS had stayed in business, it would still be there to challenge those in the federal government who would tighten the noose around the neck of the welfare poor. It would still be there as watchdog to keep the local employment and welfare bureaucracies honest. And it would still be reminding the public of the promise, yet unfulfilled, of using TANF policy as a way of lifting families out of poverty rather than simply dumping them off the welfare rolls.

In time there will be new organizations like DCCSOS. They will start with a handful of social workers or welfare mothers or regular citizens so upset about an issue that, for a time at least, they will put aside other concerns and focus their time and energy on that issue. Or it could start with a handful of students reading this book.

# Bibliography

Aberbach, J. D., Putnam, R. D., & Rockman, B.A. 1981. *Bureaucrats and Politicians in Western Democracies.* Cambridge, MA: Harvard University Press.

Arnold, R. D. 1979. *Congress and the Bureaucracy: A Theory of Influence.* New Haven: Yale University Press.

Aronson, E. 1980. *The Social Animal.* 3rd ed. San Francisco: Freeman.

Bachrach, P., & Baratz, M. S. 1970. *Power and Poverty: Theory and Practice.* New York: Oxford University Press.

Bibby, J. F. (Ed.) 1983. *Congress Off the Record.* Washington: American Enterprise Institute.

Block, F., Cloward, R. A., Ehrenreich, B., & Piven, F. P. 1987. *The Mean Season: The Attack on the Welfare State.* New York: Pantheon Books.

Brown, P. 1985. *The Transfer of Care: Psychiatric Deinstitutionalization and Its Aftermath.* London: Routledge and Kegan Paul.

Chu, F. D., & Trotter, S. 1974. *The Madness Establishment: Ralph Nader's Study Group Report on the National Institute of Mental Health.* New York: Grossman.

Clausen, R. 1973. *How Congressmen Decide: A Policy Focus.* New York: St. Martin's Press.

Compton, B. R., & Galaway, B. 1989. *Social Work Process,* 4th ed. Belmont, CA: Wadsworth.

Curtis, K. 2001. Welfare Dependency in Delaware: A Study of the State's Program Reform and Advocacy for Change. *Journal of Poverty* 5(2): 45-66.

de Figueiredo, J. M., & Silverman, B. S. 2002. Academic Ear Marks and the Return to Lobbying. Working Paper No. 43. USC-Caltech Center for the Study of Law and Politics. Los Angeles, CA.

Deutsch, M., & Gerard, H. 1955. A Study of Normative and Informational Social Influences on Individual Judgment. *Journal of Abnormal and Social Psychology* 51: 629-636.

Eisner, R. 1986. *How Real Is the Federal Deficit?* New York: Free Press.

Festinger, L. 1957. *A Theory of Cognitive Dissonance.* Stanford, CA: Stanford University Press.

Finney, J. W. 1976. Senator's Young Aide Offers an Insight Into Lobbying. *The New York Times* (July 28).

Fitzgerald, E., & McNutt, J. 1999. Electronic Advocacy in Policy Practice: A Framework for Teaching Technologically Based Practice. *Journal of Social Work Education* 35(3): 331-341.

*Lobbying for Social Change*
© 2006 by The Haworth Press, Inc. All rights reserved.
doi:10.1300/5782_13

Fitzgerald, T. 2005. Short on Bucks, but Long on Blogs. *Philadelphia Inquirer* (May 11), pp. B1, B6.

Frank, T. 2004. *What's the Matter with Kansas? How Conservatives Won the Heart of America*. New York: Metropolitan Books.

Germani, G. 1966. Social and Political Consequences of Mobility. In *Social Structure and Mobility in Economic Development*. Eds. N. J. Smelser & S. M. Lipset. Chicago: Aldine, pp. 364-394.

Gibbs, L. M. 1982. *Love Canal: My Story*. Albany, NY: SUNY Press.

Gilbert, M. A. 1979. How to Win an Argument. New York: McGraw-Hill.

Gruber, J. E. 1987. *Controlling Bureaucracies: Dilemmas in Democratic Governance*. Berkeley, CA: University of California Press.

Hayes, C. 2005. How to Turn Your Red State Blue. *In These Times* (April 18), pp.16-17.

Heilbroner, R. L., & Thurow, L. C. 1975. *The Economic Problem*, 4th ed. Englewood Cliffs, NJ: Prentice-Hall.

Hurwitz, J. 1986. Issue Perception and Legislative Decision Making. *American Political Science Quarterly* 14: 150-185.

Kingdon, J. W. 1973. *Congressmen's Voting Decisions*. New York: Harper and Row.

Kleinkauf, C. 1981. A Guide to Giving Legislative Testimony. *Social Work* 26: 297-303.

Lakoff, G. 2002. *Moral Politics: How Liberals and Conservatives Think*, 2nd ed. Chicago: University of Chicago Press.

Lamendola, L. 1977. Welfare: Governor Eager to Sign "Able-Bodied" Measure. *Newark Star-Ledger* (October 19), p. 13.

Lecky, P. 1961. *Self-Consistency: A Theory of Personality*, 2nd ed. Hamden, CT: Shoe String Press.

Levine, A. G. 1982. *Love Canal: Science, Politics, and People*. Lexington, MA: Lexington Books.

Luker, K. 1984. *Abortion and the Politics of Motherhood*. Berkeley, CA: University of California Press.

Mahaffey, M. 1982. Lobbying and Social Work. In *Practical Politics: Social Work and Political Responsibility*. Eds. M. Mahaffey & J. W. Hanks. Silver Spring, MD: National Association of Social Workers.

McCroskey, J. C. 1968. *An Introduction to Rhetorical Communication: The Theory and Practice of Public Speaking*. Englewood Cliffs, NJ: Prentice-Hall.

McLuhan, M. 1964. *Understanding Media: The Extensions of Man*. New York: McGraw-Hill.

Meyer, J. A. 1988. Don't Risk America's Job Creation Boom. *The New York Times* (August 14), p. 2F.

Murray, C. 1984. *Losing Ground: American Social Policy, 1950-1980*. New York: Basic Books.

Nader, R., & Brownstein, R. 1980. Beyond the Love Canal: Bureaucracy Has Compounded the Chemical Mess. *The Progressive* 44(5): 28-31.

*New York Times, The.* 1988. Make Work Pay More than Welfare (August 14), p. 2F.

*New York Times, The.* 1989. Senators Examine Baker on Tuesday (January 16), p. A2.

Nixon, R. M. 1974. *Public Papers of the Presidents: Richard Nixon; Containing the Public Messages, Speeches and Statements of the President.* Washington, DC: U.S. Government Printing Office.

Paige, C. 1983. *The Right to Lifers: Who They Are, How They Operate, and Where They Get Their Money.* New York: Summit Books.

Paletz, D. L., & Entman, R. M. 1981. *Media Power Politics.* New York: Free Press.

Pallack, M. S., & Cummings, W. 1976. Commitment and Energy Conservation. *Personal and Social Psychology Bulletin,* 2: 27-30.

Perelman, C., & Olbrechts-Tyteca, L. 1969. *The New Rhetoric.* Trans. J. Wilkinson & P. Weaver. South Bend, IN: University of Notre Dame Press.

Piven, F. F., & Cloward, R. A. 1971. *Regulating the Poor: The Functions of Public Welfare.* New York: Pantheon.

Potter, N. 1987. Personal communication.

Ray, D. 1982. The Sources of Voting Cues in Three State Legislatures. *Journal of Politics,* 44:1074-1087.

Richan, W. C. 1983. Obstructive Politics in an Anti-Welfare Era. In *Social Work in a Turbulent World.* Ed. M. Dinerman. Silver Spring, MD: National Association of Social Workers.

Richan, W. C. 1987. Government Policies and Black Progress: The Role of Social Research in Public Policy Debates. *Social Work* 32: 353-356.

Richan, W. C. 1988. *Beyond Altruism: Social Welfare Policy in American Society.* New York: The Haworth Press.

Rieke, R. D., & Sillars, M. O. 1995. *Argumentation and the Decision Making Process.* New York: John Wiley & Sons.

*Secaucus Home News.* 1977. It Costs More to Work Welfare Recipients (March 18), p. 2.

Shapiro, F. C. 1972. "Right to Life" has a message for New York State Legislators. *New York Times Magazine* (August 20).

Sharwell, G. R. 1978. How to Testify Before a Legislative Committee. In *Toward Human Dignity.* Ed. J. W. Hanks. New York: National Association of Social Workers.

Smelser, N. J., & Lipset, S. M. (Eds.) 1966. *Social Structure and Mobility in Economic Development.* Chicago: Aldine.

Songer, D. R., et al. 1985. Voting Cues in Two State Legislatures: A Further Application of the Kingdon Model. *Social Science Quarterly* 66: 983-990.

*Statistical Abstract of the United States.* Annual. Washington, DC: U.S. Government Printing Office.

Stein, I. 1975. Industry Effects of Government Expenditures: An Input-Output Study. Washington, DC: U.S. Department of Commerce, Bureau of Economics. COM-75-11157.

Tallmer, M. 1981. Hooker's Other Love Canals: Chemical Dumping As a Corporate Way of Life. *The Progressive* 45(11): 35-42.

Tedeschi, J., Schlenker, B., & Bonoma, T. V. 1971. Cognitive Dissonance: Private Ratiocination or Public Spectacle? *American Psychologist* 26: 685-695.

U.S. House of Representatives, Committee on Ways and Means, Subcommittee on Public Assistance and Unemployment Compensation. 1987. *Hearings to Examine Proposals to Reform the Federal-State Welfare System.* January 28, February 19, and March 4, 6, 10, 11, and 13. 100th Congress, 1st Session. Washington, DC: U.S. Government Printing Office.

U.S. Senate, Committee on Environment and Public Works, Subcommittees on Environmental Pollution and Resource Protection. 1979. *Hazardous and Toxic Waste Disposal Field Hearings.* May 18, Niagara Falls, NY, and June 29, San Francisco, CA. 96th Congress, 1st Session. Washington, DC: U.S. Government Printing Office.

Whiteman, D. 1985. The Fate of Policy Analysis in Congressional Decision Making: Three Types of Use in Committees. *Western Political Quarterly* 38: 294-311.

Yorke, I. 1978. *The Technique of Television News.* London: Focal Press.

Zeigler, H., & Baer, M. A. 1969. *Lobbying: Interaction and Influence in American State Legislatures.* Belmont, CA: Wadsworth.

Zuesse, E. 1981. Love Canal: The Truth Seeps Out. *Reason* (February): 16-33.

# Index

### Order a copy of this book with this form or online at:
http://www.haworthpress.com/store/product.asp?sku=5782

# LOBBYING FOR SOCIAL CHANGE
## Third Edition

_____ in hardbound at $59.95 (ISBN-13: 978-0-7890-3165-5; ISBN-10: 0-7890-3165-5)

_____ in softbound at $32.95 (ISBN-13: 978-0-7890-3166-2; ISBN-10: 0-7890-3166-3)

*299 pages plus index*

Or order online and use special offer code HEC25 in the shopping cart.

COST OF BOOKS_____

POSTAGE & HANDLING_____
*(US: $4.00 for first book & $1.50
for each additional book)*
*(Outside US: $5.00 for first book
& $2.00 for each additional book)*

SUBTOTAL_____

IN CANADA: ADD 6% GST_____

STATE TAX_____
*(NJ, NY, OH, MN, CA, IL, IN, PA, & SD
residents, add appropriate local sales tax)*

**FINAL TOTAL**_____
*(If paying in Canadian funds,
convert using the current
exchange rate, UNESCO
coupons welcome)*

☐ **BILL ME LATER:** (Bill-me option is good on
US/Canada/Mexico orders only; not good to
jobbers, wholesalers, or subscription agencies.)
☐ Check here if billing address is different from
shipping address and attach purchase order and
billing address information.

Signature_____

☐ **PAYMENT ENCLOSED: $**_____

☐ **PLEASE CHARGE TO MY CREDIT CARD.**

☐ Visa ☐ MasterCard ☐ AmEx ☐ Discover
☐ Diner's Club ☐ Eurocard ☐ JCB

Account #_____

Exp. Date_____

Signature_____

Prices in US dollars and subject to change without notice.

NAME_____
INSTITUTION_____
ADDRESS_____
CITY_____
STATE/ZIP_____
COUNTRY_____ COUNTY (NY residents only)_____
TEL_____ FAX_____
E-MAIL_____

May we use your e-mail address for confirmations and other types of information? ☐ Yes ☐ No
We appreciate receiving your e-mail address and fax number. Haworth would like to e-mail or fax special
discount offers to you, as a preferred customer. **We will never share, rent, or exchange your e-mail address
or fax number.** We regard such actions as an invasion of your privacy.

*Order From Your Local Bookstore or Directly From*
**The Haworth Press, Inc.**
10 Alice Street, Binghamton, New York 13904-1580 • USA
TELEPHONE: 1-800-HAWORTH (1-800-429-6784) / Outside US/Canada: (607) 722-5857
FAX: 1-800-895-0582 / Outside US/Canada: (607) 771-0012
E-mail to: orders@haworthpress.com

**For orders outside US and Canada,** you may wish to order through your local
sales representative, distributor, or bookseller.
For information, see http://haworthpress.com/distributors

*(Discounts are available for individual orders in US and Canada only, not booksellers/distributors.)*
PLEASE PHOTOCOPY THIS FORM FOR YOUR PERSONAL USE.
http://www.HaworthPress.com                    BOF06